第 1 版前言

机电工程专业英语是机械设计制造及自动化、材料成形与控制工程及汽车工程等专业的一门重要基础课，对于机电工程专业的本科、专科学生以及从事相关专业工作的科技人员来说，熟练掌握专业英语对于促进国际交流，了解国内外本专业的最新发展动态是十分必要的，并且有着越来越重要的意义。随着我国加入 WTO，与国外的技术交流越来越多，专业英语的学习更为迫切。为了满足机械设计制造及自动化、汽车工程等专业的教学需求，我们编写了《机电工程专业英语》一书。

机电工程是一门交叉学科，内涵丰富，涉及面广。本书内容包括力学、机械零件与机构、机械设计、机器人技术、汽车构造和工作性能、机械加工及成形技术、自动化技术及现代设计制造。其主要特色有：

1. 本书由浅入深，由简到繁，循序渐进，同时本教材选材广泛，内容丰富，语言规范，难度适中，便于自学。

2. 本书由基础知识篇、综合提高篇两部分组成。课文"原型"均选用国外原版报纸、杂志、教材、论著、会议论文和实用文件，从而使学生从不同角度、不同层次、不同侧面、不同渠道接触和吸收专业英语知识；使专业英语语言的语料具有"原汁原味"的真实性；使学生现在所学的专业英语知识和所获取的专业英语技能在将来更具有实用性。通过本教材的学习，学生们不仅可以熟练地掌握本专业常用的及与本专业相关的英语单词、词组及其用法，而且可以深化本专业的知识，为今后的学习和工作打下良好基础。

3. 在本书所有的课文后均附有参考译文。参考译文的目的在于"帮助学生理解和掌握专业英语的词汇、句式和功能意念等方面知识"。翻译时注意采取尽可能使译文在词语含义、词语顺序和句子结构等方面与原文保持一致的翻译方法，以便学生预习和自学。

4. 本书在编写过程中注意以学生为中心，以自主学习为主，让学生课内与课外结合，学习和应用结合，在课文中插入了一些示意图或构造图，通俗易懂，同时训练学生把基础阶段学到的语言知识在机电专业领域中应用、巩固、扩展和提高，更好地适应未来的工作需求。

本书由赵运才教授、何法江教授任主编，钟利萍、王丽君、杨春杰任副主编，参加编写的有方晓丽、石玉祥、朱林、田宏宇、匡江红、么永强，由严珩志教授担任主审。由于时间和编者水平有限，书中错误和不当之处在所难免，欢迎广大读者不吝指正。

编　者
2007 年 2 日

目　　录

Lesson 1　Introduction to Mechanical Design ·· 1
　1.1　Text ··· 1
　1.2　Words and Phrases ··· 4
　1.3　Complex Sentence Analysis ··· 4
　1.4　Exercise ·· 5
　　　1.4.1　Translate the following paragraphs ··· 5
　　　1.4.2　Choose the proper answer to fill in the blank and translate the sentences ·············· 5

Lesson 2　Mechanisms ·· 7
　2.1　Text ··· 7
　2.2　Words and Phrases ··· 9
　2.3　Complex Sentence Analysis ··· 9
　2.4　Exercise ·· 10

Lesson 3　Machine Parts (Ⅰ) ··· 11
　3.1　Text ··· 11
　3.2　Words and Phrases ··· 13
　3.3　Complex Sentence Analysis ··· 14
　3.4　Exercise ·· 15
　　　3.4.1　Translate the Following paragraphs ··· 15
　　　3.4.2　Write the name of the following parts and brief description of the roller chain on the structure and assembly relations ················· 16

Lesson 4　Machine Parts (Ⅱ) ·· 17
　4.1　Text ··· 17
　4.2　Words and Phrases ··· 19
　4.3　Complex Sentence Analysis ··· 21
　4.4　Exercise ·· 21

Lesson 5　Engineering Graphic in the Third – angle Projection ······················ 23
　5.1　Text ··· 23
　5.2　Words and Phrases ··· 26
　5.3　Complex Sentence Analysis ··· 27
　5.4　Exercise ·· 27

Lesson 6   Introduction to CAD/CAM/CAPP 29
  6.1   Text 29
  6.2   Words and Phrases 31
  6.3   Complex Sentence Analysis 32
  6.4   Exercise 33

Lesson 7   A Discussion on Modern Design Optimization 34
  7.1   Text 34
  7.2   Words and Phrases 37
  7.3   Complex Sentence Analysis 38
  7.4   Exercise 39

Lesson 8   Using Dynamic Simulation in the Development of Construction Machinery ... 40
  8.1   Text 40
  8.2   Words and Phrases 45
  8.3   Complex Sentence Analysis 46
  8.4   Exercise 46

Lesson 9   Engineering Tolerance 47
  9.1   Text 47
  9.2   Words and Phrases 50
  9.3   Complex Sentence Analysis 50
  9.4   Exercise 51

Lesson 10   Numerical Control 53
  10.1   Text 53
  10.2   Words and Phrases 55
  10.3   Complex Sentence Analysis 56
  10.4   Exercise 57

Lesson 11   Introduction to Heat Pipe Technology in Machining Process ... 58
  11.1   Text 58
  11.2   Words and Phrases 61
  11.3   Complex Sentence Analysis 61
  11.4   Exercise 62

Lesson 12   Introduction to Material Forming 63
  12.1   Text 63
  12.2   Words and Phrases 66
  12.3   Complex Sentence Analysis 67
  12.4   Exercise 68

Lesson 13 Material Forming Processes ... 69
13.1 Text ... 69
13.2 Words and Phrases ... 73
13.3 Complex Sentence Analysis ... 74

Lesson 14 Introduction to Mould ... 75
14.1 Text ... 75
14.2 Words and Phrases ... 78
14.3 Complex Sentence Analysis ... 79
14.4 Exercise ... 79

Lesson 15 Mould Design and Manufacturing ... 81
15.1 Text ... 81
15.2 Words and Phrases ... 83
15.3 Complex Sentence Analysis ... 84
15.4 Exercise ... 85

Lesson 16 Heat Treatment of Metal ... 86
16.1 Text ... 86
16.2 Words and Phrases ... 88
16.3 Complex Sentence Analysis ... 89
16.4 Exercise ... 90

Lesson 17 Virtual Manufacturing ... 91
17.1 Text ... 91
17.2 Words and Phrases ... 93
17.3 Complex Sentence Analysis ... 93
17.4 Exercise ... 94

Lesson 18 Fluid and Hydraulic System ... 95
18.1 Text ... 95
18.2 Words and Phrases ... 97
18.3 Complex Sentence Analysis ... 98
18.4 Exercise ... 98

Lesson 19 Product Test and Quality Control ... 99
19.1 Text ... 99
19.2 Words and Phrases ... 101
19.3 Complex Sentence Analysis ... 101
19.4 Exercise ... 102

Lesson 20　Introduction of Automobile Engine ·············· 103
 20.1 Text ·· 103
 20.2 Words and Phrases ··· 106
 20.3 Complex Sentence Analysis ································ 107
 20.4 Exercise ·· 107

Lesson 21　The Automobile Components ······················ 108
 21.1 Text ·· 108
 21.2 Words and Phrases ··· 111
 21.3 Complex Sentence Analysis ································ 111
 21.4 Exercise ·· 112

Lesson 22　Mechatronics ·· 113
 22.1 Text ·· 113
 22.2 Words and Phrases ··· 115
 22.3 Complex Sentence Analysis ································ 116
 22.4 Exercise ·· 117

Lesson 23　Industrial Robots ···································· 118
 23.1 Text ·· 118
 23.2 Words and Phrases ··· 121
 23.3 Complex Sentence Analysis ································ 121
 23.4 Exercise ·· 122

Lesson 24　An Army of Small Robots ·························· 123
 24.1 Text ·· 123
 24.2 Words and Phrases ··· 125
 24.3 Complex Sentence Analysis ································ 126
 24.4 Exercise ·· 127

Lesson 25　Introduction to MEMS ······························ 128
 25.1 Text ·· 128
 25.2 Words and Phrases ··· 129
 25.3 Complex Sentence Analysis ································ 130
 25.4 Exercise ·· 130

Lesson 26　Dialogue—At CIMT ································ 131
 26.1 Text ·· 131
 26.2 Words and Phrases ··· 133
 26.3 Complex Sentence Analysis ································ 134
 26.4 Exercise ·· 134

Lesson 27　How to Write a Scientific Paper ·········· 136
    27.1　Text ··· 136
    27.2　Words and Phrases ····················· 139
    27.3　Complex Sentence Analysis ·········· 140
    27.4　Exercise ·································· 141

附录 A　关于科技英语翻译 ····················· 142

附录 B　怎样写科技论文的英文摘要 ·········· 143

附录 C　课文参考译文 ··························· 157

参考文献 ··· 217

Lesson 1　Introduction to Mechanical Design

1.1　Text

[1]Machinery design is either to formulate an engineering plan for the satisfaction of a specified need or to solve an engineering problem. It involves a range of disciplines in materials, mechanics, heat, flow, control, electronics and production.

【机械结构：大本钟】

Machinery design may be simple or enormously complex, easy or difficult, mathematical or nonmathematical, it may involve atrivial problem or one of great importance. Good design is the orderly and interesting arrangement of an idea to provide certain results or effects. A well-designed product is functional, efficient, and dependable. Such a product is less expensive than a similar poorly designed product that does not function properly and must constantly be repaired.

People who perform the various functions of machinery design are typically called industrial designers. He or she must first carefully define the problem, using an engineering approach, to ensure that anyproposed solution will solve problem. [2]It is important that the designer begins by identifying exactly some satisfactory solutions, and to distinguish between them in order to identify the best. So, industrial designers must have creative imagination, knowledge of engineering, production techniques, tools, machines, and materials to design a new product for manufacture, or to improve an existing product.

In the modern industrialized world, the wealth and living standards of a nation are closely linked with their capabilities to design and manufacture engineeringproducts. It can be claimed that the advancement of machinery design and manufacturing can remarkably promote the overall level of a country's industrialization. Our country is playing a more and more vital role in the global manufacturing industry. To accelerate such an industrializing process, highly skilled design engineers having extensive knowledge and expertise are needed.

Machinery Components

The major part of a machine is the mechanical system. [3]And the mechanical system is decomposed into mechanisms, which can be further decomposed into mechanical components. In this sense, the mechanical components are the fundamental elements of machinery. On the whole, mechanical components can be classified as universal and special components. Bolts, gear, and chains are the typical examples of the universal components, which can be used extensively in different machines across various

【机械系统：轮子与轮轴】

industrial sectors. Turbine blades, crankshaft and aircraft propeller are the examples of the special components, which are designed for some specific purposes.

MechanicalDesign Process

Product design requires much research and development. Many concepts of an idea must be studied, tried, refined, and then either used ordiscarded. Although the content of each engineering problem is unique, the designers follow the similar process to solve the problems. The complete process is often outlined as in Fig. 1.1.

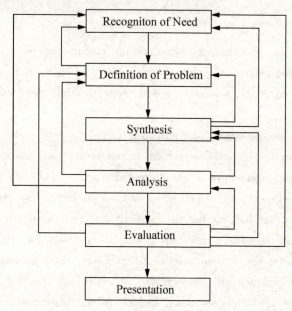

Fig. 1.1 Design Process Model

Recognition of Need

Sometimes, design begins when a designer recognizes a need and decides to do something about it. The need is often not evident at all. Recognition is usually triggered by a particular adverse circumstance or a set of random circumstances, which arise almost simultaneously. Identification of need usually consists of an undefined and vague problem statement.

Definition of Problem

Definition of problem is necessary to fully define and understand the problem, after which it is possible to restate the goal in a more reasonable and realistic way than the original problem statement. Definition of the problem must include all the specifications for the thing that is to be designed. Obvious items in the specifications are the speeds, feeds, temperature limitations, maximum range, expected variation in the variables, and dimensional and weight limitations.

Synthesis

The synthesis is one in which as many alternative possible design approaches are sought, usually without regard for their value or quality. This is also sometimes called the ideation and invention step in which the largest possible number of creative solutions is generated. The synthesis activity includes the specification of material, addition of geometric features, and inclusion of greater dimensional detail to the aggregate design.

Analysis

Analysis is a method of determining or describing the nature of something by separating it into its parts. In the process, the elements, or nature of the design, are analyzed to determine the fit between the proposed design and the original design goals.

Evaluation

Evaluation is the final proof of a successful design and usually involves the testing of a prototype in the laboratory. Here we wish to discover if the design really satisfies the needs.

The above description may give anerroneous impression that this process can be accomplished in a linear fashion as listed. On the contrary, iteration is required within the entire process, moving from any step back to any previous step.

Presentation

Communicating the design to others is the final, vital presentation step in the design process. Basically, there are only three means of communication. These are the written, the oral, and the graphical forms. A successful engineer will be technically competent and versatile in all three forms of communication. The competent engineer should not be afraid of the possibility of not succeeding in a presentation. In fact, the greatest gains are obtained by those willing to risk defeat.

Contents of Machinery Design

Machinery design is an important technological basic course in mechanical engineering education. Its objective is to provide the concepts, procedures, data, and decision analysis techniques necessary to design machine elements commonly found in mechanical devices and systems; to develop engineering students' competence of machine design that is the primary concern of machinery manufacturing and the key to manufacture good products.

【终极超级汽车的设计】

【轮胎的制作过程】

Machinery design covers the following contents:

(1) Provides an introduction to the design process, problem formulation, safety factors.

(2) Reviews the material properties and static and dynamic loading analysis, including beam, vibration and impact loading.

(3) Reviews the fundamentals of stress and defection analysis.

(4) Introduces static failure theories and fracture-mechanics analysis for static loads.

(5) Introduces fatigue-failure theory with the emphasis on stress-life approaches to high-cycle fatigue design, which is commonly used in the design of rotation machinery.

(6) Discusses thoroughly the phenomena of wear mechanisms, surface contact stresses, and

surface fatigue.

(7) Investigates shaft design using the fatigue-analysis techniques.

(8) Discusses fluid-film and rolling-element bearing theory and application.

(9) Gives a thorough introduction to the kinematics, design and stress analysis of spur gears, and a simple introduction to helical, bevel, and worm gearing.

(10) Discusses spring design including helical compression, extension and torsion springs.

(11) Deals with screws and fasteners including power screw and preload fasteners.

(12) Introduces the design and specification of disk and drum clutches and brakes.

1.2　Words and Phrases

machinery [məˈʃiːnəri]	n.	[总称] 机器，机械
trivial [ˈtriviəl]	adj.	琐细的，平常的，微不足道的
mechanism [ˈmekənizəm]	n.	机构
chain [tʃein]	n.	链（条），一连串，一系列
turbine blade		涡轮机叶片
crankshaft [ˈkræŋkʃɑːft]	n.	曲轴
propeller [prəˈpelə]	n.	推进者，推进物，尤指轮船、飞机上的螺旋推进器
discard [disˈkɑːd]	v.	丢弃，抛弃，摒弃
recognition [ˌrekəgˈniʃən]	n.	识别
trigger [ˈtrigə]	v.	引发，引起，触发
vague [veig]	adj.	含糊的，不清楚的
synthesis [ˈsinθəsis]	n.	综合
ideation [ˌaidiˈeiʃən]	n.	构思能力，思维能力，构思过程
aggregate [ˈægrigit]	adj.	合计的，集合的
prototype [ˈprəutətaip]	n.	样机，原型
erroneous [iˈrəunjəs]	adj.	错误的，不正确的
iteration [ˌitəˈreiʃən]	n.	反复
competent [ˈkɔmpitənt]	adj.	有能力的，胜任的
versatile [ˈvəːsətail]	adj.	通用的，万能的，多才多艺的

1.3　Complex Sentence Analysis

［1］Machinery design is either to formulate an engineering plan for the satisfaction of a specified need or to solve an engineering problem.

① either…or…：或……或……。

② formulate：明确地表达，阐明。

Introduction to Mechanical Design Lesson 1

机械设计用以阐明满足某种特殊需要的工程计划或解决具体的工程问题。

[2] It is important that the designer begins by identifying exactly some satisfactory solutions, and to distinguish between them in order to identify the best.

对于设计者来说,一开始就能准确判定出令人满意的设计方案,并能加以区别以便选择一个最好的,这一点很重要。

[3] And the mechanical system is decomposed into mechanisms, which can be further decomposed into mechanical components.

① be decomposed into: 被分解为。

② which 引导一个定语从句,在从句中做主语,指前面的 mechanisms。

机械系统可以分解为机构,机构又可以进一步分解为机械零件。

1.4　Exercise

1.4.1　Translate the following paragraphs

　　The practice of design can be one of the most exciting and fulfilling activities that an engineer can undertake. There is a strong sense of satisfaction and pride in seeing the results of one's creative efforts emerge into actual products and processes that benefit people. To do design well requires a number of characteristics. The design engineer should not only have adequate technical training, but must also be a person of sound judgment and wide experience, qualities which are usually acquired only after considerable time has been spent in actual professional work. A start in this direction can be made with a good teacher while the student is still at the university. However, the beginning designer must expect to get a substantial portion of this training after leaving school through further reading and study, and especially by being associated with other competent engineers. The more any one engineer knows about all phrases of design, the better. Design is an exacting profession, but highly fascinating when practiced against a broad background of knowledge.

1.4.2　Choose the proper answer to fill in the blank and translate the sentences

　　1. They are using a (　　) shovel to clear up the streets.

　　2. Many products are made by (　　).

　　3. There is not a (　　) who hasn't had this problem.

　　4. Machinery design involves a range of disciplines in materials, (　　), heat, flow, control, electronics and production.

　　5. The Allies finally smashed the Nazi war (　　).

A. Machinery: *n.* [U] Machines or machine parts in general.
1. 机器；机械
2. 机械装置
3. 方法
4. 制造舞台效果的装置
5. 文学手段；（文学作品的）情节

B. Mechanical: *adj.* of or pertaining to machines or tools.
1. 机械的，用机械的 [Z]
2. 似机械的，呆板的，无表情（或感情）的，无意识的
3. 机械学的，力学的；物理的

C. Machine: *n.* [C] A system formed and connected to alter, transmit, and direct applied forces to accomplish a specific objective.
1. 机器；机械
2. 计算机
3. 汽车；自行车；飞机
4. 机构；操纵组织的核心集团
5. 机器人似的工作的人；没有感情或意志的人

D. Mechanic: *n.* A worker skilled in making, using, or repairing machines.
机械工，修理工，技工 [C]

E. Mechanics: *n.* The analysis of the action of forces on matter or material systems.
1. 力学；机械学 [J]
2. 技术性的部分；技术；技巧 [K]

Lesson 2   Mechanisms

2.1   Text

A mechanism is the members combination more than two or two connections with the members to realize the regulation motion made up by way of the activity. They are the component of machinery. Activity connections between two members that have the relative motion are called the motion pairs. All motion pairs contacts with planes are called lower pairs and all motion pairs contacts with points or lines are called high pairs. [1] The motion specific property of mechanism chiefly depends on the relative size between the members, and the character of motion pairs, as well as the mutual disposition method etc. The member is used to support the members of motion in the mechanism to be called the machine frame and used as the reference coordinate to study the motion system. The member that possesses the independence motion is called motivity member. The member except machine frame and motivity member being compelled to move in the mechanism is called driven member. The independent parameter (coordinate number) essential for description or definite mechanism motion is called the free degree of mechanism. For gaining the definite relative motion between the members of mechanism, it is necessary make the number of motivity members of mechanism equal the number of free degrees.

【简单的机构】

Mechanisms may becategorized in several different ways to emphasize their similarities and differences. One such grouping divides mechanisms into planar, spherical, and spatial categories. All three groups have many things in common; [2] the criterion which distinguishes the groups, however, is to be found in the characteristics of the motions of the links.

A planar mechanism is one in which all particles describe plane curves in space and all these curves lie in parallel planes; i.e. the loci of all points are plane curves parallel to a single common plane. [3] This characteristic makes it possible to represent the locus of any chosen point of a planar mechanism in its true size and shape on a single drawing or figure. The motion transformation of any such mechanism is called coplanar. The plane four-bar linkage, the plate cam and driven parts, and the slider-crank mechanism are familiar examples of planar mechanism. The vast majority of mechanism in use today is planar. The following Fig. 2.1 is cam mechanism.

A cam is a machine member that drives a follower through a specified motion. By the proper design of a cam, any desired motion to a machine member can be obtained. As such, cams are widely used in almost all machinery. They include internal combustion engines, a variety of machine tools, compressors and computers. In general, a cam can be designed in two ways.

【凸轮的应用】

(1) The profile of a cam is designed to give a desired motion to the follower.

(2) To choose a suitable profile to ensure a satisfactory performance by the follower.

A rotary cam is a part on a machine, which changes cylindrical motion to straight-line motion. The purpose of a cam is to transmit various kinds of motion to other parts of a machine.

Practically every cam must be designed and manufactured to fit special requirements. Though each cam appears to be quite different from the other, all of them work in similar ways. In each case, as the cam is rotated or turned, another part is connected with the cam, called a follower, is moved either right or left, up and down, or in and out. The follower is usually connected to other parts on the machine to accomplish the desired action. If the follower loses contact with the cam, it will fail to work.

Cams are classified according to their basic shapes. Fig. 2.1 illustrates four different types of cams.

(1) Plate (Disc) Cam.

(2) Translation Cam.

(3) Cylindrical Cam.

(4) Face Cam.

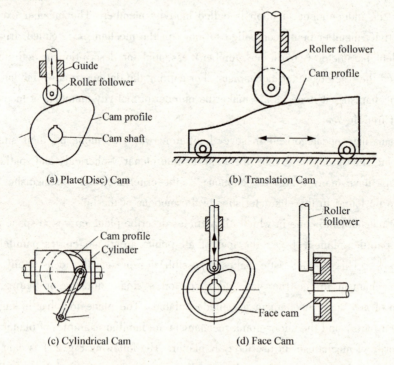

Fig. 2.1 Types of Cams

Planar mechanisms utilizing only lower pairs are called planar linkages mechanisms, they may include only revolute and prismatic pairs. Although a planar pair might theoretically be included, this would impose no constraint and thus be equivalent to an opening in the kinematics chain. Planar motion also requires that axes of all prismatic pairs and all revolute axes be normal to the plane motion.

2.2 Words and Phrases

mechanism	n. 机构
motion pairs	运动副
activity connection	活动连接
lower pair	低副
high pair	高副
disposition [dispəˈziʃən]	n. 配置；排列
machine frame	机座，机架
coordinate [kəuˈɔːdinit]	n. 坐标
motivity member	原动件
parameter [pəˈræmitə]	n. 参变量，参数
driven member	从动件
free degree	n. 自由度
categorize [ˈkætigəraiz]	v. 分类
category [ˈkætigəri]	n. 种类，逻辑范畴
planar [ˈpleinə]	adj. 平面的
spherical [ˈsferikəl]	adj. 球的，球面的
spatial [ˈspeiʃəl]	adj. 空间的
loci [ˈləusai]	n. [locus 的复数形式] 点的轨迹
constraint	n. 约束
prismatic pair	移动副

2.3 Complex Sentence Analysis

[1] The motion specific property of mechanism chiefly depends on the relative size between the members, and the character of motion pairs, as well as the mutual disposition method etc.

机构的运动特性主要取决于构件间的相对大小、运动副的性质以及相互配置方式等。

① specific property：特性。
② as well as：不但……而且；和……一样；和；也，表示递进或并列关系。

[2] The criterion which distinguishes the groups, however, is to be found in the

characteristics of the motions of the links.

然而，区别分类的标准在于连杆装置的运动特性。

① which 引导定语从句，修饰 criterion。
② to be found 为不定式被动语态。
③ links 译为"连杆装置"。

[3] This characteristic makes it possible to represent the locus of any chosen point of a planar mechanism in its true size and shape on a single drawing or figure.

有了这一特点，就能够在单个图形或图像上，以实际的尺寸和形状来绘出平面机构的任意选择点的轨迹。

① makes it possible：使……可能。
② represent：描绘，展现。
③ planar mechanism：平面机构。
④ in size and shape：在大小和形状方面。

2.4　Exercise

Translate the lineate phrases and fill in the brackets

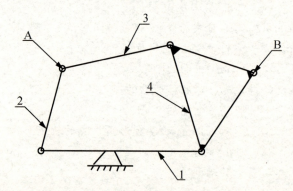

该机构为<u>平面四连杆机构</u>（　　　），
1 为<u>机架</u>（　　　），
2 为<u>原动件</u>（　　　），
3、4 为<u>从动件</u>（　　　），
A 为<u>回转副</u>（　　　），属于<u>低副</u>（　　　），
B 为<u>固定连接</u>（　　　）。
<u>构件</u>（　　　）4 中的<u>焊接符号</u>（　　　）表示 4 为一个构件。
该机构的<u>自由度数</u>（　　　）必须等于原动件数，才能实现确定的<u>运动</u>（　　　）。

Lesson 3   Machine Parts (I)

3.1   Text

Gears

[1] Gears are direct contact bodies, operating in pairs, that transmit motion and force from one rotating shaft to another, or from a shaft to a slide (rack), by means of successively engaging projections called teeth.

Tooth profiles. The contacting surfaces of gear teeth must be aligned in such a way that the drive is positive; i.e., the load transmitted must not depend on frictional contact. As shown in the treatment of direct contact bodies, this requires that the common normal to the surfaces not to pass through the pivotal axis of either the driver or the follower.

【齿轮与链传动】

As it is known as direct contact bodies, cycloidal and involute profiles provide both a positive drive and a uniform velocity ratio; i.e., conjugate action.

Basic relations. The smaller of a gear pair is called the pinion and the larger is the gear. When the pinion is on the driving shaft the pair acts as a speed reducer; When the gear drives, the pair is a speed increaser. Gears are more frequently used to reduce speed than to increase it.

If a gear having N teeth rotates at n revolutions per minute, the product $N*n$ has the dimension "teeth per minute". This product must be the same for both members of a mating pair if each tooth acquires a partner from the mating gear as it passes through the region of tooth engagement.

For conjugate gears of all types, the gear ratio and the speed ratio are both given by the ratio of the number of teeth on the gear to the number of teeth on the pinion. If a gear has 100 teeth and a mating pinion has 20, the ratio is $100/20 = 5$. Thus the pinion rotates five times as fast as the gear, regardless of the speed of the gear. Their point of tangency is called the pitch point, and since it lies on the line of centers, it is the only point at which the tooth profiles have pure rolling contact. Gears on nonparallel, non-intersecting shafts also have pitch circles, but the rolling-pitch-circle concept is not valid.

Gear types are determined largely by the disposition of the shafts; This means that if a specific disposition of the shafts is required, the type of gear will more or less be fixed. On the other hand, if a required speed change demands a certain type, the shaft positions will also be fixed.

Spur gears and helical gears. A gear having tooth elements that are straight and parallel to its axis is known as a spur gear. A spur pair can be used to connect parallel shafts only.

[2] If an involute spur pinion were made of rubber and twisted uniformly so that the ends rotated about the axis relative to one another, the elements of the teeth, initially straight and parallel to the axis, would become helices. The pinion then in effect would become a helical gear.

Worm and bevel gears. In order to achieve line contact and improve the load carrying capacity of the crossed axis helical gears, the gear can be made to curve partially around the pinion, in somewhat the same way that a nut envelops a screw. The result would be a cylindrical worm and gear. Worms are also made in the shape of an hourglass, instead of cylindrical, so that they partially envelop the gear. This results in a further increase in load-carrying capacity.

Worm gears provide the simplest means of obtaining large ratios in a single pair. They are usually less efficient than parallel-shaft gears, however, because of an additional sliding movement along the teeth.

V-belt

The rayon and rubber V-belt are widely used for power transmission. Such belts are made in two series: the standard V-belt and the high capacity V-belt. The belts can be used with short center distances and are made endless so that difficulty with splicing devices is avoided.

First, cost is low, and power output may be increased by operating several belts side by side. All belts in the drive should stretch at the same rate in order to keep the load equally divided among them. When one of the belts breaks, the group must usually be replaced. The drive may be inclined at any angle with tight side either top or bottom. Since belts can operate on relatively small pulleys, large reductions of speed in a single drive are possible.

Second, the included angle for the belt groove is usually from 34° to 38°. The wedging action of the belt in the groove gives a large increase in the tractive force developed by the belt.

Third, pulley may be made of cast iron, sheet steel, or die-cast metal. [3] Sufficient clearance must be provided at the bottom of the groove to prevent the belt from bottoming as it becomes narrower from wear. Sometimes the larger pulley is not grooved when it is possible to develop the required tractive force by running on the inner surface of the belt. The cost of cutting the grooves is thereby eliminated. Pulleys are on the market permit an adjustment in the width of the groove. The effective pitch diameter of the pulley is thus varied, and moderate changes in the speed ratio can be secured.

【自行车上的齿轮】

Chain Drives

The first chain-driven or "safety" bicycle appeared in 1874, and chains were used for driving the rear wheels on early automobiles. [4] Today, as the result of modern design and production methods, chain drives that are much superior to their prototypes are available, and these have contributed greatly to the development of efficient agricultural machinery, well-drilling equipment, and mining and construction machinery. Since about 1930 chain drives have become increasingly popular, especially for power saws, motorcycle, and escalators etc.

Machine Parts (I) Lesson 3

There are at least six types of power-transmission chains; three of these will be covered in this article, namely the roller chain, the inverted tooth, or silent chain, and the bead chain. The essential elements in a roller-chain drive are a chain with side plates, pins, bushings (sleeves), and rollers, and two or more sprocket wheels with teeth that look like gear teeth. Roller chains are assembled from pin links and roller links. A pin link consists of two side plates connected by two pins inserted into holes in the side plates. The pins fit tightly into the holes, forming what is known as a press fit. A roller link consists of two side plates connected by two press-fitted bushings, on which two hardened steel rollers are free to rotate. When assembled, the pins are a free fit in the bushings and rotate slightly, relative to the bushings when the chain goes on and leaves a sprocket.

Standard roller chains are available in single strands or in multiple strands. In the latter type, two or more chains are joined by common pins that keep the rollers in the separate strands in proper alignment. The speed ratio for a single drive should be limited to about 10∶1; the preferred shaft center distance is from 30 to 35 times the distance between the rollers and chain speeds greater than about 2500 feet (800 meters) per minute are not recommended. Where several parallel shafts are to be driven without slip from a single shaft, roller chains are particularly well suited.

An inverted tooth, or silent chain is essentially an assemblage of gear racks, each with two teeth, pivotally connected to form a closed chain with the teeth on the inside, and meshing with conjugate teeth on the sprocket wheels. The links are pin-connected flat steel plates usually having straight-sided teeth with an included angle of 60°. As many links are necessary to transmit the power and they are connected side by side. Compared with roller-chain drives, silent-chain drives are quieter, operate successfully at higher speeds, and can transmit more load for the same width. Some automobiles have silent-chain camshaft drives.

Bead chains provide an inexpensive and versatile means for connecting parallel or nonparallel shafts when the speed and power transmitted are low. The sprocket wheels contain hemispherical or conical recesses into which the beads fit. The chains look like key chains and are available in plain carbon and stainless steel and also in the form of solid plastic beads molded on a cord. Bead chains are used on computers, air conditioners, television tuners, and Venetian blinds. The sprockets may be steel, die-cast zinc or aluminum, or molded nylon.

3.2 Words and Phrases

gear	n.	齿轮
slide	n.	滑块
rack	n.	齿条
projection [prəˈdʒekʃən]	n.	凸出，凸起部分
cycloidal [saiˈklɔidəl]	adj.	摆线的

cycloidal profile		摆线轮廓
involute ['invəluːt]	adj.	渐开线的
involute profile		渐开线轮廓
conjugate ['kɔndʒugit]	adj.	共轭的
pinion ['pinjən]	n.	小齿轮
dimension [di'menʃən]	n.	量纲
mate [meit]	v.	啮合
engagement [in'geidʒmənt]	n.	啮合
tangency ['tændʒənsi]	n.	接触
pitch [pitʃ]	n.	齿节
intersect [ˌintə'sekt]	v.	相交，交叉
disposition [ˌdispə'ziʃən]	n.	排列，配置
helical gear		螺旋齿轮，斜齿轮
spur gear		正齿轮，直齿轮
worm [wəːm]	n.	蜗轮，蜗杆
bevel gear		伞形齿轮，锥齿轮
hourglass ['auəglɑːs]	n.	沙漏
V-belt		V型带
pulley ['puli]	n.	（皮带）轮
groove [gruːv]	n.	沟，槽
tractive ['træktiv]	adj.	牵引的
clearance ['kliərəns]	n.	间隙
chain drive		链传动
prototype ['prəutətaip]	n.	模型，原型机
saw [sɔː]	n.	锯
escalator ['eskəleitə]	n.	自动扶梯
roller chain		套筒滚子链条，滚子链
bead chain		滚珠链条
bushing ['buʃiŋ]	n.	套筒
sprocket ['sprɔkit]	n.	链轮
strand [strænd]	n.	排，列
venetian blind		威尼斯百叶窗，软百叶窗
die-cast		压铸

3.3 Complex Sentence Analysis

[1] Gears are direct contact bodies, operating in pairs, that transmit motion and force from one rotating shaft to another, or from a shaft to a slide (rack), by means of

successively engaging projections called teeth.

齿轮是直接接触的实体，成对使用，在称为齿的凸起的连续啮合作用下，齿轮将运动和力从一根转轴传递到另一根转轴上，或者将运动和力从一根轴传递到滑块（齿条）上。

① operating in pairs：分词短语，修饰前面的 Gears。
② that 引导的从句，修饰前面的 Gears。
③ by means of 表示"借助"、"通过"的意思。

[2] If an involute spur pinion were made of rubber and twisted uniformly so that the ends rotated about the axis relative to one another, the elements of the teeth, initially straight and parallel to the axis, would become helices.

假设一渐开线直齿轮是用橡胶制成的，并且能够均匀扭转，那么，两端就会绕着轴线做相对的转动，这样，开始是直的并平行于轴线的小齿轮上的齿，就变成了螺旋形。

① were made of："由……组成"。
② so that 引导结果状语从句。
③ parallel to："平行于……"。

[3] Sufficient clearance must be provided at the bottom of the groove to prevent the belt from bottoming as it becomes narrower from wear.

① at the bottom of…在……的底部
② prevent…from wear：防止磨损

[4] Today, as the result of modern design and production methods, chain drives that are much superior to their prototypes are available, and these have contributed greatly to the development of efficient agricultural machinery, well-drilling equipment, and mining and construction machinery.

如今，随着现代设计和制造方法的改进，链传动的应用越来越广泛，大大提高了农业机械、钻探设备、矿业和建筑机械的效率。

① superior to 表示"优于"的意思。
② and 引导的是一句并列句。

3.4　Exercise

3.4.1　Translate the Following paragraphs

A gear having tooth elements that are straight and parallel to its axis is known as a spur gear. A spur pair can be used to connect parallel shafts only. Parallel shafts, however, can also be connected by gears of another type, and a spur gear can be mated with a gear of a different type.

Helical gears have certain advantages; for example, when connecting parallel shafts they have a higher load-carrying capacity than spur gears with the same tooth numbers and cut with the same cutter. Helical gears can be also be used to connect nonparallel, non-intersecting shafts at any angle to one another. Ninety degrees is the most common angle at which such gears are used.

Worm gears provide the simplest means of obtaining large ratios in a single pair. They are usually less efficient than parallel shaft gears, however, because of an additional sliding movement along the teeth. Because of their similarity, the efficiency of a worm and gear depends on the same factors as the efficiency of a screw.

3.4.2 Write the name of the following parts and brief description of the roller chain on the structure and assembly relations

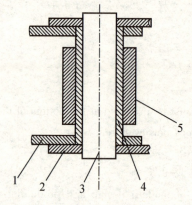

Fig. 3.1 Structure

Lesson 4　Machine Parts (II)

4.1　Text

Fastener

【刀片的更换】

[1] Fasteners are devices which permit one part to be joined to a second part and, hence, they are involved in almost all designs.

There are three main classifications of fasteners, which are described as follows:

(1) Removable. This type permits the parts to be readily disconnected without damaging the fastener. An example is the ordinary nut-and-bolt fastener.

(2) Semi permanent. For this type, the parts can be disconnected, but some damage usually occurs to the fastener. One such example is a cotter pin.

(3) Permanent. When this type of fastener is used, it is intended that the parts will never be disassembled. Examples are riveted joints and welded joints.

The importance of fasteners can be realized when referring to any complex product. In the case of the automobile, there are literally thousands of parts which are fastened together to produce the total product. The failure or loosening of a single fastener could result in a simplenuisance such as a door rattle or in a serious situation such as a wheel coming off. Such possibilities must be taken into account in the selection of the type of fastener for the specific application.

Nuts, bolts, and screws are undoubtedly the most common means of joining materials. Since they are so widely used, it is essential that these fasteners attain maximum effectiveness at the lowest possible cost.

An ordinary nut loosens when the forces of vibration overcome those of friction. In a nut and lock washer combination, the lock washer supplies an independent locking feature preventing the nut from loosening. The lock washer is useful only when the bolt might loosen because of a relative change between the length of the bolt and the parts assembled by it. [2] This change in the length of the bolt can be caused by a number of factors—creep in the bolt, loss of resilience, difference in thermal expansion between the bolt and the bolted members, or wear. In the above static cases, the expanding lock washer holds the nut under axial load and keeps the assembly tight. When relative changes are caused by vibration forces, the lock washer is not nearly as effective.

Rivets are permanent fasteners. They depend on deformation of their structure for their holding action. Rivets are usually stronger than the thread-type fastener and are more economical on a first-cost basis. Rivets are driven either hot or cold, depending upon the mechanical properties of the rivet material. Aluminum rivets, for instance, are cold-driven, since cold working improves the strength of aluminum. Most large rivets are hot-driven, however.

Shaft

Virtually all machines contain shafts. The most common shape for shafts is circular and the cross section can be either solid or hollow (hollow shafts can result in weight saving).

Shafts are mounted in bearings and transmit power through such devices as gears, pulleys, cams and clutches. These devices introduce forces which attempt to bend the shaft; hence, the shaft must be rigid enough to prevent overloading of the supporting bearings. [3] In general, the bending deflection of a shaft should not exceed 0.01 in. per ft. of length between bearing supports.

For diameters less than 3 in., the usual shaft material is cold-rolled steel containing about 0.4 percent carbon. Shafts are either cold-rolled or forged in sizes from 3 in. to 5 in.. For sizes above 5 in., shafts are forged and machined to size. Plastic shafts are widely used for light load applications. One advantage of using plastic is safety in electrical applications, since plastic is a poor conductor of electricity.

Another important aspect of shaft design is the method of directly connecting one shaft to another. This is accomplished by devices such as rigid and flexible couplings.

Bearing

A bearing can be defined as a member specifically designed to support moving machine components. The most common bearing application is the support of a rotating shaft that is transmitting power from one location to another. Since there is always relative motion between a bearing and mating surface, friction is involved. In many instances, such as the design of pulleys, brakes, and clutches, friction is desirable. However, in the case of bearings, the reduction of friction is one of the prime considerations: Friction results in loss of power, the generation of heat, and increased wear of mating surfaces.

The concern of a machine designer with ballbearings and roller bearings is fivefold as follows: (1) Life in relation to load; (2) stiffness, i.e. deflections under load; (3) friction; (4) wear; (5) noise. For moderate loads and speeds the correct selection of a standard bearing on the basis of load rating will usually secure satisfactory performance. The deflection of the bearing elements will become important where loads are high, although this is usually of less magnitude than that of the shafts or other components associated with the bearing. [4] Where speeds are high special cooling arrangements become necessary which may increase frictional drag. Wear is primarily associated with the introduction of contaminants, and sealing arrangements must be chosen with regard to the hostility of the environment.

Notwithstanding the fact that responsibility for the basic design of ball bearings and roller bearings rests with the bearing manufacturer, the machine designer must form a correct appreciation of the duty to be performed by the bearing and be concerned not only with bearing selection but with the conditions for correct installation.

The fit of the bearing races onto the shaft or onto the housings is of critical importance because of their combined effect on the internalclearance of the bearing as well as preserving the desired degree of interference fit. Inadequate interference can induce serious trouble from fretting corrosion. The inner race is frequently located axially by abutting against a shoulder. A radius at this point is essential for the avoidance of stress concentration and ball races are provided with a radius or chamfer to allow space for this.

Ajournal bearing, in its simplest form, is a cylindrical bushing made of a suitable material and containing properly machined inside and outside diameters. The journal is usually the part of a shaft or pin that rotates inside the bearing, as shown in Fig. 4. 1.

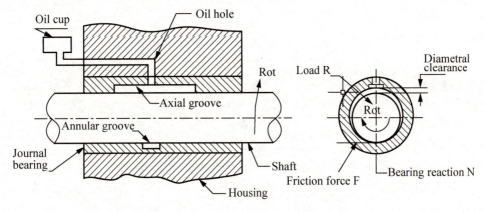

Fig. 4. 1 Journal Bearing

Journal bearings operate with sliding contact, to reduce the problems associated with sliding friction in journal bearings, alubricant is used in conjunction with compatible mating materials. When selecting the lubricant and mating materials, one must take into account bearing pressures, temperatures and also rubbing velocities. The principle function of the lubricant in sliding contact bearings is to prevent physical contact between the rubbing surfaces. Thus the maintenance of an oil film under varying loads, speeds and temperature is the prime consideration in sliding contact bearings.

4.2 Words and Phrases

device	[di'vais]	n. 器件；设备；装置
fastener	['fɑːsnə]	n. 紧固件，紧固零件
classification	[ˌklæsifi'keiʃən]	n. 分类，类别
removable	[ri'muːvəbl]	adj. 可移动的，可拆的
semipermanent	[ˌsemi'pəːmənənt]	adj. 半永久性的

cotter pin	开口销，开尾销
rivet ['rivit]	n. 铆钉；v. 铆；铆接
weld [weld]	v. 焊接，熔接
nuisance ['nju:sns]	n. 障碍，损害
rattle ['rætl]	v. & n. 发出喀啦声，硬物质的撞击声
nut [nʌt]	n 螺帽
bolt [bəult]	n. 螺钉，螺栓 v. 用螺栓连接
screw [skru:]	n. 螺钉，螺旋丝杆
lock washer	锁紧垫圈，止动垫圈，防松垫圈
resilience [ri'ziliəns]	n. 弹力，弹性
aluminum [ˌæju'minjəm]	n. 铝（金属元素符号）
shaft [ʃɑ:ft]	n. 轴
bearing ['bɛəriŋ]	n. 轴承，支承，支撑点，支座
gear [giə]	n. 齿轮
cam [kæm]	n. 凸轮，靠模
clutch [klʌtʃ]	v. & n. 抓住，离合器
cold-roll	v. & n. 冷轧，冷轧机
forge [fɔ:dʒ]	v. & n. 锻造，打制
flexible ['fleksəbl]	adj. 柔软的，适用性强
friction ['frikʃən]	n. 摩擦
brake [breik]	v. 破坏，折断，损坏
wear [wɛə]	v. & n. 磨损，耗损
arrangement [ə'reindʒmənt]	n. 布置，排列
contaminant [kən'tæminənt]	n. 杂质，污染物质
sealing arrangement	密封装置
hostility [hɔs'tiliti]	n. 敌意，恶劣
appreciation [əˌpri:ʃi'eiʃən]	n. 评价，欣赏
interference [ˌintə'fiərəns]	n. 干涉，过盈
fretting ['fretiŋ]	n. 微振磨损
corrosion	n. 腐蚀
abut [əbʌt]	v. 邻接，倚靠
stress concentration	应力集中
shoulder	n. 轴肩
chamfer ['tʃæmfə]	v. & n. 倒角，倒圆，开槽
journal bearing	滑动轴承
cylindrical [ˌsilin'drikəl]	adj. 圆筒状的，柱状的
lubricant ['lju:brikənt]	n. 润滑剂，润滑材料
compatible [kəm'pætəbl]	adj. 相适用，和谐的，一致的

4.3 Complex Sentence Analysis

[1] Fasteners are devices which permit one part to be joined to a second part and, hence, they are involved in almost all designs.

紧固件可以将一个零件与另一个零件相连接。因此，几乎在所有的设计中都要用到紧固件。

① which 引导定语从句修饰 devices。

② to be joined to a second part 第一个不定式 to 表示目的。be joined to 是介词词组，to 表示"到"的意思。

③ are involved in 表示"涉及"、"包括"的意思。

[2] This change in the length of the bolt can be caused by a number of factors-creep in the bolt, loss of resilience, difference in thermal expansion between the bolt and the bolted members, or wear.

这种螺栓长度的变化可由多种因素引起——螺栓内部蠕变、弹性丧失、螺栓与被连接件间的热膨胀差异或磨损。

① factors-creep 是复合词，表示"引起蠕变的因素"。

② loss of resilience 表示"弹性丧失"。

[3] In general, the bending deflection of a shaft should not exceed 0.01 in. per ft. of length between bearing supports.

一般来说，在两个轴承支承之间，轴在每英尺长度上的弯曲变形不应该超过 0.01 英寸。

① 0.01 in. per ft. 表示"每英尺长度上为 0.01 英寸"。

ft 是 foot（英尺）的简写；in 是 inch（英寸）的简写。

② between bearing supports 中 between 表示两者之间，可译为在两轴承支承之间。

[4] Where speeds are high special cooling arrangements become necessary which may increase frictional drag.

在高转速场合下需要有专门的冷却装置，这可能会增大摩擦阻力。

which may increase frictional drag 修饰主语 cooling arrangements。

4.4 Exercise

Translate the Following Paragraphs

A bearing is a connector that permits the connected members to either rotate or translate (more to and from) relative to one another but prevents them from separating in the direction in which loads are applied. In many cases one of the members is fixed, and the bearing acts as a support for the moving member.

Sliding bearing are the simplest to construct and, considering the multitude of pin-jointed devices and structures in use, are probably the most commonly used.

The essential parts of a ball bearing—the inner and outer ring, the balls, and the separator. The inner ring is mounted on a shaft and has a groove in which the balls ride. The outer ring is usually the stationary part of the bearing and also contains a groove to guide and support the balls. The separator prevents contact between the balls and thus reduces friction, wear, and noise from the regions where sliding conditions would occur.

Lesson 5　Engineering Graphic in the Third-angle Projection

5.1　Text

Preface

[1] Graphics comes to our vocabulary from the Greek word grapho, whose extended meaning is "drafting" or "drawing", the drawing is the primary medium for developing and communicating technical ideas. Engineering drawings provide an exact and complete description of objects. In addition to a description of the shape of an object, an engineering drawing gives all further information needed to manufacture the object drawn, such as dimensions, tolerances, and so on. So it is often said the engineering drawing is the common language of engineering. Every engineer must master this language. The main tasks of engineering graphics:

To learn the knowledge of the projections;

To cultivate the drawing making and drawing reading abilities;

To cultivate and develop the spatial analysis and spatial visualization abilities.

As a common language of engineering, the drawing is use to direct the production and make the technical interchange. So, it is necessary to specify, in a unified way, drafting practices, such as the layout of drawings, dimensioning, and so on.

Formation of Three-projection Views

Three projection planes system: Since it is impossible to determine the position of a point with its only one projection, more projection planes are added. Usually, three projection planes perpendicular to each other are used in orthographic projection. They are horizontal projection plane, frontal projection plane and profile projection plane, denoted by H, V, W, respectively.

【3D 投影技术】

The third-angle projection: Three projection planes divide space into eight parts or quadrants numbered from 1 to 8, as shown in Fig. 5.1. [2] According to the Chinese National Standard of Technical Drawings, the first-angle projection is used to make engineering drawings while in some other countries, such as in the USA and Canada, the third-angle projection is used. In this paper we focus on the third-angle projection.

Formation of three-projection views: In first angle, an object is placed in quadrant 1, and observer always looks through the object towards the projection plane. But in third-angle, the object is placed in quadrant 3, and observer always looks through the projection plane towards the object. In third-angle projection, projection plane is assumed transparent, so form into views. The symbols of the first-angle and the third-angle projection in the following Fig. 5.2.

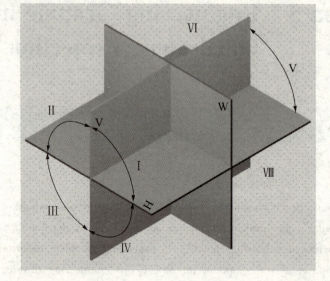

Fig. 5.1　Projection planes

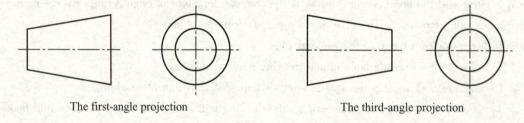

The first-angle projection　　　　　　　　The third-angle projection

Fig. 5.2　The Symbols of the Different Angle Projection

Composite Objects

Projection rules of an object: The front and top views are aligned vertically to show the width of the object; The right and left views are aligned horizontally to show the height of the object; The top and right views have the same depth of the object.

Drawingthree views:

(1) Analyzing-shape method: Any composite object can be broken into a combination of some primary geometric object. Any of these basic shapes can be positive, classified to the superposition style and the cutting style.

(2) Select the projection: Because the front view is the most important one in the three views, it is very important to select adequate projection direction to form the front view.

(3) Drawing steps: Locate the axis lines, center-lines of symmetry and base lines; draw the base with H pencil; check the drawing and darken the lines.

Reading the composite views:

Points of reading views: Break the object into its individual basic shapes; when reading views at least two views should be read simultaneously; master the meanings of lines and areas in views.

Methods to read views:

(1) Analyzing shape method: Break the object down into its basic geometric solids.

(2) Analyzing lines and planes method: Break the object into various surfaces and lines.

For example, like the following Fig. 5.3, the three views of a Composite Object.

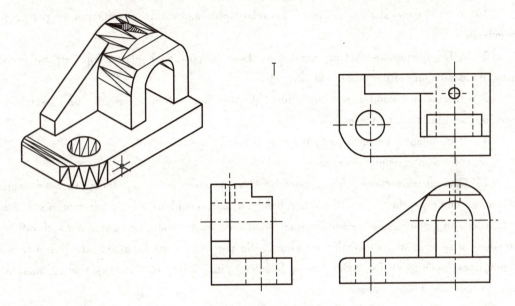

Fig. 5.3 Three Views of Composite Object

Detail Drawings

Detail drawings: It is a drawing that indicates the construction, size, and technical requirements of a part. It describes its shape, gives the dimensions, provide all the information needed to make the part.

The contents of a detail drawing:

(1) A sufficient number of views to give a complete shape description of the exterior and interior constructions of the part.

(2) All the dimensions needed for manufacturing the part.

(3) Technical requirements including tolerances, geometric tolerances, surface roughness, material specification, heat treatments, and so on.

Selection of views: To meet the requirements of making a clear and complete shape description of the object, the first thing to decide before starting to draw is which views are needed and the best way to position the part on the drawing.

(1) Selection of main view: The characteristic shape principle; the functioning position principle; the machining position principle.

(2) Selection of other views: To limit the number of views to the minimum necessary and

sufficient principle; to avoid the use of hidden lines principle; to avoid unnecessary repetition of details principle.

Assembly Drawings

Assembly drawings: A drawing that shows the parts of a machine or machine unit assembled in their relative working position is called an assembly drawing.

The contents of an assembly drawing are as follows:

(1) A set of views showing the positional relationship and mutual operation of the parts being assembled.

(2) A few dimensions that are needed to show the positional relationship between critical parts, the positioning of the product at site, etc.

(3) Technical requirements including all the information necessary for assembling, checking, and maintaining the machine.

(4) Item numbers for each part, the item list, and the title block.

Conventions in assembly drawings:

(1) General conventions: In an assembly drawing there is no gap shown between contact surfaces or mating surfaces. On the other hand, a gap should be shown between non contact surfaces or non mating surfaces; section lines of adjacent parts should be carried out with different directions or spaces; in an assembly drawing, solid parts cut along their axis are shown without section lines; such as shafts, axles, rods, handles, pins, keys, etc. Screws, bolts, nuts, and their washers also keep its shape.

(2)[3] Special conventions: Representation of making the cut along joint face or taking some parts apart; representation of showing parts separately; representation of using phantom lines; exaggerated representation; simplified representation.

5.2　Words and Phrases

graphics ['græfiks]　　　　n. 制图，图学
drafting ['drɑːftiŋ]　　　　n. 草图，制图
drawing [drɔːin]　　　　　n. 绘图，制图，图样
projection [prə'dʒekʃən]　　n. 投影
dimension [di'menʃən]　　　n. 尺寸；v. 给……标注尺寸
spatial analysis　　　　　　空间分析
spatial visualization　　　　空间想象
horizontal projection　　　　水平投影
frontal projection　　　　　正投影
profile projection　　　　　侧投影
quadrant ['kwɔdrənt]　　　n. 象限

center-lines of symmetry	对称中心线
composite object	组合体
detail drawing	零件图
assembly drawing	装配图
phantom line	假想线

5.3 Complex Sentence Analysis

[1] Graphics comes to our vocabulary from the Greek word grapho, whose extended meaning is "drafting" or "drawing", the drawing is the primary medium for developing and communicating technical ideas.

图学一词来源于希腊语 grapho，其延伸意义为"绘图"或"图样"。图样是开发和交流技术思想的主要工具。

[2] According to the Chinese National Standard of Technical Drawings, the first-angle projection is used to make engineering drawings while in some other countries, such as in the USA and Canada, the third-angle projection is used.

依据中国机械制图国家标准，制图采用第一角投影，而其他一些国家像美国和加拿大则采用第三角投影。

[3] Special conventions: Representation of making the cut along joint face or taking some parts apart; representation of showing parts separately; representation of using phantom lines; exaggerated representation; simplified representation.

特殊规定：沿结合面剖切或把某些零件拆开的画法；单独表示零件画法；使用假想线画法；夸大画法；简化画法。

5.4 Exercise

Translate the Following Paragraphs

Similar to an offset in that the cutting-plane line staggers, however, it differs in that the cutting-plane line is offset at some angle other than 90°. When the section is taken the sectional view is drawn as if the cutting-plane is rotated to the plane perpendicular to the line of sight. This is why the right side sectional view may sometimes be elongated (depending on the shape).

Exercise:

Drawing the front view to aligned section.

The Fig. 5.4 is the topic and Fig. 5.5 is the answer.

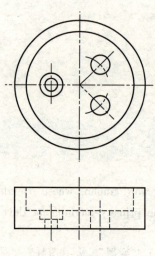
Fig. 5.4 The Topic

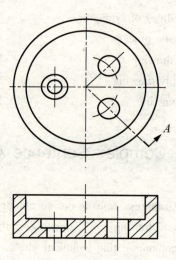
Fig. 5.5 The Answer

Lesson 6　Introduction to CAD/CAM/CAPP

6.1　Text

Throughout the history of our industrial society, many inventions have been patented and whole new technologies have evolved. [1] Perhaps the single development that has impacted manufacturing more quickly and significantly than any previous technology is the digital computer. Computers are being used increasingly for both design and detailing of engineering components in the drawing office.

[2] Computer-aided design (CAD) is defined as the application of computers and graphics software to aid or enhance the product design from conceptualization to documentation. CAD is most commonly associated with the use of an interactive computer graphics system, referred to as a CAD system. Computer-aided design systems are powerful tools and are used in the mechanical design and geometric modeling of products and components.

There are several good reasons for using a CAD system to support the engineering designfunction:

(1) To increase the productivity.
(2) To improve the quality of the design.
(3) To uniform design standards.
(4) To create a manufacturing data base.
(5) To eliminate inaccuracies caused by hand-copying of drawings and inconsistency between drawings.

Models in CAD can be classified as being two-dimensional models, two-and-half- dimensional models, or three-dimensional models. A 2-D model represents a flat part and a 3-D model provides representation of a generalized part shape (as shown in Fig. 6.1). A $2\frac{1}{2}$-D model can be used to represent a part of constant section with no side-wall details. [3] The major advantage of a $2\frac{1}{2}$-D model is that it gives a certain amount of 3-D information about a part without the need to create the database of a full 3-D model.

After a particular design alternative has been developed, some form of engineering analysis must often be performed as a part of the design process. [4] The analysis may take the form stress-strain calculations, heat transfer analysis, dynamic simulation etc. Some examples of the software typically offered on CAD systems are mass properties and Finite Element Method (FEM) analysis.

Mass properties involve the computation of such features of a solid object as its volume, surface area, weight, and center of gravity. FEM analysis is available on most CAD systems to aid in heat transfer, stress-strain analysis, dynamic characteristics, and other engineering computations. Presently, many CAD systems can automatically generate the 2-D or 3-D FEM meshes which are essential to FEM analysis.

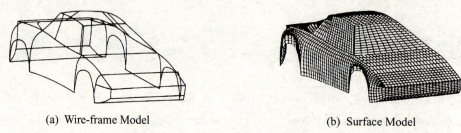

(a) Wire-frame Model   (b) Surface Model

Fig. 6.1 Three-dimension Models

CAM can be defined as computer aided preparation manufacturing including decision-making, process and operational planning, software design techniques, and artificial intelligence, and manufacturing with different types of automation (NC machine, NC machine centers, NC machining cells, NC flexible manufacturing systems), and different types of realization (CNC single unit technology, DNC group technology).

TheCAM covers group technology, manufacturing database, automated and tolerance. Fig. 6.2 illustrates the general scope of CAM.

When a design has frozen, manufacturing can begin. Computers have an

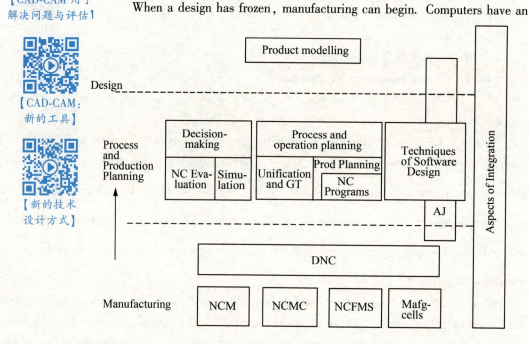

Fig. 6.2 The General Scope of CAM

important role to play in many aspects of production. Modern shipbuilding fabricates structures from welded steel plates that are cut from a large steel sheet. Computer-controlled flame cutters are often used for this task and the computer is used to calculate the optimum layout of the components to minimize waste metal.

Computer aided process planning (CAPP) can be defined as the functions which use computers to assist the work of process planners. The levels of assistance depend on the different strategies employed to implement the system. [5] Lower level strategies only use computers for storage and retrieval of the data for the process plans which will be constructed manually by process planners, as well as for supplying the data which will be used in the planner's new work. In comparison with lower level strategies, higher level strategies use computers to automatically generate process plans for some work pieces of simple geometrical shapes. Sometimes a process planner is required to input the data needed or to modify plans which do not fit specific production requirements well. The highest level strategy, which is the ultimate goal of CAPP, generates process plans by computer, which may replace process planners, when the knowledge and expertise of process planning and working experience have been incorporated into the computer programs. [6] The database in a CAPP system based on the highest level strategy will be directly integrated with conjunctive systems, e.g. CAD and CAM. CAPP has been recognized as playing a key role in CIMS (Computer integrated manufacturing system)

【CAD 的创造性两个珠宝商的故事I】

【CAD 的创造性两个珠宝商的故事II】

【CAD 的创造性两个珠宝商的故事III】

【CAD 的创造性两个珠宝商的故事IV】

6.2 Words and Phrases

evolve [iˈvɔlv]　　　　　　　　　　v. （使）发展，（使）进展，（使）进化
conceptualization [kənˌseptjuəlaiˈzeiən]　n. 化为概念，概念化
documentation [ˌdɔkjumenˈteiʃən]　n. 文件
inconsistency [ˌinkənˈsistənsi]　n. 不兼容性
NC. Numerical Control　　　　数字控制
CNC. Computer Numerical Control　计算机数字控制
interactive [ˌintərˈæktiv]　　　adj. 交互式的
wire-frame models　　　　　　线框模型
surface models　　　　　　　　表面模型
solid models　　　　　　　　　实体模型
stress-strain　　　　　　　　　应力-应变
fabricate [ˈfæbrikeit]　　　　　v. 构成，伪造，虚构
incorporate [inˈkɔːpəreit]　　　adj. 合并的，一体化的

6.3 Complex Sentence Analysis

[1] Perhaps the single development that has impacted manufacturing more quickly and significantly than any previous technology is the digital computer.

① that has impacted manufacturing more quickly and significantly than any previous technology 是定语从句,修饰 development。

② 全句可翻译成:与以前出现的任何科学技术相比,对工程制造业冲击最快、影响更大的是数字计算机。

[2] Computer-aided design (CAD) is defined as the application of computers and graphics software to aid or enhance the product design from conceptualization to documentation.

① be defined as:定义成,定义为。

例如,Teachers are defined as those who do some teaching at school。

② to aid or enhance the product design from conceptualization to documentation 为本句的目的状语;from conceptualization to documentation 为介词短语作定语修饰前面的 design,其字面的解释是从概念到文件,其实指的就是产品设计过程。

[3] The major advantage of a $2\frac{1}{2}$-D model is that it gives a certain amount of 3-D information about a part without the need to create the database of a full 3-D model.

① that 引导的是表语从句。

② without 引导的介词短语在整个句子中充当状语,例如:

I wouldn't have accomplished the designated task without your help.

[4] The analysis may take the form stress-strain calculations, heat transfer analysis, dynamic simulation etc. Some examples of the software typically offered on CAD systems are mass properties and Finite Element Method (FEM) analysis.

① 这里的 take 应译为,包括,包含。

② stress-strain:应力—应变;dynamic simulation:动力学仿真,simulation:仿真,计算;Finite Element Method (FEM):有限元方法,是一种对物体进行物理特性分析的方法,目前被广泛地应用在机械学、传热学、电磁学等领域。

[5] Lower level strategies only use computers for storage and retrieval of the data for the process plans which will be constructed manually by process planners, as well as for supplying the data which will be used in the planner's new work.

① as well as:也,又,介词性词组,常引导名词、代词,或相当于名词性的短语;

② for supplying the data which will be used in the planner's new work,与 for storage and retrieval of the data for the process plans which will be constructed manually by process planners 作用相当,都是 use computers 的目的。

[6] The database in a CAPP system based on the highest level strategy will be directly integrated with conjunctive systems, e.g. CAD and CAM.

based on the highest level strategy, 过去分词短语作定语前面的 system; based on, 基于, 建立在, 在句中可作状语或定语, 试比较:

based on the experimental results, it could be inferred that a heat pipe has a strong ability to transfer heat.

We do believe the facts based on the experiments.

6.4 Exercise

Translate the Following Paragraphs

AutoCAD is a computer-aided drafting and design system implemented on a personal computer. It supports a large number of devices. Device drivers come with the system and include most of the digitizers, printer/plotters, video display boards, and plottersavailable on the market.

AutoCAD supports 2-D drafting and 3-D wire-frame models. The system is designed as a single-user CAD package. The drawing elements are lines, poly-lines of any width, arcs, circles, faces, and solids. There are many ways to define a drawing element. For example, a circle can be defined by the center and its radius, three points, and two end points of its diameter. The system always prompts the user for all options.

Of course, the prompt can be turned off by advanced users. Annotation and dimensioning are also supported. Text and dimension symbols can be placed anywhere on the drawing, at any angle, and at any size. A variety of fonts and styles are also available.

Lesson 7　A Discussion on Modern Design Optimization

7.1　Text

　　The integration of optimization techniques with Finite Element Analysis (FEA) and CAD is having pronounced effects on the product design process. [1] This integration has the power to reduce design costs by shifting the burden from the engineer to the computer. Furthermore, the mathematical rigor of a properly implemented optimization tool can add confidence to the design process. Generally, an optimization method controls a series of applications, including CAD software as well as FEA automatic solid meshers and analysis processors. This combination allows for shape optimizations on CAD parts or assemblies under a wide range of physical scenarios including mechanical and thermal effects.

　　Modern optimization methods perform shape optimizations on components generated within a choice of CAD packages. Ideally, there is seamless data exchange via direct memory transfer between the CAD and FEA applications without the need for file translation. Furthermore, if associativity between the CAD and FEA software exists, any changes made in the CAD geometry are immediately reflected in the FEA model. In the approach taken by ALGOR, the design optimization process begins before the FEA model is generated. The user simply selects which dimension in the CAD model needs to be optimized and the design criterion, which may include maximum stresses, temperatures or frequencies. The analysis process appropriate for the design criteria is then performed. The results of the analysis are compared with the design criterion, and, if necessary without any human intervention, the CAD geometry is updated. [2] Care is taken such that the FEA model is also updated using the principle of associativity, which implies that constraints and loads are preserved from the prior analysis. The new FEA model, including a new high-quality solid mesh, is now analyzed, and the results are again compared with the design criterion. This process is repeated until the design criterion is satisfied. Fig. 7.1 shows the procedure of shape optimization.

Introduction

　　The typical design process involves iterations during which the geometry of the part(s) is altered. In general, each iteration also involves some form of analysis in order to obtain viable engineering results. Optimal designs may require a large number of such iterations, each of which is costly, especially if one considers the value of an engineer's time. The principle behind design optimization applications is to relieve the engineer of the laborious task by automatically conducting these iterations. At first glance, it may appear that design optimization is a means to replace the engineer and his or her expertise from the design loop. This is certainly not the case because any design optimization application cannot infer what should be optimized, and what are the design variables, the quantities or parameters that can be changed in order to achieve an optimum design. Thus, design optimization applications are simply another tool available to the engineer. The usefulness of this tool is gauged by its ability to efficiently identify the optimum.

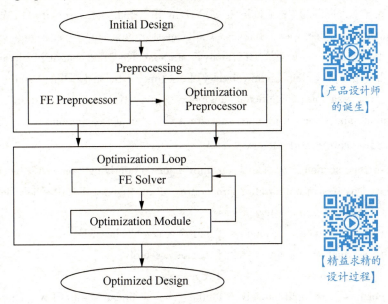

Fig. 7.1 Procedure of Shape Optimization

Design optimization applications tend to be numerically intensive because they must still perform the geometrical and analysis iterations. [3] Fortunately, most design optimization problems can be cast as a mathematical optimization problem for which there exist many efficient solution methods. The drawback to having many methods is that there usually exists an optimum mathematical optimization method for a given problem. This complexity should be remedied by the design optimization application by giving the engineer not only a choice of methods, but also a suggestion as to which approach is most appropriate for his or her design problem.

In this paper, we focus on the design optimization of mechanical parts or assemblies. In this case, a typical optimized quantity is the maximum stress experienced. Typical design variables include geometric quantities, such as the thickness of a particular part. The design of the part or assembly is initiated within a CAD software application. If the component warrants an engineering

analysis, the engineer will generally opt to apply finite element analysis (FEA) in order to model or simulate its mechanical behavior. The FEA results, such as the maximum stress, can be used to ascertain the validity of the design. During the design process, the engineer may alter parameters or characteristics of the CAD and/or FEA models, including some of the physical dimensions, the material or how the part or assembly is loaded or constrained. Associativity between the CAD and FEA software should allow the engineer to alter the model in either application, and have the other automatically reflect these changes. For example, if the thickness of a part is changed or a hole is added in the CAD software, the FEA model's mesh should automatically reflect those changes. Under most circumstances, engineers will employ linear static FEA to obtain the stresses. This analysis approach has the benefit of yielding a solution for FEA models with many elements in relatively little time. Obviously, linear static FEA has drawbacks as well. For example, significant engineering expertise may be required when estimating the magnitude and direction of loads that are a consequence of motion.

Background and Theory

In this section, we focus on the theory underlying some of the mathematical methods employed by design optimization procedures. But, first we describe how the optimization problem arises. Consider a three-step process:

(1) Generation of geometry of part or assembly in CAD;

(2) Creation of FEA model of part or assembly;

(3) Evaluation of results of FEA models.

For now, we limit ourselves to the case of linear static FEA. Therefore, the results are comprised of deflections and stresses at one instance. The manual design process involves all three steps, with the results being used to evaluate whether the design is appropriate. If the design is found inadequate, changes are made to steps (1) or (2) or both. It is clear from this description that the output of the FEA results is what should be optimized, and that any input to the CAD or FEA models can be viewed as a design variable. A design optimization algorithm conducts many FEA runs, each one with a different set of values for the design parameters. Before the manual design approach can be transformed into a design optimization algorithm, there must be associativity between the CAD and FEA applications. The rational behind this requirement is best explained using an example. Consider the initial design stage when the engineer applies constraints on a particular surface of the FEA model; it can be safely assumed that this surface coincides with a surface in the CAD model. Now, if the design optimization algorithm decides to alter the geometry of the CAD surface, then the FEA model must automatically reflect these changes, and apply the constraints on the new representation of this surface. Thus, associativity is required in order to achieve this automatic communication between the CAD and FEA models. Having defined the design optimization problem for mechanical systems, we now describe the mathematics used to solve these problems.

Most optimization problems are made up of three basic components.

(1) An objective function which we want to minimize (or maximize). For instance, in designing an automobile panel, we might want to minimize the stress in a particular region.

(2) A set of design variables that affect the value of the objective function. In the automobile panel design problem, the variables used define the geometry and material of the panel.

(3) A set of constraints that allow the design variables to have certain values but exclude others. In the automobile panel design problem, we would probably want to limit its weight.

It is possible to develop an optimization problem without constraints. Some may argue that almost all problems have some form of constraints. For instance, the thickness of the automotive panel cannot be negative. Although in practice, answers that make good sense in terms of the underlying physics, such as a positive thickness, can often be obtained without enforcing constraints on the design variables.

Benefits and Drawbacks

The elimination or reduction of repetitive manual tasks has been the impetus behind many software applications. Automatic design optimization is one of the latest applications used to reduce man-hours at the expense of possibly increasing the computational effort. It is even possible that an automatic design optimization scheme may actually require less computational effort than a manual approach. This is because the mathematical rigor on which these schemes are based may be more efficient than a human-based solution. Of course, these schemes do not replace human intuition, which can occasionally significantly shorten the design cycle.[4] One definite advantage of automated methods over manual approaches is that software applications, if implemented correctly, should consider all viable possibilities. That is, no variable combination of the design parameters is left unconsidered. Thus, designs obtained using design optimization software should be accurate to within the resolution of the overall method.

7.2　Words and Phrases

optimization [ˌɔptimaiˈzeiʃən]	n. 最佳化，最优化
finite element analysis (FEA)	有限元分析
computer aided design (CAD)	计算机辅助设计
burden [ˈbəːdn]	n. 担子，负担，责任，义务
rigor [ˈrigə]	n. 严格，严密，精确
mesh [meʃ]	n. 网孔，网格，网状物
scenario [siˈnɑːriəu]	n. [意大利语] 方案，情况
seamless [ˈsiːmlis]	adj. 无缝的，无伤痕的
criterion [kraiˈtiəriən]	n. 标准，规范，准则，判据
iteration [ˌitəˈreiʃən]	n. 反复，迭代

geometry [dʒiˈɔmitri]	n.	几何学，几何图形（形状），表面形状
gauge [geidʒ]	v.	判断，测试，测定，测量
intensive [inˈtensiv]	adj.	强化的，加强的
cast [kɑːst]	v.	计算，派（角色），分类整理
assembly [əˈsembli]	n.	组合，装配，部件，汇编
variable [ˈvɛəriəbl]	n.	可变物，变量 adj. 可变的，变量的
warrant [ˈwɔrənt]	v.	成为……的证据，保证，证明……是正确的
yield [jiːld]	v.	产出，产生，提供，给予，得出
expertise [ˌekspəˈtiːz]	n.	专家的意见，专门知识，经验；专家
underlying [ˌʌndəˈlaiiŋ]	adj.	（做）基础的，根本的，在下面的
linear [ˈliniə]	adj.	线的，直线的，线性的
function [ˈfʌŋkʃən]	n.	功能，作用，职责，[数] 函数
constraint [kənˈstreint]	n.	约束，强制，局促
impetus [ˈimpitəs]	n.	推动力，促进，刺激，激励
scheme [skiːm]	n.	计划，阴谋，方案，图解

7.3 Complex Sentence Analysis

[1] This integration has the power to reduce design costs by shifting the burden from the engineer to the computer.

① power：能力，has the power to 翻译成"能够"。
② 注意 power 在作为"能力"时和 ability 的区别，和 ability 相比 power 更强调"本能，智能和体能"，试比较：

Some animals have the power to see in the dark.
He has a strong ability to deal with the business.

[2] Care is taken such that the FEA model is also updated using the principle of associativity, which implies that constraints and loads are preserved from the prior analysis.

① 主句很短，such that 引导状语从句。
② which 引导非限定性定语从句，which 代表前面这个句子的意思。
③ 此外上述句子，还可写成以下两种形式：

Care is taken such that the FEA model is also updated using the principle of associativity, as implies that constraints and loads are preserved from the prior analysis.
As implies that constraints and loads are preserved from the prior analysis, Care is taken such that the FEA model is also updated using the principle of associativity.

[3] Fortunately, most design optimization problems can be cast as a mathematical optimization problem for which there exist many efficient solution methods.

① cast：派（角色），此处 be cast as 转译为"看成"。

② for which…：介词 + which 引导的定语从句修饰其前面的 problem。试比较：
At an instant, the energy in the control volume includes therate at which thermal and mechanical energy enters and leave through the control surface.

[4] One definite advantage of automated methods over manual approaches is that software applications, if implemented correctly, should consider all variable possibilities.

① advantage…over…：与……相比的优越性
② that 引导表语从句，其中 if implemented correctly 是插入短语。

7.4　Exercise

Translate the Following Paragraphs

Optimization is concerned with finding the best possible solution, formally referred to as the optimal solution, to a particular problem (for example, a design problem). The term optimization is often used very loosely in general speech, for our purposes it has a precise meaning: the action of finding the best possible solution to a problem as defined by an unambiguous criterion: the cost function.

Generally, there is more than one solution to a design problem, and the first solution is not necessarily the best. The need for optimization is inherent in the design process. A mathematical theory of optimization has become highly developed and is being applied to design where design functions can be expressed by mathematical equations or with finite element computer modeling. Optimization techniques may require considerable depth of knowledge and mathematical skill to select the appropriate optimization techniques and work through it to a solution. The growing acceptance of the Taguchi method comes from its applicability to a wide variety of problems with a methodology that is not highly mathematical.

Byoptimal design we mean the best of all feasible designs. Optimization is the process of maximizing a desired quantity or minimizing an undesired one. Optimization theory is the body of mathematics that deals with the properties of maxima and minima and how to find maxima and minima numerically.

Lesson 8   Using Dynamic Simulation in the Development of Construction Machinery

8.1   Text

Introduction

【隧道钻机制造者】

[1] The general motives for "Virtual Prototyping" are probably familiar to all engineers: Stricter legal requirements (e.g. with regard to exhaust emissions and sound) and tougher customer demands (e.g. with regard to performance and handling) lead to more advanced, complex systems, which are harder to optimize. With traditional methods, development will cost more and need more time. In contrast to this, increased competition demands lower development cost and shorter project times.

"Virtual Prototyping" has been generally adopted in the vehicle industry as a major step towards solving this conflict both on the consumer side (cars) and on the commercial side (trucks and buses as shown in Fig. 8.1). Having started with simulation of sub-systems, the state-of-the-art is simulation of complete vehicles, mostly for evaluation of handling, comfort, and durability but also for crash-tests.

Fig. 8.1   Multi-body Model of a Volvo L220E Wheel Loader, Loading Gravel

[2] One reason for the off-road equipment industry lagging behind can be found in the size of these companies: Being significantly smaller, broad investments in the latest CAE tools (together with the necessary training) take longer until amortization. The other, and probably more important reason is that the products are very different to those of the on-road vehicle industry—not only geometrically (size), but topologically (sub-systems of various domains and their interconnections).

Using Dynamic Simulation in the Development of Construction Machinery   Lesson 8

Cases have recently been published where complete machines were simulated for evaluation of the simulation technique itself, sub-systems, comfort-related aspects, or durability. This paper too, will deal with dynamic simulation of complete machines, but for analysis and optimization of overall performance and related aspects. The focus will be on wheel loaders with hydrodynamic transmissions, but most findings (and questions) will be also applicable to other off-road machinery.

【挖掘机】

Design Process and Visualization

The aim of the present project isevolution of the current product development process, rather than revolution by means of Design Science. The research question is therefore how to augment the existing design process with dynamic simulation. [3] As mentioned before, the focus is on analysis and optimization of overall performance and related aspects.

The revised design process has to fulfil the following non-optional targets: Lead to development of compared with today. Saved resources (time, money, and people) can then be spent on optimizing one or all of the aspects mentioned in the first item in the list.

(1) Products of at least equal high performance, efficiency, and operateability;
(2) With increased robustness;
(3) In a shorter time;
(4) At a lower development cost.

In an earlier project, a valuable lesson has been learned: Speed matters when it comes to iterations, especially in the concept phase. When Volvo's old loading unit calculation program was to be replaced by a more modern version, this was done with a proprietary simulation system, which was based on a multi-body system (MBS) and a modern database. The development was done in-house. This new simulation system has proved to be more flexible, more accurate, and especially more efficient for the user, except for some pre-study engineers, who used the superior speed of the old calculation program to brute-force optimize loading unit geometries. Since the new system obtains results by multi-body simulation, rather than calculation of hard-coded explicit equations, one run takes a couple of seconds longer than with the old program. Brute—force optimizations of the old type are no longer time efficient. If this had been known before, i.e. if it had been included in the project targets, one could have developed a special downscaled version, that was less accurate but faster. Introduction of the new system forced those pre-study engineers to abandon a time-efficient technique that worked well.

A similar risk can be seen with this research project: The current initial (static) calculation loop (as shown in Fig. 8.2) is fast and reasonably accurate. The shortcoming today is rather that the dynamic behaviour of the complete machine is first evaluated by testing a functional prototype, followed by testing a "real" prototype. Therefore a moderately revised process is proposed.

As practiced today, the process starts with feeding the product targets into the initial static calculation loop. If no satisfactory solution can be found, the targets need to be revised. The next step is described as "Dynamically augmented, static calculations" (see below for an explanation).

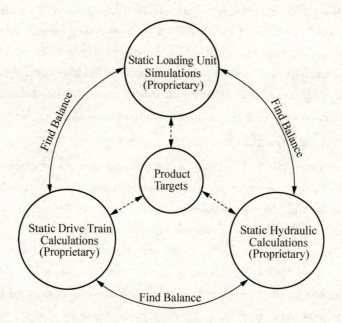

Fig. 8.2 Initial Calculation Loop for Balancing the Main System

Here, as well as in the next step "Dynamic simulation of complete machine", non-fulfilled product targets do not necessarily lead to a reiteration, as long as the deviation can be approved. Since product targets will probably never cover all product properties (including dynamic behaviour), this checkpoint will give the whole process some flexibility. [4] Only if the deviation is too high will a new static calculation loop need to be started (with the original product targets as input). If no alternative layout candidate can be calculated, the product targets need to be revised. Since simulating complete machines can take a long time, a quick check on whether the solution from the initial loop is dynamically feasible, would be of great help. This is supposed to be done in the second step "Dynamically augmented, static calculations". Concrete methods still need to be developed. However, one example can be given (applies to machines with hydrodynamic transmissions and LS-hydraulics): a critical phase in a so-called "short loader cycle" (or V-cycle) is when the machine, coming backwards with a full bucket, changes direction towards the load receiver (e.g. an articulated hauler or a dump truck). During that time, there is a close interaction between the main subsystems.

(1) In order to reverse the machine, the operator lowers the engine speed (otherwise the gear shifting will be jerky and the transmission couplings might wear out prematurely). Less torque is available at lower speeds. Additionally, the engine response is worse at lower speeds, mainly due to inertia of the turbo charger (and smoke limiter settings, as explained earlier).

(2) When switching gears from reverse to forward, the loader is still rolling backwards. This forces an abrupt change of rotational direction of the torque converter's turbine wheel, thus greatly increasing the slip, which leads to a sudden increase in torque demand from the engine.

(3) Some operators do not stop lifting the loading unit while reversing, thus requiring high

oil flow throughout the whole process. The oil flow is proportional to the hydraulic pump's displacement and shaft speed, and the load-sensing pumps can be assumed to be directly connected to the engine crankshaft. Thus, at lower engine speeds and high demand of oil flow, the displacement goes towards maximum (simply put). The amount of torque that a pump demands of the engine is proportional to its displacement and hydraulic pressure. Since the loader's bucket is full and due to the loading unit's geometry, hydraulic pressure is high. With displacement at maximum, this too leads to an increased torque demand.

Both drive train and hydraulics thus suddenly apply higher load to an already weakened engine. All depends on the time scale of these three concurrent phenomena, which is why a satisfactory answer can only be given by a detailed dynamic simulation (or testing of a real machine, i.e. a functional prototype). However, an approximate, less time-consuming first approach is possible: given the loader speed when switching gears from reverse to forward, and given the engine speed at that time, the maximum slip between the pump wheel and the turbine wheel of the torque converter can be calculated, and thus the maximum demanded engine torque (by using the torque converter's specifications). In the worst case scenario, hydraulic pressure and pump displacement can be assumed to be maximal. Together with the engine speed, this gives the second engine torque demand. If the sum of both torque demands is larger than the available steady-state engine torque at that speed, the proposed system layout will almost certainly lead to dynamic problems. If the available steady-state engine torque is considerably larger than the sum of both torque demands, the system will most probably function as intended. [5] To check the case in between, it is important to consider that due to factors such as turbo charger inertia and smoke limiter mentioned before, an accelerating engine seldom has full steady-state torque at lower engine speeds. Therefore, checking against the static torque curve might give a false sense of security.

What is needed is adynamic engine torque curve, measured at a typical less gap between static and dynamic torque at lower acceleration (red, dashed curve).

Due to faster boost pressure build-up relative to engine speed acceleration rate. Assuming the engine is released to low idle during reversing (worstcase); the acceleration rate is simply obtainable as the speed difference from the engines max torque speed to low idle, divided by a typical time for the reversal phase. Using a text bench with an electro-magnetic brake, an engine run-up with a forced acceleration as described above can be performed. The amount of available torque during that phase equals the necessary braking torque (as shown in Fig. 8.3).

In Fig. 8.3, the red, dashed curves represent a test, where the engine was allowed to accelerate less. In theory, this should not only generate more available torque because the rotating parts consume less torque for acceleration, but also because there is more time for turbo boost pressure to be built up. As can be seen in the first diagram, the engine torque itself does not increase faster in time for the case with less forced acceleration. Instead, confirming the theory, more torque is available relative

【塔吊】

to engine speed, expressed as a smaller gap between static and dynamic torque curve for the slower acceleration. If the engine were allowed to accelerate sufficiently slowly, the dynamic torque curve (bold line style) would follow the static one (thin line style).

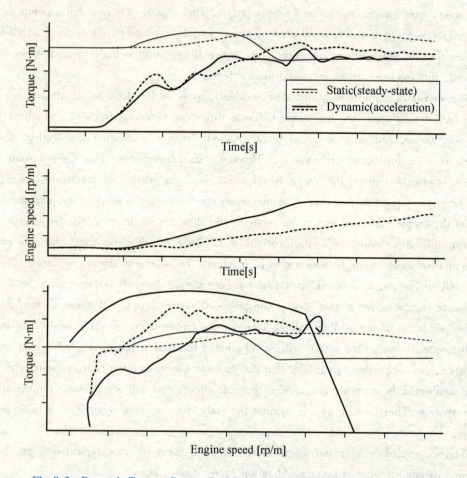

Fig. 8.3 Dynamic Torque Curve of a Modern, Turbo—Charged Diesel Engine

In order to quickly sort out system layout candidates that will lead to dynamic problems, more such checking methods need to be developed, together with refinement of the existing rules of thumb.

Taking a critical look at the proposed revised design process, even if it has been labeled as "evolutionary rather than revolutionary" in the beginning of this section, it implies a bigger change than might be obvious at first glance. With its introduction, functional prototypes are only built to verify system layouts that have passed both steps that check the dynamic behaviour. These steps are given the great responsibility of deciding whether a certain system layout can be further pursued or is to be sent back for reiteration. The worst scenario would be to reject cases that actually would work in reality, but nobody will ever know since only approved cases enter the functional prototype phase. To avoid this and to build confidence, there has to be a smooth transition between current practice and the proposed process.

Conclusion and Outlook

This paper presented the joint research by Volvo Wheel Loaders andLinköping University on simulation of complete machines for analysis and optimization of overall performance. The motivation on the side of the industrial partner is to develop products of equally high performance, efficiency and operatability, but with more robustness regarding these aspects, in a shorter time and at a lower total development cost. A revised product development process (with regard to the research topic) has been proposed. Examples of areas for future research have also been presented. Research in the immediate future will focus on a definition of operatability (including quantification), as well as practical simulation problems (such as defining modules and physically motivated and intuitive interfaces between them).

In a longer perspective, a measure of complexity needs to be developed. Research will be done on how to optimize operatability, which will also include a look at control strategies.

8.2 Words and Phrases

dynamic [daiˈnæmik]	adj. 动力的，动力学的，动态的
dynamic simulation	动态仿真
prototype [ˈprəutətaip]	n. 原型；模型；典型；榜样；样机
Virtual Prototyping	虚拟原型机
off-road [ˌɔːfˈrəud]	adj. 道路之外的，越野的
lag [læg]	v. 缓缓而行，滞后；v. 落后于，押往监狱，加上外套
amortization [əˌmɔːtiˈzeiʃən]	n. 摊销，分期偿付，分期偿还
topologically [ˌtɔpəˈlɔdʒik(əl)i]	adv. 拓扑地
optimization [ˌɔptimaiˈzeiʃən]	n. 最佳化，最优化
hydrodynamic [ˈhaidrəudaiˈnæmik]	adj. 水力的，水压的，液力的，流体动力学的
augment [ɔːˈgment]	v. 增加，增大；n. 增加
operatability [ˌɔpəˈreitəbiliti]	n. 操作性能
robustness [rəˈbʌstnis]	n. 强[健]壮，雄壮；健全；耐用，坚固
proprietary [prəˈpraiətəri]	adj. 专利的，独占的，有财产的，私有的
downscale [ˈdaunˌskeil]	v. 缩减……规模；按比例缩减，减少
reiteration [riːˌitəˈreiʃən]	n. 重复，反复
checkpoint [ˈtʃekpɔint]	n. 关卡，公路检查站，边境检查站，检查点
jerky [ˈdʒəːki]	adj. 急拉的，急动的
concurrent [kənˈkʌrənt]	adj. 同时，兼，并行地
scenario [siˈnɑːriəu]	n. 游戏的关，某一特定情节
intuitive [inˈtjuː(ː)itiv]	adj. 直觉的，本能的；天生的
perspective [pəˈspektiv]	n. 透视图，远景，前途，观点，看法，观察

8.3　Complex Sentence Analysis

[1] The general motives for "Virtual Prototyping" are probably familiar to all engineers.

be familiar to = be known to（某人或某物）对……是熟悉的

e.g. The food and the climate here are familiar to me.

我对这儿的饮食和气候比较熟悉。

试比较：be familiar with（某人）熟悉……。

[2] One reason for the off-road equipment industry lagging behind can be found in the size of these companies.

该句中 lagging behind 作定语修饰前面的 industry，意思是"落后，滞后"。

[3] As mentioned before, the focus is on analysis and optimization of overall performance and related aspects.

此句中，as 替代 the focus is on analysis and optimization of overall performance and related aspects。

[4] Only if the deviation is too high will a new static calculation loop need to be started (with the original product targets as input).

当 only 引导副词、副词性词组和状语句子时，后面所跟的主句一般需倒装。

试比较：Only then did I realize made such a big mistake.

只是在那时，我才认识到我犯了一个多么大的错误。

Only when one loses health doeshe know its value.

只有当人们身体不好时才认识到健康的重要性。

[5] To check the case in between, it is important to consider that due to factors such as turbo charger inertia and smoke limiter mentioned before, an accelerating engine seldom has full steady-state torque at lower engine speeds.

in between：在中间，在……之间；挡路。

8.4　Exercise

Translate the Following Paragraph

As shown earlier, off-road equipment consists of systems from various domains, and most of them need to be taken into account when simulating performance of complete machines, which is usually a collaborative activity. As noted by many researchers, engineers have often already chosen one domain-specific simulation program that they are familiar with. Instead of forcing migration to one monolithic simulation system that can be used in several domains (but offers only limited functionality in the individual domain), a better approach is to couple the specialized, single-domain tools. This has the advantage that both pre- and post-processing are done decentralized, in the engineer's domain-specific tools. J. Larsson develops a technique for such co-simulation and applies it to a model of a complete wheel loader. The present research project will use this approach and further develop it.

Lesson 9　Engineering Tolerance

9.1　Text

Introduction

A solid is defined by its surface boundaries. [1] Designers typically specify a component's nominal dimensions such that it fulfils its requirements. In reality, components cannot be made repeatedly to nominal dimensions, due to surface irregularities and the intrinsic surface roughness. [2] Some variability in dimensions must be allowed to ensure manufacture is possible. However, the variability permitted must not be so great that the performance of the assembled parts is impaired. The allowed variability on the individual component dimensions is called the tolerance.

Component Tolerances

Control of dimensions is necessary in order to ensure assembly and interchangeability of components. Tolerances are specified on critical dimensions that affect clearances and interferences fits. One method of specifying tolerances is to state the nominal dimension followed by the permissible variation, so a dimension could be stated as 40.000 mm ± 0.003 mm. [3] This means that the dimension should be machined so that it is between 39.997 mm and 40.003 mm. Where the variation can vary either side of the nominal dimension, the tolerance is called a bilateral tolerance. For a unilateral tolerance, one tolerance is zero, e.g. $40_0^{+0.006}$.

【自行车的制造过程 I】

【自行车的制造过程 II】

【自行车的制造过程 III】

Most organizations have general tolerances that apply to dimensions when an explicit dimension is not specified on a drawing. For machined dimensions a general tolerance may be ± 0.5 mm. So a dimension specified as 15.0 mm may range between 14.5 mm and 15.5 mm. Other general tolerances can be applied to features such as angles, drilled and punched holes, castings, forgings, weld beads and fillets.

[4] When specifying a tolerance for a component, reference can be made to previous drawings or general engineering practice. Tolerances are typically specified in bands as defined in British or ISO standards. Table 9-1 gives a guide for the general applications of tolerances. For a given tolerance, e.g. H7/s6, a set of numerical values is available from a corresponding chart for the size of component under consideration. The following (Table 9-1) is the specific examples for a shaft or cylindrical spigot fitting into a hole.

Table 9-1 Example of Tolerance Bands and Typical Applications

Class	Description	Characteristic	ISO code	Assembly	Application
Clearance	Free running fit	Good for large temperature variations, high running speeds or heavy journal pressures	H9/d9	Noticeable clearance	Multiple bearing shafts, hydraulic position in cylinder, removable levers, bearing for rollers
	Close running fit	For running on accurate machines and accurate location at moderate speeds and journal pressures	H8/f7	Clearance	Machine tool main bearings, crankshaft and connecting rod bearings, shaft sleeves, clutch sleeves, guide blocks
	Sliding fit	When parts are not intended to run freely, but must more and turn and locateaccurately	H7/g6	Push fit without noticeable Clearance	Push on gear wheels and clutches, connecting rod bearings, indicator pistons
	Locationclearance fit	Provides snug fit for location of stationary parts, but can be freely assembled	H7/h6	Hand pressure with lubrication	Gears, tailstock sleeves, adjusting rings, loose bushes for piston bolts and pipe line
Transition	Location transition fit	For accurate location (compromise between clearance and interference fit)	H7/k6	Easily tapped with hammer	Pulleys, clutches, gears, fly wheels, fixed hand wheels and permanent levers
	Location transition fit	For more accurate location	H7/n6	Needs pressure	Motor shaft armatures, toothed collars on wheels
Interference	Locational interference fit	For parts requiring rigidity and alignment with accuracy of location	H7/p6	Needs pressure	Split journal bearings
	Medium drive fit	Forordinary steel parts or shrink fits on light sections	H7/s6	Needs pressure or temperature difference	Clutch hubs, bearings, bushes in blocks, wheels, connecting rods. Bronze collars on grey cast iron hubs

Standard Fits for Holes and Shafts

A standard engineering task is to determine tolerances for a cylindrical component, e.g. a shaft, fitting or rotating inside a corresponding cylindrical component or hole. The tightness of fit will depend on the application. [5] For example, a gear located onto a shaft would require a "tight" interference fit, where the diameter of the shaft is actually slightly greater than the inside diameter of the gear hub in order to be able to transmit the desired torque. Alternatively, the diameter of a journal bearing must be greater than the diameter of the shaft to allow rotation. [6] Given that it is not economically possible to manufacture components to exact dimensions, some variability in sizes of both the shaft and hole dimension must be specified. However, the range of variability should not be so large that the operation of the assembly is impaired. Rather than having an infinite variety of tolerance dimensions that could be specified, national and international standards have been produced defining bands of tolerances, examples of which are listed in Table 9-1, e. g. H11/c11. To turn this information into actual dimensions corresponding tables exist, defining the tolerance levels for the size of dimension under consideration. In order to use this information the following list and Fig. 9.1 give definitions used in conventional tolerance. Usually the hole-based system is used, as the results in a reduction in the variety of drill, reamer, broach and gauge tooling required.

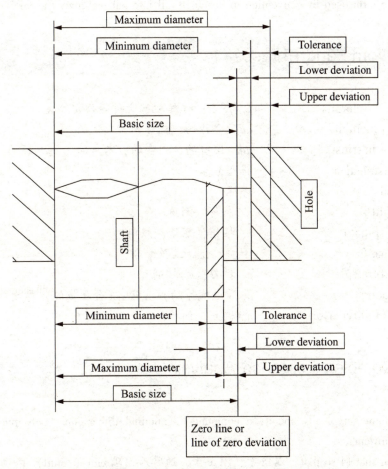

Fig. 9.1 The Definitions Used in Conventional Tolerance

Size: a number expressing in a particular unit the numerical value of a dimension.

Actual size: the size of a part as obtained by measurement.

Limits of size: the maximum and minimum sizes permitted for a feature.

Maximum limit of size: the greater of the two limits of size.

Minimum limit of size: the smaller of the two limits of size.

Basic size: the size by reference to which the limits of size are fixed.

Deviation: the algebraic difference between a size and the corresponding basic size.

Actual deviation: the algebraic difference between the actual size and the corresponding basic size.

Upper deviation: the algebraic difference between the maximum limit of size and the corresponding basic size.

Lower deviation: the algebraic difference between the minimum limit of size and the corresponding basic size.

Tolerance: the difference between the maximum limit of size and the minimum limit of size.

Shaft: the term used by convention to designate all external features of a part.

Hole: the term used by convention to designate all internal features of a part.

9.2 Words and Phrases

tolerance [ˈtɔlərəns]	n. 公差；v. 给机器部件等规定公差
nominal [ˈnɔminl]	adj. 公称的，标称的，额定的
intrinsic [inˈtrinsik]	adj. 固有的，内在的，本质的
normal distribution	正态分布
weld bead	焊缝
fillet [ˈfilit]	n. 圆角，倒角
spigot [ˈspigət]	n. 插销，塞子，阀门
interference fit	干涉配合，过盈配合
broach [brəutʃ]	n. 拉刀；v. 拉削
gauge [geidʒ]	n.（电线等的）直径；（金属板的）厚度；量具
deviation [ˌdiːviˈeiʃən]	n. 偏差，偏移

9.3 Complex Sentence Analysis

[1] Designers typically specify a component's nominal dimensions such that it fulfils its requirements.

such that 同 so that 以便于、以至于，通常后面跟 can (could) + 动词原形。

[2] Some variability in dimensions must be allowed to ensure manufacture is possible.

在这个句子中，to ensure manufacture is possible 是 Some variability 的主语补足语，同时，manufacture is possible 为 ensure 的宾语从句。

e.g. A lot of students will be allowed to do whatever is good for them.

人们允许大多数学生做对他们有益的事情。

[3] This means that the dimension should be machined so that it is between 39. 997 mm and 40. 003 mm.

在该句中，mean 的中文意思是"意味着"。实际上，当 mean 为动词时需注意以下两个结构。

① mean to do something：计划做某事、打算做某事，主语通常是人。

e. g. I meant to have seen you, but I was too busy at that time.

我原打算去看你的，但是那时实在太忙。

② mean doing something：意味着做某事，主语通常是物。

e. g. What he said at the meeting meant his finishing the task given by himself。

他在会上的发言意味着他将独自地完成所分配的任务。

[4] When specifying a tolerance for a component, reference can be made to previous drawings or general engineering practice.

在这个句子中，When specifying a tolerance for a component 相当于 When we are specifying a tolerance for a component，由于 specify 的逻辑主语就是主句的主语，同时该时间状语的主要谓语动词是 be，按照英语语法规则，可将 we are 省去。

[5] Forexample, a gear located onto a shaft would require a "tight" interference fit, where the diameter of the shaft is actually slightly greater than the inside diameter of the gear hub in order to be able to transmit the desired torque.

① 在这个句子中，located onto a shaft 为过去分词短语作定语，其作用相当于一个定语从句。

② where the diameter of the shaft is actually slightly greater than the inside diameter of the gear hub in order to be able to transmit the desired torque 为非限定性定语从句修饰前面的 a "tight" interference fit。

e. g. The man followed by a lot of students is a professor studying simulation technology.

身后有许多学生跟着的那名男子是一位从事仿真技术研究的教授。

I like living inHefei, where a lot of universities are located.

我喜欢生活在合肥，那儿有许多大学。

[6] Given that it is not economically possible to manufacturecomponents to exact dimensions, some variability in sizes of both the shaft and hole dimension must be specified.

在句中，Given = provided，意为"假定"。

e. g. Given that all we want has been prepared, what on earth should we do next?

假定我们所需要的一切都准备好了，那么下一步我们究竟应该做些什么呢？

9. 4 Exercise

Translate the Following Paragraphs

Computers are usedextensively in most engineering functions. Engineering is a profession in which a knowledge of the natural sciences is applied with judgment to develop ways of using the materials and forces of nature. Typical engineering functions using CAPACS (computer-aided production and control systems) are design, process planning, analysis and optimization, synthesis, evaluation and documentation, simulation, modeling, and quality control planning. Using CAPACS in engineering increases the productivity of engineers and improves the quality of designs.

Forexample, the application of computers to an engineering design process is performed by a CAD system. Engineers can design and thoroughly test concepts quickly and simply from one workstation. Computers permit engineers to take a concept from its original design through testing to numerical control (NC) output, or a combination of steps in between. They perform complex scientific and engineering computations rapidly with high accuracy, calculate physical properties before actual parts are made and provide a fast, easy method to create model of even the most complex parts.

The computer hasinfluenced the way products are designed, documented and released for production. As technology develops, engineering operation becoming more and more automated are relieving the engineer of many tedious manual calculations.

Lesson 10 Numerical Control

10.1 Text

[1] Numerical control (NC) is a form of programmable automation in which the processing equipment is controlled by means of numbers, letters, and other symbols. The numbers, letters, and symbols are coded in an appropriate format to define a program of instructions for a particular work part or job. The instructions are provided by either of the two binary coded decimal systems: the Electronic Industries Association (EIA) code, or the American Standard Code for Information Interchange (ASCII). ASCII-coded machine control units will not accept EIA coded instructions and vice versa. Increasingly, however, control units are being made to accept instructions in either code. [2] Automation operation by NC is readily adaptable to the operation of all metalworking machines. Lathes, milling machines, drill presses, boring machines, grinding machines, turret punches, flame or wire-cutting and welding machines, and even pipe benders are available with numerical controls.

BasicComponents of NC

A numerical control system consists of the following three basic components:
(1) Program instructions.
(2) Machine control unit.
(3) Processing equipment.

The program instructionsare the detailed step by step commands that direct the processing equipment. [3] In its most common form, the commands refer to positions of a machine tool spindle with respect to the worktable on which the part is fixed. More advanced instructions include selection of spindle speeds, cutting tools, and other functions.

The machine control unit (MCU) consists of the electronics and control hardware that reads and interprets the program of instructions and convert it into mechanical actions of the machine tool or other processing equipment.

The processing equipment is the component that performs metal process. In the most common example of numerical control, it is used to perform machining operations. The processing equipment consists of the worktable and spindle as well as the motors and controls needed to drive them.

Types of NC

There are two basic types of numerical control systems: point to point and contouring.

Point to point control system, also called positioning, are simpler than contouring control system. Its primary purpose is to move a tool or workpiece from one programmed point to another. Usually the machine function, such as a drilling operation, is also activated at each point by command from the NC Program. Point to point systems are suitable for hole machining operations such as drilling, countersinking, counterboring, reaming, boring and tapping. Hole punching machines, spotwelding machines, and assembly machines also use point to point NC systems.

Contouring system, also known as the continuous path system, positioning and cutting operations are both along controlled paths but at different velocities. Because the tool cuts as it travels along a prescribed path, accurate control and synchronization of velocities and movements are important. The contouring system is used on lathes, milling machines, grinders, welding machinery, and machining centers. Movement along the path, or interpolation, occurs incrementally, by one of several basic methods. There are a number of interpolation schemes that have been developed to deal with the various problems that are encountered in generating a smooth continuous path with a contouring type NC system. They include linear interpolation, circular interpolation, helical interpolation, parabolic interpolation and cubic interpolation. In all interpolations, the path controlled is that of the center of rotation of the tool. Compensation for different tools, different diameter tools, or tools wear during machining, can be made in the NC program.

Programming for NC

[4] A program for numerical control consists of a sequence of directions that causes an NC machine to carry out a certain operation, machining being the most commonly used process. Programming for NC may be done by an internal programming department, on the shop floor, or purchased from an outside source. Also, programming may be done manually or with computer assistance.

The program contains instructions and commands. Geometric instructions pertain to relative movements between the tool and the workpiece. Processing instructions pertain to spindle speeds, feeds, tools, and so on. Travel instructions pertain to the type of interpolation and slow or rapid movements of the tool or worktable. Switching commands pertain to on/off position for coolant supplies, spindle rotation, direction of spindle rotation, tool changes, workpiece feeding, clamping, and so on. The first NC programming language was developed by MIT developmental work on NC programming systems in the late 1950s and called APT (Automatically Programmed Tools).

DNC and CNC

The development of numerical control was a significant achievement in batch and job shop manufacturing, from both a technological and a commercial viewpoint. There have been two enhancements and extensions of NC technology, including:

(1) Direct numerical control.
(2) Computer numerical control.

Numerical Control Lesson 10

Direct numerical control can be defined as a manufacturing system in which a number of machines are controlled by a computer through direct connection and in real time. The tape reader is omitted in DNC, thus relieving the system of its least reliable component. Instead of using the tape reader, the part program is transmitted to the machine tool directly from the computer memory. In principle, one computer can be used to control more than 100 separate machines. (One commercial DNC system during the l970s boasted a control capability of up to 256 machine tools.) The DNC computer is designed to provide instructions to each machine tool on demand. When the machine needs control commands, they are communicated to it immediately.

【CNC与金属切割】

【CNC与切割车床】

Since the introduction of DNC, there have been dramatic advances in computer technology. The physical size and cost of a digital computer has been significantly reduced at the same time that its computational capabilities have been substantially increased. In numerical control, the result of these advances has been that the large hard-wired MCUs of conventional NC have been replaced by control units based on the digital computer. Initially, minicomputers were utilized in the early 1970s. As further miniaturization occurred in computers, minicomputers were replaced by today's microcomputers.

Computer numerical control is an NC system using dedicated microcomputer as the machine control unit. Because a digital computer is used in both CNC and DNC, it is appropriate to distinguish between the two types of system. There are three principal differences:

(1) DNC computers distribute instructional data to, and collect data from, a large number of machines. CNC computers control only one machine, or a small number of machines.

(2) DNC computers occupy a location that is typically remote from the machines under their control. CNC computer are located very near their machine tools.

(3) DNC software is developed not only to control individual pieces of production equipment, but also to serve as part of a management information system in the manufacturing sector of the firm. CNC software is developed to augment the capabilities of a particular machine tool.

10.2 Words and Phrases

numerical control 数字控制
instruction [inˈstrʌkʃən] n. 指令
binary [ˈbainəri] adj. 二进制
lathe [leið] n. 车床
mill [mil] v. 铣
drill [dril] v. 钻
bore [bɔː] v. 镗

grind	[graind]	v.	磨
turret	[ˈtʌrit]	n.	转盘
punch	[pʌntʃ]	n.	冲床
flame	[fleim]	n.	(电)火花
wire-cutting			线切割
pipe bender			弯管机
spindle	[ˈspindl]	n.	主轴
contour	[ˈkɔntuə]	n.	轮廓
workpiece	[ˈwəːkpiːs]	n.	工件
countersink	[ˈkauntəsiŋk]	n.	钻(沉头)孔
counterbore	[kauntəˈbɔː]	n.	镗(沉头)孔
ream	[riːm]	n.	铰孔
tapping	[ˈtæpiŋ]	n.	攻螺纹
spotwelding			点焊
synchronization	[ˌsiŋkrənaiˈzeiʃən]	n.	同步
interpolation	[inˌtəːpəuˈleiʃən]	n.	插补
parabolic	[ˌpærəˈbɔlik]	adj.	抛物线的
compensation	[kɔmpenˈseiʃən]	n.	补偿
pertain	[pə(ː)ˈtein]	v.	合适
coolant	[ˈkuːlənt]	n.	冷却液
clamping	[ˈklæmpiŋ]	n.	夹紧
miniaturization	[minitʃəraiˈziaʃən]	n.	小型化
dedicated	[ˈdedikeitid]	adj.	专用的

10.3　Complex Sentence Analysis

[1] Numerical control (NC) is a form of programmable automation in which the processing equipment is controlled by means of numbers, letters, and other symbols.

数控技术是一种利用程序实现自动控制的技术，加工制造设备采用数控技术后能由数字、字符和符号等进行控制。

① a form of…"一个……的形式"。

② in which…引导的是定语从句，修饰前面的 programmable automation。

③ by means of "通过……"，"使用……方法"。

[2] Automation operation by NC is readily adaptable to the operation of all metalworking machines. Lathes, milling machines, drill presses, boring machines, grinding machines, turret punches, flame or wire-cutting and welding machines, and even pipe benders are available with numerical controls.

数控加工制造目前已经广泛地应用于几乎所有的金属加工机床：车床，铣床，钻床，镗床，磨床，回转冲床，电火花或线切割机床以及焊接机床，甚至弯管机也可采用数控加工技术。

① is adaptable to… "可适用于……"。
② are available with… "用……有效"。

[3] In its most common form, the commands refer to positions of a machine tool spindle with respect to the worktable on which the part is fixed.

最常用的指令形式可以使机床刀具主轴位于工作台上的具体位置，工作台是用于固定加工零件的。

① refer to…表示"指……"的意思。
② with respect to…表示"相对于……"的意思。
③ on which 引导的是定语从句，修饰前面的 worktable。

[4] A program for numerical control consists of a sequence of directions that causes an NC machine to carry out a certain operation, machining being the most commonly used process.

数控系统（NC）的程序包括使数控（NC）机床进行操作和机加工中最常用的一系列指令。

① consist of 表示为"包含"的意思。
② that 引导的从句修饰前面的 directions。
③ machining 是一个名词，表示"机械加工"的意思。
④ being 是一个分词短语结构形式。

10.4　Exercise

Translate the Following Paragraphs

Numerical control may be defined as a method of accurately managing the movement of machine tools by a series of programmed numerical data which activate the motors of the machine tool. There is nothing complex or magical about this system. It is based on the simple fundamental that combines automatic measurement of machine table slide will move with a series of programmed instructions.

The numerically controlled machine is supplied with detailed information regarding the part by means of punched tape. The machine decodes this punched information and electronic devices activate the various motors on the machine tool, causing them to position the work and follow specific machining instructions. The measuring and recording devices incorporated into numerically controlled machine tools assure that the part being manufactured will be accurate. Numerically controlled machines minimize the possibility of human error which existed before their development.

Over recent years, the have been great improvements to NC systems. In many cases, the tape reader on NC machines is bypassed and the machine receives its instructions directly from a computer. However students should be made aware of the basics of NC before being exposed to the more recent developments of computerized numerical control (CNC) and direct numerical control (DNC).

Lesson 11　Introduction to Heat Pipe Technology in Machining Process

11.1　Text

【激光切割】

【喷水切割与电蚀切割】

In any machining processes, most of the input energy is converted into heat in the cutting zone. This results in increases in tool and work-piece temperatures. Elevated temperature can significantly shorten the tool life. Excessive heat accumulated in the tool and work-piece can contribute to thermal distortion and poor dimensional control of the work-piece. In addition, high tool temperatures promote the formation of BUE (built-up edge) on the tool tip.

[1] In a drilling process, tool temperatures are particularly important because the chips, which absorb much of the cutting energy, are generated in a confined space and remain in contact with the tool for a relatively long time compared with any other machining operation. As a result, drill temperatures are much higher than in any other process under similar conditions. The most common cooling method is the use of cutting fluids flooding through the cutting zone. In machining operations, three types of cutting fluids are commonly used: oil with additives such as sulfur, chlorine, and phosphorus, emulsions, and synthetics containing inorganic and other chemicals. Used coolant from machining processes is harmful to both environment and human health. Chemical substances that provide the lubrication function in the machining process are toxic to the environment if the cutting fluid is released to soil and water. The chemical substances in coolant caused serious health problems to workers who are exposed to the coolant in both liquid and mist form. Ding and Hong have proposed replacing the conventional fluids with cryogenic fluids such as liquid nitrogen or carbon dioxide. Although this method shows some promise in increasing tool life and obviates the need for cutting fluid removal and disposal, many technical issues, including safety remain unresolved. Recently, there has been a strong global trend towards the minimization of cutting fluids because they have been demonstrated to be primary sources of industrial pollution. [2] In order for machining process to run dry, an effective cooling method, other than flooding by a coolant, is desirable to remove the heat accumulated in drill tool.

Heat pipes have been proved as an effective alternative to conventional methods of removing heat from a drill tip allowing drilling operations to be carried out in a dry and "green" fashion. The components of a heat pipe are a sealed container (pipe wall and end caps), a wick structure, and a small amount of working fluid in equilibrium with its own vapor. Fig. 11.1 illustrates the physical configuration of the heat-pipe. Typically, a heat pipe can be divided into three sections: evaporator section, adiabatic (transport) section and condenser section. The external heat load on the evaporator section causes the working fluid to vaporize.

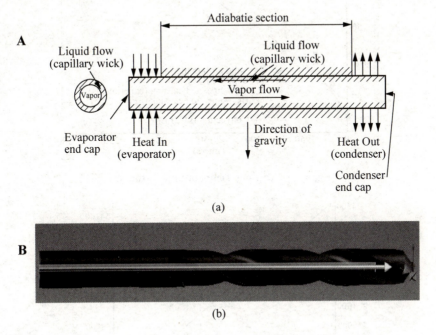

Fig. 11.1　(a) Schematic of a Heat Pipe, (b) Location of Heat Pipe Inside Drill

The resulting vapor pressure drives the vapor through the adiabatic section to the condenser section, where the vapor condenses, releasing its latent heat of vaporization to the low temperature environment. The condensed working fluid is then pumped back by capillary pressure generated by the meniscus in the wick structure. Transport of heat can be continuous as long as there is enough capillary pressure generated to drive the condensed liquid back to the evaporator.

[3] From the heat transfer point of view, the authors Jen *et al.* did much work to prove the feasibility and effectiveness of the heat pipe in the drilling operation, which could be summarized as follows:

(1) Both numerical studies and initial experiments show that the use of a heat pipe inside the drill reduces the temperature field significantly (as shown in Fig. 11.2).

(2) The closer the heat pipe gets to the tip, the more effective it gets in taking the heat away from the drill tip. The stresses in the drill don't increase significantly with increase in the length of the heat pipe, but the manufacturing concerns would restrict the length of the heat pipe (as shown in Fig. 11.3).

(3) The diameter of the heat pipe affects more the stress levels in the drill than the maximum temperatures reached in the drill. The diameter doesn't affect the maximum temperature experienced in the drill, but it does affect the temperature distribution (as shown in Fig. 11.4).

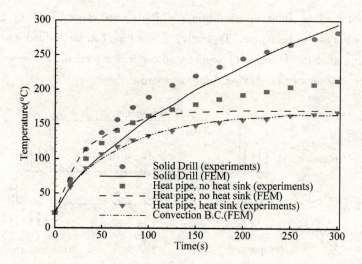

Fig. 11.2　Drilling Temperatures in the Tip

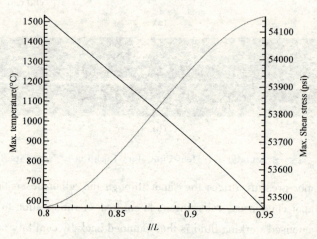

Fig. 11.3　Effect of l/L Ratio

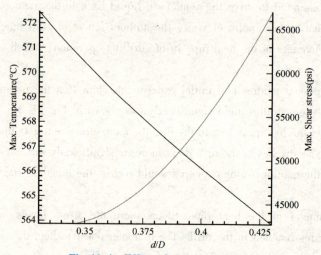

Fig. 11.4　Effect of change of d/D

Introduction to Heat Pipe Technology in Machining Process Lesson 11

11.2 Words and Phrases

cutting zone　　　　　　　　　切削区域
workpiece ['wəːkpiːs]　　　　　n. 工件，工作件
thermal distortion　　　　　　热变形，热扭曲
cutting fluid　　　　　　　　　切削液
additive ['æditiv]　　　　　　adj. 附加的，加成的，添加的；n. 添加剂
sulfur [sʌlfə]　　　　　　　　n. [化] 硫磺；vt. 用硫磺处理
chlorine ['klɔːriːn]　　　　　n. [化] 氯
phosphorus [flɔsfərəs]　　　　n. [化] 磷
emulsion [iˈmʌlʃən]　　　　　n. 乳状液；[医] 乳剂；[摄] 感光乳剂
cryogenic [ˌkraiəuˈdʒenik]　　adj. 低温学的，低温的，低温存储的
meniscus [miˈniskəs]　　　　　n. 新月，半月板，（液柱的）弯月面

11.3 Complex Sentence Analysis

[1] In a drilling process, tool temperatures are particularly important because the chips, which absorb much of the cutting energy, are generated in a confined space and remain in contact with the tool for a relatively long time compared with any other machining operation.

① which absorb much of the cutting energy, 非限制性定语从句修饰 chips。
② compared with any other machining operations, 过去分词作定语修饰 time, 试比较：The approaches proved by the experiments in the lab have been widely employed in industries.

[2] In order for machining process to run dry, an effective cooling method, other than flooding by a coolant, is desirable to remove the heat accumulated in drill tool.

① machining process to run dry, 干式机械加工过程，run 为连系动词，dry 作表语。
② other than: 与……不同；与……不同方式
　　You can't get there other than by swimming.

[3] From the heat transfer point of view, the authors Jen *et al*. did much work to prove the feasibility and effectiveness of the heat pipe in the drilling operation.

① From the heat transfer point of view: 从传热的角度。
② From…point of view: 从……的角度。试比较，froma static point of view, from dynamic point of view.

11.4　Exercise

Translate the Following Paragraphs

The operation of a heat pipe can be analyzed using a fundamental thermodynamic cycle for the working fluid, in which the thermal energy is converted to kinetic energy. The basic thermodynamic cycle can be studied using a temperature-entropy diagram. As expected from the second law, the conversion of the thermal energy to kinetic energy is associated with heat rejection at a temperature below the high temperature reservoir in the system where the efficiency is less than 100%. Note that a heat pipe can never be completely isothermal because this would violate the second law. If the thermal conductivity is measured based on the temperature difference in the system with the same amount of heat transferred, the thermal conductivity of the heat pipe system is much larger than pure conduction in the solid rod with the same dimension of the heat pipe. This is because the heat transfer mechanism in the heat pipe is due to the latent heat of evaporation and condensation. Although a thermodynamic approach can give a good insight into the performance of a heat pipe, this analysis is very limited and we need to appeal to heat transfer and fluid mechanics to solve the problem quantitatively. Fluid flow analysis is used to describe the axial liquid pressure drop in the wick structure; the maximum capillary pumping head and the vapor flow in the vapor channel. This analysis in combination with the heat transfer analysis can be used to model the heat transfer and fluid flow in the evaporator and condenser, as well as forced convection in the vapor channel. With these detailed analyses, an optimum operation condition can be found, and used in the design to further improve the performance of the heat pipe cooling.

Lesson 12　Introduction to Material Forming

12.1　Text

Material Forming Processes as a System

The term material forming refers to a group of manufacturing methods by which the given shape of a workpiece (a solid body) is converted to another shape without change in the mass or composition of the material of the workpiece.

【旋转成型】

Classification of manufacturing processes: Material forming is used synonymously with deformation or deforming and comprises the methods in group II of the manufacturing process classification shown below. The manufacturing processes are divided into six main groups.

Group I—Primary forming: Original creation of a shape from the molten or gaseous state or from solid particles of undefined shape, that is, creating cohesion between particles of the material.

Group II—Deforming: Converting a given shape of a solid body to another shape without change in mass or material composition, that is, maintaining cohesion.

Group III—Separating: Machining or removal of material, that is, destroying cohesion.

Group IV—Joining: Uniting of individual workpieces to form filling subassemblies, filling and impregnating of workpieces, and so on, that is, increasing cohesion between several workpieces.

Group V—Coating: Application of thin layers to a workpiece, for example, galvanizing, painting, coating with plastic foils, that is, creating cohesion between substrate and coating.

Group VI—Changing the material properties: Deliberately changing the properties of the workpiece in order to achieve optimum characteristics at a particular point in the manufacturing process. [1] These methods include changing the orientation of micro-particles as well as their introduction and removal, such as by diffusion, that is, rearranging, adding, or removing particles.

In manufacturing technology, particularly in groups I to IV, we are continually faced with the problem of how to manufacture most economically a particular technical product, with specific tolerance requirements, surface structure, and material properties.

Cold Forming and Hot Forming

[2] By applying a stress that exceeds the original yield strength of metallic material, we have strain hardened or cold worked the metallic material, while simultaneously deforming it. This is the basis for many manufacturing techniques, such as wire drawing. Fig. 12.1 illustrates several manufacturing processes that make use of both cold-working and hot-working processes.

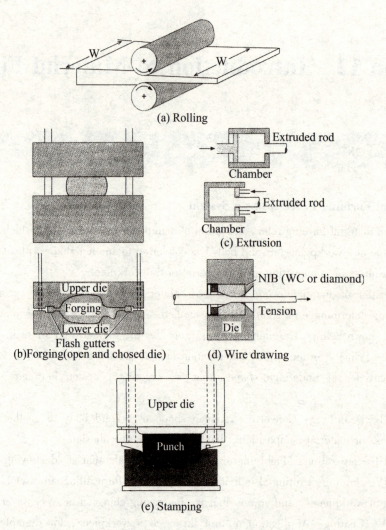

Fig. 12.1 Metal Forming Processes That Make Use of Cold Working As Well As Hot Working

Many techniques are used tosimutaneously shape and strengthen a material by cold working (Fig. 12.1). For example, rolling is used to produce metal plate and sheet. Forging deforms the material into a die cavity, producing relatively complex shapes such as automotive crankshafts or connecting rods. In drawing, a metallic rod is pulled through a die to produce a wire or fiber. In extrusion, a material is pushed through a die to form products of uniform cross-sections, including rods, tubes, or aluminum trims for doors or windows. Deep drawing is used to form the body of aluminum beverage cans. Stretch forming and bending as well as other processes are used to shape material. Thus, cold working is an effective way of shaping metallic materials while simultaneously increasing their strength. We can obtain excellent dimensional tolerances and surface finishes by the cold working processes. Note that many of the processes such as rolling, can be conducted using both cold and hot working.

We can deform a metal into a useful shape by hot working rather than cold working. As described previously, hot working is defined as plastically deforming the metallic material at above the recrystallization temperature. Hot working is well-suited for forming large parts, since the metal has a low yield strength and high ductility at elevated temperatures. In addition, HCP metals such as magnesium have more slip systems at hot-working temperature; the high ductility permits larger deformation than are possible by cold working. For example, a very thick plate can be reduced to a thin sheet in a continuous series of operations.

An advantage of hot working is that the imperfection of materials can be eliminated during the process: Some imperfection in the original material may be eliminated or their effects minimized; gas pores can be closed and welded shut; composition differences in the metal can be reduced; the structure of metals can be refined and controlled by recrystallization. Therefore, mechanical and physical properties of metals can be improved obviously.

Principles of Plastic Forming

Plasticity theory is the foundation for the numerical treatment of metal forming processes. Materials science and metallurgy can explain the origins of the plastic state of metallic bodies and its dependence on various parameters, such as process speed, prior history, temperature, and so on. The essentially older plasticity theory deals with the calculation of stresses, forces, and deformation.

Plasticity theory is rather based on macroscopically observed phenomena, in other words, on the properties of materials which can be observed and measured directly in deformation processes, such as the tension and compression tests. This leads to the following simple description of the plastic state.

[3] Plasticity is the capacity of a material to change its shape permanently under the action of forces when the corresponding stress state reaches a material-dependent critical magnitude called yield strength or initial flow stress. As seen from the results of the tension test, when the stress is below the yield strength, the deformation disappears upon unloading: the material behaves elastically. If the stress exceeds the yield strength, permanent deformation will be formed. Upon unloading, the workpiece has a form that is different from its initial one. It is then said to have been plastically or permanently deformed, or, if a definite final shape was sought, it has been (trans) formed. Materials which behave in an elastic-plastic manner can, after having been permanently deformed, again be loaded until the flow stress is reached without additional permanent deformation setting in. This increase in the flow stress as a result of prior deformation is called strain hardening or work hardening.

Work hardening can be balanced by the dynamic softing processes of recovery and recrystallization.

The original cold-worked microstructure is composed of deformed grains containing a large number of tangled dislocations. When we first heat the metal, the additional thermal energy permits the dislocation to move and form the boundaries of a polygonized subgrain structure. The dislocation density, however, is virtually unchanged. This low temperature treatment removes the residual stresses due to cold working without causing a change in dislocation density is called recovery.

When a cold worked metallic material is heated above a certain temperature (recrystallization temperature), rapid recovery eliminates the residual stresses and produce the polygonized dislocation structure. New small grains then nucleate at the cell boundaries of the polygonized structure, eliminating most of the dislocations. Because the number of dislocations is greatly reduced, the recrystallized metal has low strength and high ductility. The process of formation of new grains by heat treating a cold-worked material is known as recrystallization. Recrystallization may be followed by grain growth if the temperature is sufficiently high.

Methods Used in Material Forming

The following classification of the deformation methods into five groups is based mainly on the important differences in effective stresses. No simple descriptions of stress states are possible since, depending on the kind of operation, different stress states may occur simultaneously, or they may change during the course of the deforming operation. Therefore, the predominant stresses are chosen as the classification criteria. The five groups of material-forming processes may then be defined as follows: (1) Compressive forming (forming under compressive stresses): German standard covers the deformation of a solid body in which the plastic state is achieved mainly by uni- or multiaxial compressive loading. (2) Combined tensile and compressive forming (forming under combined tensile and compressive stresses). (3) Tensile forming (forming under tensile stresses). (4) Forming by bending (forming by means of bending stresses). (5) Forming by shearing (forming under shearing stresses).

12.2　Words and Phrases

synonymously [siˈnɔnimǝsli]	adv. 同义地
cohesion [kəuˈhiːʒən]	n. 结合，凝聚，[物理]内聚力结合
subassembly [ˈsʌbəˈsembli]	n. 部件，组件
impregnate [ˈimpregneit; (US) impregnet]	v. 使充满，使怀孕；注入，灌输
	adj. 充满的，怀孕的
stamping [ˈstæmpiŋ]	n. 冲压，压印，模压，模锻
rolling [ˈrəuliŋ]	n. 轧制，旋转，翻滚
	a. 旋转的，转动的，摇摆的，起伏的
forging [ˈfɔːdʒiŋ]	n. 锻造，锻炼；锻件
crankshaft [ˈkræŋkʃɑːft]	n. 曲轴，机轴
cavity [ˈkæviti]	n. 洞，空穴，型腔
connecting rod	连杆
drawing [ˈdrɔːiŋ]	n. 拉拔，制图，图画

Introduction to Material Forming Lesson 12

extrusion [eksˈtruːʒən]	n. 挤压，挤出，推出
deep drawing	拉深
stretch forming	拉伸变形
bending	n. 弯曲（变形）
HCP metals	密排六方金属
imperfection [ˌimpəˈfekʃən]	n. 缺陷，不完整性，非理想性
gas pores	气孔
galvanise [ˈgælvənaiz]	v. & n. <英=galvanize> 电镀
foil [fɔil]	n. 箔，金属薄片，烘托，衬托；v. 贴箔于……，衬托，阻止
substrate [ˈsʌbstreit]	n. (=substratum) 底层，下层，[地] 底土层，基础
deliberately [diˈlibərətli]	adv. 有目的地，故意地
metallurgy [meˈtælədʒi]	n. 冶金，冶金学，冶金术
macroscopically [ˌmækrəˈskɔpikli]	adv. 宏观上
recovery	n. 回复
recrystallization	n. 再结晶
tangled	adj. 紊乱的；复杂的
dislocation	n. 位错
polygonized subgrain structure	多边形亚晶结构
grain growth	晶粒长大
predominant [priˈdɔminənt]	adj. 卓越的，支配的，主要的，突出的，有影响的
shearing stress	剪应力

12.3 Complex Sentence Analysis

[1] These methods include changing the orientation of micro-particles as well as their introduction and removal, such as by diffusion, that is, rearranging, adding, or removing particles

① as well as：和、还有
这些方法包括改变微粒的取向，以及通过扩散产生或消除这些微粒，即重排、增加或消除微粒。

② rearranging：重排

[2] By applying a stress that exceeds the original yield strength of metallic material, we have strain hardened or cold worked the metallic material, while simultaneously deforming it.

① have strain hardened：产生形变硬化

② while simultaneously：而同时

[3] Plasticity is the capacity of a material to change its shape permanently under the action of forces when the corresponding stress state reaches a material-dependent critical magnitude called yield strength or initial flow stress

① under the action of：在……作用下
② critical magnitude：临界值
③ flow stress：流变应力

12.4 Exercise

Translate the Following Paragraphs

The so-called ceramic group of cutting tools represents the most recent development in cutting tool materials. They consist mainly of sintered oxides, usually aluminum oxide, and are almost invariably in the form of clamped tips. Because of the comparative cheapness of ceramic tips and the difficulty of grinding them without causing thermal cracking, they are made as throw-away inserts.

Ceramic tools are a post-war introduction and are not yet in general factory use. Their most likely applications are in cutting metal at very high speeds, beyond the limits possible with carbide tools. Ceramics resist the formation of a built-up edge and in consequence produce good surface finishes. Since the present generation of machine tools is designed with only sufficient power to exploit carbide tooling, it is likely that, for the time being, ceramics will be restricted to high-speed finish machining where there is sufficient power available for the light cuts taken. The extreme brittleness of ceramic tools has largely limited their use to continuous cuts, although their use in milling is now possible.

As they are poorer conductors of heat than carbides, temperatures at the rake face are higher than in carbide tools, although the friction force is usually lower. To strengthen the cutting edge, and consequently improve the life of the ceramic tool, a small chamfer or radius is often stoned at the cutting edge, although this increases the power consumption.

Lesson 13　Material Forming Processes

13.1　Text

In this section, a short description of the process examples about material forming will be given. But assembly and joining processes are not described here.

Forging

Forging can be characterized as: mass conserving, solid state of work material (metal), and mechanical primary basic process-plastic deformation.[1] Technically, forging may be defined as the process of giving metal increased utility by shaping it, refining it, and improving its mechanical properties through controlled plastic deformation under impact or pressure.

【锻造和冲压】

A wide variety of forging processes are used, and Fig. 13.1 (a) shows the most common of these: drop forging. The metal is heated to a suitable working temperature and placed in the lower die cavity. The upper die is then lowered so that the metal is forced to fill the cavity. [1]Excess material is squeezed out between the die faces at the periphery as flash, which is removed in a later trimming process. When the term forging is used, it usually means hot forging. Cold forging has several specialized names. The material loss in forging processes is usually quite small. Normally, forged components require some subsequent machining, since the tolerances and surfaces obtainable are not usually satisfactory for a finished product. Forging machines include drop hammers and forging presses with mechanical or hydraulic drives. These machines involve simple translatory motions.

Rolling

Rolling can be characterized as: mass conserving, solid state of material, mechanical primary basic process-plastic deformation. Rolling is extensively used in the manufacturing of plates, sheets, structural beams, and so on. Fig. 13.1 (b) shows the rolling of plates or sheets. An ingot is produced in casting and in several stages it is reduced in thickness, usually while hot. Since the width of the work material is kept constant, its length is increased according to the reductions. After the last hot-rolling stage, a final stage is carried out cold to improve surface quality and tolerances and to increase strength. In rolling, the profiles of the rolls are designed to produce the desired geometry.

Powder Compaction

Powder compaction can be characterized as: mass conserving, granular state of material, mechanical basic process-flow and plastic deformation. In this context, only compaction of metal powders is mentioned, but generally compaction of molding sand, ceramic materials, and so on, also belong in this category.

In the compaction of metal powders [as shown in Fig. 12.1 (c)] the die cavity is filled with a measured volume of powder and compacted at pressures typically around 500 N/mm^2. During this pressing phase, the particles are packed together and plastically deformed. Typical densities after compaction are 80% of the density of the solid material. Because of the plastic deformation, the particles are "welded" together, giving sufficient strength to withstand handling. After compaction, the components are heat-treated-sintered-normally at 70% ~ 80% of the melting temperature of the material. The atmosphere for sintering must be controlled to prevent oxidation. The duration of the sintering process varies between 30 min and 2 h. the strength of the components after sintering can, depending on the material and the process parameters, closely approach the strength of the corresponding solid material.

The die cavity, in the closed position, corresponds to the desired geometry. Compaction machinery includes both mechanical and hydraulic presses. The production rates vary between 6 and 100 components per minute.

Casting

Casting can be characterized as: mass conserving, fluid state of material, mechanical basic process-filling of the die cavity. Casting is one of oldest manufacturing methods and one of the best known processes. The material is melted and poured into a die cavity corresponding to the desired geometry [as shown in Fig. 13.1 (d)]. The fluid material takes the shape of the die cavity and this geometry is finally stabilized by the solidification of the material.

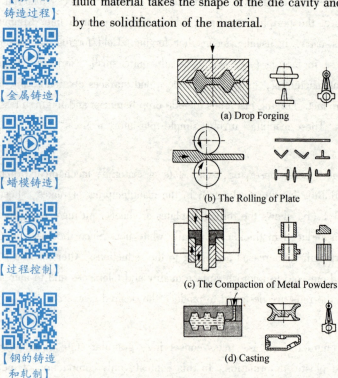

Fig. 13.1　Mass-conserving Processes in the Solid State of the Work Material

The stages or steps in a casting process are the making of a suitable mold, the melting of the material, the filling or pouring of the material into the cavity, and the solidification. Depending on the mold material, different properties and dimensional accuracies are obtained. Equipment used in a casting process includes furnaces, mold-making machinery, and casting machines.

Turning

Turning can be characterized as: mass reducing, solid state of work material, mechanical primary basic process-fracture. The turning process, which is the best known and most widely used mass-reducing process, is employed to manufacture all types of cylindrical shapes by removing material in the form of chips from the work material with a cutting tool [as shown in Fig. 13.2 (a)]. The work material rotates and the cutting tool is fed longitudinally. The cutting tool is much harder and more wear resistant than the work material. A variety of types of lathes are employed, some of which are automatic in operation. The lathes are usually powered by electric motors which, through various gears, supply the necessary torque to the work material and provide the feed motion to the tool.

【机械加工工艺】

A wide variety of machining operations or processes based on the same metal-cutting principle are available; among the most common are milling and drilling carried out on various machine tools. By varying the tool shape and the pattern of relative work-tool motions, many different shapes can be produced [as shown in Fig. 13.2 (b) and (c)].

EDM

Electrical discharge machining (EDM) can be characterized as: mass reducing, solid state of work material, thermal primary basic process-melting and evaporation [as shown in Fig. 13.2 (d)]. In EDM, material is removed by the erosive action of numerous small electrical discharges (sparks) between the work material and the tool (electrode), the latter having the inverse shape of the desired geometry. [3] Each discharge occurs when the potential difference between the work material and the tool is large enough to cause a breakdown in the fluid medium, fed into the gap between the tool and work piece under pressure, producing a conductive spark channel. The fluid medium, which is normally mineral oil or kerosene, has several functions. It serves as a dielectric fluid and coolant, maintains a uniform resistance to the flow of current, and removes the eroded material. The sparking, which occurs at rate of thousands of times per second, always occurs at the point where the gap between the tool and work piece is smallest and develops so much heat that a small amount of material is evaporated and dispersed into the fluid. The material surface has a characteristic appearance composed of numerous small craters.

ECM

Electrochemical machining (ECM) can be characterized as: mass reducing, solid state of work material, chemical primary basic process-electrolytic dissolution [as shown in Fig. 13.2 (e)]. Electrolytic dissolution of the work piece is established through an electric circuit, where the work material is made the anode, and the tool, which is approximately the inverse shape of the desired geometry, is made the cathode. The electrolytes normally used are water-based saline solutions (sodium chloride and sodium nitrate in 10% ~ 30% solutions). The voltage, which usually is in the range 5V ~ 20V, maintains high current densities, $0.5A/mm^2 \sim 2A/mm^2$, giving a relatively high removal rate, $0.5cm^3/min \cdot 1000A \sim 6cm^3/min \cdot 1000A$, depending on the work material.

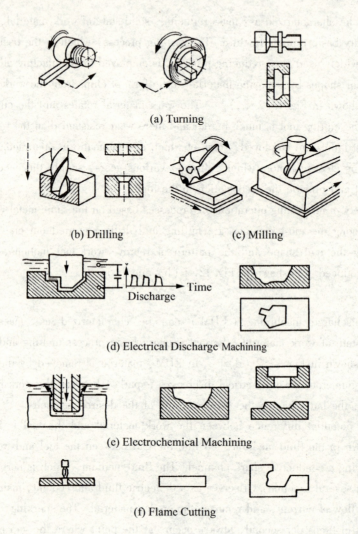

Fig. 13.2 Mass-reducing Processes in the Solid State of the Work Material

Flame Cutting

Flame cutting can be characterized as: mass reducing, solid state of work material, chemical primary basic process-combustion [as shown in Fig. 13.2 (f)]. In flame cutting, the material (a ferrous metal) is heated to a temperature where combustion by the oxygen supply can start. Theoretically, the heat liberated should be sufficient to maintain the reaction once started, but because of heat losses to the atmosphere and the material, a certain amount of heat must be supplied continuously. A torch is designed to provide heat both for starting and maintaining the reaction. Most widely used is the oxyacetylene cutting torch, where heat is created by the combustion of acetylene and oxygen. The oxygen for cutting is normally supplied through a center hole in the tip of the torch.

The flame cutting process can only by used for easily combustible materials. For other materials, cutting processes based on the thermal basic process-melting have been developed (are cutting, are plasma cutting, etc.). This is the reason cutting under both thermal and chemical basic processes.

Fine Blanking

Fine blanking is a technique used for production of blanks perfectly flat and with a cut edge which is comparable to a machined finish. This quick and easy process is worthy of serious thought when the number of parts justifies the cost of a blanking tool especially when consideration is given to the fact that operations such as shaving are eliminated.

One of the fine blanking methods is that in which the punch has a round edge and a small clearance. This is best used for blanks but appears to give less satisfactory results when used for producing holes. In this method the radius on the edge of a die is selected according to the type hardness and thickness of a particular material coupled also to the shape of a profile on the component. The minimum radius that will impart a good result on a component is an essential feature and this radius can vary from 0.3 to 2 mm according to conditions.

The question of punch and die clearances is a vital point with this design of tool and they are always much closer than those used for conventional blanking tools. As a general guide, a total clearance of 0.01 to 0.03 mm will give good results and emphasis is made of the point that these are total clearances and not each side of a hole or blank.

13.2　Words and Phrases

squeeze [skwiːz]　　　　　　 v. 压榨，挤，挤榨
ingot [ˈiŋgət]　　　　　　　　 n. [冶] 锭铁，工业纯铁
profile [ˈprəufail]　　　　　　 n. 剖面，侧面，外形，轮廓
ceramic [siˈræmik]　　　　　 adj. 陶器的
sintering [ˈsintəriŋ]　　　　　v. 烧结
oxidation [ˌɔksiˈdeiʃən]　　　 n. [化] 氧化
solidification [səˌlidifiˈkeiʃən]　n. 凝固
longitudinal [ˌlɔndʒiˈtjuːdinl]　adj. 经度的，纵向的
erosive [iˈrəusiv]　　　　　　adj. 侵蚀性的，腐蚀性的
dissolution [ˌdisəˈljuːʃən]　　 n. 分解，解散
electrolyte [iˈlektrəulait]　　　n. 电解，电解液
sodium chloride　　　　　　　氯化钠

sodium nitrate		硝酸钠
ferrous [ˈferəs]		adj. 铁的，含铁的，[化] 亚铁的
oxyacetylene [ɔksiəˈsetiliːn]		adj. [化] 氧乙炔的
acetylene [əˈsetiliːn]		n. [化] 乙炔，电石气
combustible [kəmˈbʌstəbl]		adj. 易燃的
plasma [ˈplæzmə]		n. [解] 血浆，乳浆，[物] 等离子体，等离子区
fine blanking		精密冲裁
cut edge		剪切刃
clearance		n. 间隙；(公差中的) 公隙
shaving		n. 刨削；修整
punch		n. 冲头，凸模；冲压机，冲床，打孔机；vt. 冲孔，打孔
blank		n. 落料件
producing hole		冲孔
die		n. 模具；凹模

13.3　Complex Sentence Analysis

[1] Technically, forging may be defined as the process of giving metal increased utility by shaping it, refining it, and improving its mechanical properties through controlled plastic deformation under impact or pressure.

① be defined as：被定义为……

② under impact or pressure：在冲击力或压力的作用下

[2] Excess material is squeezed out between the die faces at the periphery as flash, which is removed in a later trimming process.

① which：引导定语从句，修饰 excess material。

② flash：飞边。

③ trimming process：切边、清理过程。

[3] Each discharge occurs when the potential difference between the work material and the tool is large enough to cause a breakdown in the fluid medium, fed into the gap between the tool and work piece under pressure, producing a conductive spark channel.

① when：引导时间状语从句修饰 occurs。

② fed into…：从句修饰 fluid medium。

Lesson 14 Introduction to Mould

14.1 Text

Mould is a fundamental technological device for industrial production. Industrially produced goods are formed in moulds which are designed and built specially for them. The mould is the core part of manufacturing process because its cavity gives its shape. There are many kinds of mould, such as casting & forging dies, ceramic moulds, die-casting moulds, drawing dies, injection moulds, glass moulds, magnetic moulds, metal extruding moulds, plastic and rubber moulds, plastic extruding moulds, powder metallurgical moulds, compressing moulds, etc.

The following is the introduction of some of the moulding process and the corresponding moulds used.

Compression Moulding

Compression moulding is the least complex of the moulding processes and is ideal for large parts or low-quantity production. For low-quantity requirements it is more economical to build a compression mould than an injection mould. Compression moulds are often used for proto-typing, where samples are needed for testing fit and forming into assemblies. This allows for further design modification before building an injection mould for high-quantity production. Compression moulding is best suited for designs where tight tolerances are not required.

A compression mould is simply two plates with cavities cut into either one or both plates. Additional plates between the top and bottom plates can be included to create cavities in the moulded part. Fig. 14.1 shown below is an example of a basic two-plate single cavity mold. The mould does not require heater elements or temperature controllers. The moulding temperature is fully controlled by the pressure it is running in.

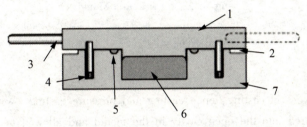

Fig. 14.1 A Compression Mould

1. top plate; 2. opening bar slot; 3. handle; 4. dowel pin & bushing; 5. flash & tear trim gate; 6. part cavity; 7. bottom plate.

Due to the simplicity of the mould, it is the most economical mould to buy. And the economical mould/tool cost keeps small quantity running affordable.

Injection Moulding

Injection moulding is the most complex of the moulding processes. Due to the more complex design of the injection mould, it is more expensive to purchase than a cast or compression mould. [1]Although tooling costs can be high, cycle time is much faster than other processes and the part cost can be low, particularly when the process is automated. [2]Injection moulding is well suited for moulding delicately shaped parts because high pressure (as much as 29000 psi) is maintained on the material to push it into every corner of the mould cavity.

Moulds used in injection moulding consist of two halves: one stationary and one movable. The stationary half is fastened directly to the stationary platen and is in direct contact with the nozzle of the injection unit during operation. The movable half of the mould is secured to the movable platen and usually contains the ejector mechanism. The use of a balanced runner system carries the plastic from the sprue to each individual cavity.

An injection mould can be a simpler two plate mould with a runner system to allow the rubber compound to be injected into each cavity from the parting line or a more complex mould with a number of plates, an ejector system and additional heating elements within the core.

Fig. 14.2 shown below are examples of basic three-plate and two-plate multi-cavity injection moulds. The moulds do not require heater elements or temperature controllers. The moulding temperature is fully controlled by the injection pressure it is running in.

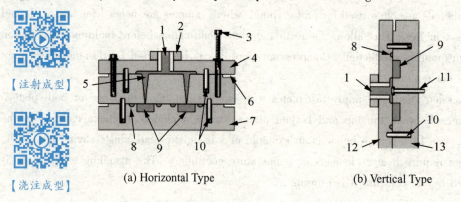

(a) Horizontal Type   (b) Vertical Type

Fig. 14.2   An Injection Mould

1. injection runner; 2. nozzle bushing; 3. stripper bolt; 4. top plate; 5. sprue; 6. opening bar slot; 7. bottom plate; 8. flash & tear trim gate; 9. part cavity; 10. dowel pin and bushing; 11. ejector; 12. fixed plate; 13. movable plate.

Cast Moulding

There are two types of casting, open casting and pressure casting. With open casting, the liquid mixture is poured into the open cavity in the mould and allowed to cure. With pressure casting, the liquid mixture is poured into the open cavity, the cap is put in place and the cavity is pressurized. Pressure casting is used for more complex parts and whenmoulding foam materials.

In principle, pressure casting is identical to injectionmoulding with a different class of materials. Cast moulding can, in fact, produce parts that have identical geometries to injection-moulded ones. In many cases, injection moulding has been a substitute for casting moulding due to decreased parts cost. However, for structural parts, particularly those parts with thick-walls, cast moulding can often be the better selection.

Because the materials flow as low-pressure liquids, tooling is generally less expensive. Low tooling costs make casting ideal for small production quantities and prototypes. It is short to medium-production runs. Liquid cast urethane compounds have outstanding resistance to abrasion, impact, and flex fatigue. Also, complex shapes and thick cross-sections can be produced in many compounds. But this process has longer cycle and cure times than othermoulding processes does. And once the material has been moulded, it can not be regrind and reused.

The construction of the mould for castmoulding is almost identical to that of moulds for injection moulding. It consists of two major sections—the ejector half and the cover half which meet at the parting line. The cavities and cores are usually machined into inserts that are fitted into each of these halves. The cover mould half is secured to stationary platen, while the ejector mould half is fastened to the movable platen. The cavity and machining core must be designed so that the mould halves can be pulled away from the solidified casting. Ejector pins are required to remove the part from the mould when it opens. Lubricants must also be sprayed into the cavities to prevent sticking.

Moulds are usually made of tool steel, mould steel ormaraging steel. [3] Since the mould materials have no natural porosity and the molten metal rapidly flows into the mould during injection, venting holes and passageways must be built into the moulds at the parting line to evacuate the air and gases in the cavity.

Extrusion Moulding

[4] Although extrusion moulds are quite simple the extrusion moulding process requires great care in the setting up and manufacture and final processing to ensure consistency of product. Pressure is forced through the die plate that has the correct profile cut into it. Variations in feed rate, temperature and pressure need to be controlled.

Unlike compression or injectionmoulding the rubber is not cured when it comes out of the mould. The raw rubber is laid out on circular or long trays (depending on the profile) and loaded into an autoclave for curing under heat and pressure.

For long continuous lengths a salt bath curing system may be used and for silicone extrusion a continuous heating line is used. The curing process used is dependent upon the quantity and profile of the extrusion required.

Most extrusion moulds are simply one round piece of steel with the profile of the intended extrusion wire cut into them. Allowances are made for the shrinkage, expansion of the intended compound. Extrusion dies are the least complex of the moulds.

These moulds are relatively cheap to build but because of the processing involved minimum run quantities will vary.

14.2　Words and Phrases

mould [məuld]	n. 模具，模（型），模塑，压模
cavity [ˈkæviti]	n. 模腔，型腔，空洞
die [dai]	n. 模（子，片，具），压模，塑模
casting & forging die	铸、锻模
ceramic mould	陶瓷模
die-casting mould	压铸模
drawing die	拉丝模
injection mould	注塑模
magnetic mould	磁铁成形模
extruding mould	挤压成形模
powder metallurgical mould	粉末冶金模
compressing mould	冲压模
moulding [ˈməuldiŋ]	n. 成形
proto-typing	初始制模
assembly [əˈsembli]	n. 装配件，组件
tolerance [ˈtɔlərəns]	n. 公差，容许
affordable [əˈfɔːdəbl]	adj. 提供得起的
fasten [ˈfɑːsn]	v. 连接，固定，夹紧
secure [siˈkjuə]	v. 固定，紧固
ejector [iˈdʒektə(r)]	n. 脱模销，推顶器
runner [ˈrʌnə(r)]	n. 浇道，流道
sprue [spruː]	n. 流道，浇道
parting line	合模线，拼缝线
core [kɔː]	n. 模芯，中间层
cure [kjuə]	v. 固化，塑化
urethane [juəriWein]	n. 聚氨酯
abrasion [əˈbreiʒən]	n. 磨蚀，磨损
flex fatigue	弯曲疲劳
insert [inˈsəːt]	n. 插件，嵌件
pin [pin]	n. 销，杆
tool steel	工具钢
maraging steel	马氏体时效钢
porosity [pɔːˈrɔsiti]	n. 多孔性，有孔性

venting hole　　　　　　　　排气孔，通风孔
evacuate [iˈvækjueit]　　　　v. 排出，抽空
autoclave [ˈɔːtəukleiv]　　　n. 高压釜
salt bath curing system　　　盐浴固化系统
silicone extrusion　　　　　 硅橡胶挤压

14.3　Complex Sentence Analysis

[1] Although tooling costs can be high, cycle time is much faster than other processes and the part cost can be low, particularly when the process is automated.
① tooling costs：模具成本。
② particularly when the process is automated：时间状语从句，译为：尤其当工艺过程为自动操作时。

[2] Injection moulding is well suited for moulding delicately shaped parts because high pressure (as much as 29000 psi) is maintained on the material to push it into every corner of the mould cavity.
① is well suited for：最适合用于。
② delicately shaped parts：外形精致的零件。
③ psi：英制压力单位，磅/平方英寸。

[3] Since the mould materials have no natural porosity and the molten metal rapidly flows into the mould during injection, venting holes and passageways must be built into the moulds at the parting line to evacuate the air and gases in the cavity.
① since 引导原因状语从句，译为：由于……。
② venting holes：排气孔。
③ parting line：合模线。

[4] Although extrusion moulds are quite simple the extrusion moulding process requires great care in the setting up and manufacture and final processing to ensure consistency of product.
① in the setting up and manufacture and final processing：在制定、制造和最后的加工过程中。
② to ensure consistency of product：动词不定式作目的状语，译为：以确保产品设计与制造相一致。

14.4　Exercise

Translate the Following Paragraphs

The most common types of moulds used in industry today are: (1) two-plate moulds, (2) three-plate moulds, (3) side-action moulds, (4) unscrewing moulds.

A two-plate mould consists of two active plates, into which the cavity and core inserts are mounted. In this mould type, the runner system, sprue, runners, and gates solidify with the part being moulded and are ejected as a single connected item. Thus the operation of a two-plate mould usually requires continuous machine attendance.

The three-plate mould consists of: (1) the stationary or runner plate, which contains thesprue and half of the runner; (2) the middle or cavity plate, which contains the other half of the runner, the gates, and cavities and is allowed to float when the mould is open; (3) the movable or core plate, which contains the cores and the ejector system. This type of mould design facilitates separation of the runner system and the part when the mould opens.

Lesson 15 Mould Design and Manufacturing

15.1 Text

CAD and CAM are widely applied in mould design and mould making. [1] CAD allows you to draw a model on screen, then view it from every angle using 3-D animation and, finally, to test it by introducing various parameters into the digital simulation models (pressure, temperature, impact, etc.). CAM, on the other hand, allows you to control the manufacturing quality. The advantages of these computer technologies are legion: shorter design times (modifications can be made at the speed of the computer), lower cost, faster manufacturing, etc. This new approach also allows shorter production runs, and to make last-minute changes to the mould for a particular part. Finally, also, these new processes can be used to make complex parts.

Computer-Aided Design (CAD) of Mould

Traditionally, the creation of drawings of mould tools has been a time-consuming task that is not part of the creative process. Drawings are an organizational necessity rather than a desired part of the process.

【CAD与模具设计】

Computer-Aided Design (CAD) means using the computer and peripheral devices to simplify and enhance the design process. CAD systems offer an efficient means of design, and can be used to create inspection programs when used in conjunction with coordinate measuring machines and other inspection equipment. CAD data also can play a critical role in selecting process sequence.

A CAD system consists of three basic components: hardware, software, users. The hardware components of a typical CAD system include a processor, a system display, a keyboard, a digitizer, and a plotter. The software component of a CAD system consists of the programs which allow it to perform design and drafting functions. The user is the tool designer who uses the hardware and software to perform the design process.

Based on the 3-D data of the product, the core and cavity have to be designed first. Usually the designer begins with a preliminary part design, which means the work around the core and cavity could change. Modern CAD systems can support this with calculating a split line for a defined draft direction, splitting the part in the core and cavity side and generating the run-off or shut-off surfaces. After the calculation of the optimal draft of the part, the position and direction of the cavity, slides and inserts have to be defined. Then, in the conceptual stage, the positions and the geometry of the mould components—such as slides, ejection system, etc.—are roughly defined. With this information, the size and thickness of the plates can be defined and the corresponding standard mould can be chosen from the standard catalog. If no standard mould fits these needs, the standard mould that comes nearest to the requirements is chosen and changed accordingly—by adjusting the constraints and parameters so that any number of plates with any size can be used in the mould. Detailing the functional components and adding the standard components complete the mould (as shown in Fig. 15.1). This all happens in 3-D. Moreover, the mould system provides functions for the checking, modifying and detailing of the part. Already in this early stage, drawings and bill of materials can be created automatically.

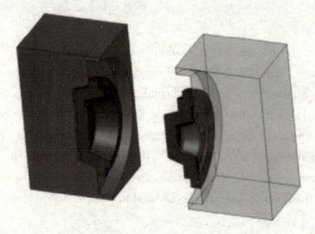

Fig. 15.1 3-D Solid Model of Mould

Through the use of 3-D and the intelligence of the mould design system, typical 2-D mistakes—such as a collision between cooling and components/cavities or the wrong position of a hole—can be eliminated at the beginning. [2] At any stage a bill of materials and drawings can be created—allowing the material to be ordered on time and always having an actual document to discuss with the customer or a bid for a mould base manufacturer.

【卡丁车油箱的设计】

The use of a special 3-D mould design system can shorten development cycles, improve mould quality, enhance teamwork and free the designer from tedious routine work. The economical success, however, is highly dependent upon the organization of the workflow. The development cycles can be shortened only when organizational and personnel measures are taken. The part design, mould design, electric design and mould manufacturing departments have to consistently work together in a tight relationship.

Computer-Aided Manufacturing (CAM) of Mould

【模具制造】

One way to reduce the cost of manufacturing and reduce lead-time is by setting up a manufacturing system that uses equipment and personnel to their fullest potential. The foundation for this type of manufacturing system is the use of CAD data to help in making key process decisions that ultimately improve machining precision and reduce non-productive time. This is called as computer-aided manufacturing (CAM). [3] The objective of CAM is to produce, if possible, sections of a mould without intermediate steps by initiating machining operations from the computer workstation.

With a goodCAM system, automation does not just occur within individual features. Automation of machining processes also occurs between all of the features that make up a part, resulting in tool-path optimization. As you create features, the CAM system constructs a process plan for you. Operations are ordered based on a system analysis to reduce tool changes and the number of tools used.

On theCAM side, the trend is toward newer technologies and processes such as micro milling to support the manufacturing of high-precision injection moulds with complex 3-D structures and high surface qualities. CAM software will continue to add to the depth and breadth of the machining intelligence inherent in the software until the CNC programming process becomes completely automatic. This is especially true for advanced multifunction machine tools that require a more flexible combination of machining operations. CAM software will continue to automate more and more of manufacturing's redundant work that can be handled faster and more accurately by computers, while retaining the control that machinists need.

[4] With the emphasis in the mould making industry today on producing moulds in the most efficient manner while still maintaining quality, mould makers need to keep up with the latest software technologies-packages that will allow them to program and cut complex moulds quickly so that mould production time can be reduced. In a nutshell, the industry is moving toward improving the quality of data exchange between CAD and CAM as well as CAM to the CNC, and CAM software is becoming more "intelligent" as it relates to machining processes—resulting in reduction in both cycle time and overall machining time. Five-axis machining also is emerging as a "must-have" on the shop floor-especially when dealing with deep cavities. And with the introduction of electronic data processing (EDP) into the mould making industry, new opportunities have arisen in mould-making to shorten production time, improve cost efficiencies and achieve higher quality.

15.2 Words and Phrases

screen [skri:n]	n. 屏幕，隔板
animation [ˌæniˈmeiʃən]	n. 动画
digital simulation model	数字模拟模型
legion [ˈliːdʒən]	n. 多，大批，无数
creative [kri(ː)ˈeitiv]	adj. 创造力的
peripheral [pəˈrifərəl]	adj. 外围的，周边的
split [split]	adj. 分割的，对分的
run-off	n. 流出口，流放口
shut-off	n. 截流，断流
ejection system	脱模系统，卸料装置
collision [kəˈliʒən]	n. 打击，碰撞

tedious [ˈtiːdiəs]	adj.	沉闷的
lead-time	n.	研制周期
tool-path	n.	方法路径
CNC		计算机数字控制
multifunction [ˌmʌltiˈfʌŋkʃən]	n.	多功能
redundant [riˈdʌndənt]	adj.	多余的，冗余的
in a nutshell		总之

15.3　Complex Sentence Analysis

［1］CAD allows you to draw a model on screen, then view it from every angle using 3-D animation and, finally, to test it by introducing various parameters into the digital simulation models (pressure, temperature, impact, etc.).

① draw, view 和 test 表示 3 个并列的操作。

② digital simulation model：数字模拟模型。

［2］At any stage a bill of materials and drawings can be created—allowing the material to be ordered on time and always having an actual document to discuss with the customer or a bid for a mould base manufacturer.

① a bill of materials：材料清单。

② allowing 和 having 引导两个现代分词短语，做伴随状语。

［3］The objective of CAM is to produce, if possible, sections of a mould without intermediate steps by initiating machining operations from the computer workstation.

① if possible：插入语，译成：如可能，是 if it is possible 的省略语，试比较：

If possible, I will visit you inChicago next month.

I will lend you some money to help you with the present difficulty if possible.

② by：通过……方式。

［4］With the emphasis in the mould making industry today on producing moulds in the most efficient manner while still maintaining quality, mould makers need to keep up with the latest software technologies-packages that will allow them to program and cut complex moulds quickly so that mould production time can be reduced.

① with：译为：随着……，引导的介词短语作状语，修饰整个句子。试比较：

With the development of the economy inChina, the people around the country are living a happy life.

② in the most efficient manner 饰 producing moulds。

③ keep up with：紧跟。

④ that：在这里引导了一个宾语从句，修饰前面的 software technologies-packages。

15.4　Exercise

Translate the Following Paragraphs

A key decision early in mold making process is determining what machining operations will be used and in what order. Machining considerations should be analyzed during the development of the CAD model. If this isn't done, the programmer may not be able to use certain machining strategies.

Each of the processes has advantages and disadvantages when producing a close tolerance mould. The proper selection of process and sequence of process will not only result in more precise dimensional control, but also will reduce manufacturing time by reducing bench work.

The worst case here is that the model may have to be modified, significantly adding to lead-time. Not allworkpieces are suitable for hard milling, for example. The smallest internal radius, the largest working depth and the hardness of the material all have to be considered when making this decision.

CAD data can be used to program electrode machining operations. Dimensional data can be downloaded to software that automates electrode design and generates simulations of electrode action so that users can test cut prior to burning. The software also allows users to try different qualities of graphite to determine the optimum grade before actual burning begins.

Lesson 16　Heat Treatment of Metal

16.1　Text

The generally accepted definition for heat treating metals and metal alloys is "heating and cooling a solid metal or alloy in a way so as to obtain specific conditions and/or properties." Heating for the sole purpose of hot working (as in forging operations) is excluded from this definition. Likewise, the types of heat treatment that are sometimes used for products such as glass or plastics are also excluded from coverage by this definition.

Transformation Curves

The basis for heat treatment is the time-temperature-transformation curves or TTT curves where, in a single diagram all the three parameters are plotted. Because of the shape of the curves, they are also sometimes called C-curves or S-curves.

To plot TTT curves, the particular steel is held at a given temperature and the structure is examined at predetermined intervals to record the amount of transformation taken place. [1] It is known that the eutectoid steel (T8) under equilibrium conditions contains, all austenite above 727℃, whereas below, It is pearlite. To form pearlite, the carbon atoms should diffuse to form cementite. The diffusion being a rate process, would require sufficient time for complete transformation of austenite to pearlite. From different samples, it is possible to note the amount of the transformation taking place at any temperature. [2] These points are then plotted on a graph with time and temperature as the axes. Through these points, transformation curves can be plotted as shown in Fig. 16.1 for eutectoid steel. The curve at extreme left represents the time required for the transformation of austenite to pearlite to start at any given temperature. Similarly, the curve at extreme right represents the time required for completing the transformation. Between the two curves are the points representing partial transformation. The horizontal lines M_s and M_f represent the start and finish of martensitic transformation.

Classification of Heat Treating Processes

【金属的热处理与特性】

In some instances, heat treatment procedures are clear cut in terms of technique and application. whereas in other instances, descriptions or simple explanations are insufficient because the same technique frequently may be used to obtain different objectives. For example, stress relieving and tempering are often accomplished with the same equipment and by use of identical time and temperature cycles. The objectives, however, are different for the two processes.

The following descriptions of the principal heat treating processes are generally arranged according to their interrelationships.

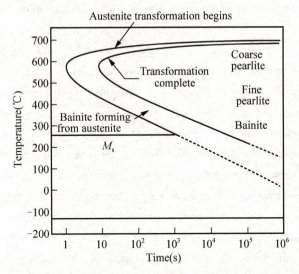

Fig. 16.1 Isothermal Decomposition Diagram of T8 Steel

Normalizing consists of heating a ferrous alloy to a suitable temperature above its specific upper transformation temperature. [3] This is followed by cooling in still air to at least some temperature well below its transformation temperature range. For low-carbon steels, the resulting structure and properties are the same as those achieved by full annealing; for most ferrous alloys, normalizing and annealing are not synonymous.

Normalizing usually is used as a conditioning treatment, notably for refining the grains of steels that have been subjected to high temperatures for forging or other hot working operations. The normalizing process usually is succeeded by another heat treating operation such as austenitizing for hardening, annealing, or tempering.

Annealing is a generic term denoting a heat treatment that consists of heating to and holding at a suitable temperature followed by cooling at a suitable rate. It is used primarily to soften metallic materials, but also to simultaneously produce desired changes in other properties or in microstructure. The purpose of such changes may be, but is not confined to, improvement of machinability, facilitation of cold work (known as in-process annealing), improvement of mechanical or electrical properties, or to increase dimensional stability. When applied solely to relieve stresses, it commonly is called stress-relief annealing, synonymous with stress relieving.

When the term "annealing" is applied to ferrous alloys without qualification, full annealing is implied. This is achieved by heating above the alloy's transformation temperature, then applying a cooling cycle which provides maximum softness. This cycle may vary widely, depending on composition and characteristics of the specific alloy.

Quenching is the rapid cooling of a steel or alloy from the austenitizing temperature by immersing the workpiece in a liquid or gaseous medium. Quenching media commonly used include water, 5% brine, 5% caustic in an aqueous solution, oil, polymer solutions, or gas (usually air or nitrogen).

Selection of a quenching medium depends largely on the hardenability of the material and the mass of the material being treated (principally section thickness).

The cooling capabilities of the above-listed quenching media vary greatly. In selecting a quenching medium, it is best to avoid a solution that has more cooling power than is needed to achieve the results, thus minimizing the possibility of cracking and warp of the parts being treated. Modifications of the term quenching include direct quenching, fog quenching, hot quenching, interrupted quenching, selective quenching, spray quenching, and time quenching.

Tempering. In heat treating of ferrous alloys, tempering consists of reheating the austenitized and quench-hardened steel or iron to some preselected temperature that is below the lower transformation temperature (generally below 1300°F or 705℃). Tempering offers a means of obtaining various combinations of mechanical properties. Tempering temperatures used for hardened steels are often no higher than 150~200℃. The term "tempering" should not be confused with either process annealing or stress relieving. Even though time and temperature cycles for the three processes may be the same, the conditions of the materials being processed and the objectives may be different.

Stress Relieving. Like tempering, stress relieving is always done by heating to some temperature below the lower transformation temperature for steels and irons. For nonferrous metals, the temperature may vary from slightly above room temperature to several hundred degrees, depending on the alloy and the amount of stress relief that is desired.

The primary purpose of stress relieving is to relieve stresses that have been imparted to the workpiece from such processes as forming, rolling, machining or welding. The usual procedure is to heat workpieces to the pre-established temperature long enough to reduce the residual stresses (this is a time-and temperature-dependent operation) to an acceptable level; this is followed by cooling at a relatively slow rate to avoid creation of new stresses.

16.2 Words and Phrases

forge [fɔːdʒ]	v. 锻造
eutectoid [juːˈtektɔid]	adj. 共析的
austenite [ˈɔːstəˌnait]	n. 奥氏体
pearlite [ˈpəːlait]	n. 珠光体
martensitic [ˌmɑːtinˈzitik]	adj. 马氏体的
stress relieving	消除应力,低温退火
tempering [ˈtempəriŋ]	n. 回火

normalizing [ˈnɔːməlaiziŋ]	n.	常化，正火
ferrous alloy		铁合金
transformation [ˌtrænsfəˈmeiʃən]	n.	变换，转换，相变
still [stil]	adj.	不动的，静止的
full annealing		完全退火
notably [ˈnəutbəli]	adv.	显著地，特别是
austenitize [ˈɔːstənətaiz]	v.	奥氏体化，使成奥氏体
denote [diˈnəut]	v.	指示，表示，概述
machinability [məˌʃiːnəˈbiliti]	n.	切削加工性，机械加工性能
facilitation [fəˌsiliˈteiʃən]	n.	便于
in-process	adj.	（加工、处理）过程中的
qualification [ˌkwɔlifiˈkeiʃən]	n.	资格，条件，限制，限定
quenching [ˈkwentʃiŋ]	n.	淬火
brine [brain]	n.	盐水
caustic [ˈkɔːstik]	adj.	腐蚀性的，碱性的
aqueous [ˈeikwiəs]	adj.	水的，水成的
warp [ˈwɔːp]	n.	翘曲，变形
glossary [ˈglɔsəri]	n.	词汇表，术语汇编
quench-hardened	adj.	淬火硬化的
process annealing		工序间退火，中间退火
fog quenching		喷雾淬火
hot quenching		高温淬火，热淬火
interrupted quenching		分级淬火
selective quenching		局部淬火
time quenching		等温淬火，控制时间淬火，即时淬火

16.3 Complex Sentence Analysis

[1] It is known that the eutectoid steel (T8) under equilibrium conditions contains, all austenite above 727℃, whereas below, it is pearlite.

共析钢（T8）在平衡条件下，在727℃以上时全为奥氏体，低于此温度则为珠光体。

① that：引导主语从句。
② eutectoid steel：共析钢。
③ below 指低于727℃。

[2] These points are then plotted on a graph with time and temperature as the axes.
① with time and temperature as the axes：axes，轴，此处为坐标轴，以时间和温度为坐标轴。

[3] This is followed by cooling in still air to at least some temperature well below its transformation temperature range.

① follow: 接着，跟着。
② 句中 this 代替上一句话的内容，先 heating a ferrous alloy…，接下来，再 cooling…。

16.4　Exercise

Translate theFollowing Paragraphs

Carburizing consists of absorption and diffusion of cartoon solid ferrous alloys by heating to some temperature above the upper transformation temperature of the specific alloy. Temperatures used for carburizing are generally in the range of 1650°F of to 1900°F (900℃ to 1040℃). Heating is done in a carbonaceous environment (liquid, solid, or gas). This produces a carbon gradient extending inward from the surface, enabling the surface layers to be hardened to a high degree either by quenching from the carburizing temperature or by cooling to room temperature followed by reaustenitizing and quenching.

Carbonitriding is a case hardening process in which a ferrous material (most often a low-carbon grade of steel) is heated above the transformation temperature in a gaseous atmosphere of such composition as to cause simultaneous absorption of carbon and nitrogen at (by) the surface and, by diffusion a concentration, gradient is created. The process is completed by cooling at a rate that produces the desired properties in the workplace.

Lesson 17 Virtual Manufacturing

17.1 Text

What is Virtual Manufacturing

[1]Virtual manufacturing (VM) is an integrated, synthetic manufacturing environment exercised to enhance all levels of decision and control in a manufacturing enterprise. VM can be described as a simulated model of the actual manufacturing setup which may or may not exist. It holds all the information relating to the process, the process control and management and product specific data. It is also possible to have part of the manufacturing plant be real and the other part virtual. Virtual manufacturing is the use of computer models and simulations of manufacturing process to aid in design and production of manufactured products.

Lawrence Associate [1996], have identified three different types of Virtual Manufacturing paradigms that use Virtual Reality technology to provide the integrated environment.

(1)[2] Design—centered VM: provides designers with the tools to design products that meet design criteria such as design for X;

(2) Production—centered VM: provides the means develop and analyze alternative production and process plans;

(3)[3] Control—centered VM: allows the evaluation of product design, production plans, and control strategy and a means to iteratively to iteratively improve all of them through the simulation of the control process.

What is the Significance of VM

VM aims at providing an integrated environment for a number of isolated manufacturing technologies such as Computer Aided Design, Computer Aided Manufacturing, and Computer Aided Process Planning, thus allowing multiple users to concurrently carry out all or some of these functions without the need for being physically close to each other. For example, a process planning engineer and a manufacturing engineer can evaluate and provide feedback to a product designer, who may be physically located in another state or country, at the same time as the design is being conceived.

Another important contribution of VM is Virtual Enterprise (VE). Lin et al. [1995]

defined a Virtual Enterprise as "rapidly configured multi—disciplinary network of small, process specific firms configured to meet a window of opportunity to design and produce a specific product." Using this technology, a group of people, or corporations can pool their expertise and resources and capitalize a market opportunity, by sharing information in a VM environment. [4] The principal advantage of this technology is its ability to provide a multi-media environment, enhancing communication at all levels in a product's life cycle.

【虚拟现实在医学方面的应用】

Applications of VM

Application of VM encompass the entire life cycle of a product. Reported developments include a virtual space decision support system by Imamura and Nomura [1994] at the Matsushita company inJapan. This system applied towards the marketing and sales of kitchen furniture, allows customers to experience a kitchen environment and evaluate alternatives and select the best combination according to preferences. Their preferences are stored as drawings and subsequently transferred to the company's production facilities.

【焊接】

Owen [1994] presented the work implemented at John Deere Company's production facility, that used Virtual Manufacturing for the installation of an arc welding production system. The project involved using a Virtual 3-D environment for design, evaluation, and testing of the robotic production system. Part of the work was carried out at John Deere's facility while part of it was done by Genesis System and Technomatrix Technologies. The VM approach helped shorten the design-to-manufacturing cycle-time.

DuPont [1994] presented an overview of Virtual Reality applications, and reported about Virtual prototyping being carried out at the Coventry School of Art and Design. These virtual prototypes are constructed in a computer at the beginning of the design process and allow the designer to perform tests on the virtual prototype such as a car beforehand, by walking around or through the design, examine its performance on a virtual road, sit in the driver's seat, and check view lines, etc. [5] Also reported were VM applications such as the virtual concurrent design and assembly of a landing gear, and simulation of side-impact collision to test vehicle safety.

Kim et al. [1994] also reported VR applications including the use of VM by designers at Boeing Aircraft Company for the ergonomic evaluation of their airplane designs for operation as well as maintenance. Another study used a VM environment to train robots. An operator's movements were recognized, interpreted and stored in the form of robotic movement commands. Shenai described the Virtual Wafer Fabrication (VWF) infrastructure which provided an framework for the optimization of key process and design variables in the development of application specific semi-conductor devices. Other application areas discussed in Larijani [1994] include machine-vision applications for diagnosis, fault detection, inspection and preventive maintenance, safety and maintenance training, ergonomic analysis. For example, new cab or shovel configurations for each Caterpillar moving equipment are tested by real drivers for possible imbalances while handling virtual bulldozers and trucks.

17.2 Words and Phrases

virtual manufacturing	虚拟制造
synthetic [sinˈθetik]	adj. 人造的，综合的，假想的
be described as	被说成，被称作
paradigm [ˈpærəˌdaim]	n. 范例，式样
Virtual Reality	虚拟现实
iteratively [ˈitərətivli]	adv. 反（重）复，迭代
concurrently [kənˈkʌrəntli]	adv. 同时，兼，并行地
Virtual Enterprise	虚拟企业
configure [kənˈfigə]	v. 使成形，使具形体，装配，配置
multi-disciplinary [ˈmʌltiˈdisiplinˌəri]	adj.（有关）多种学科的
collision [kəˈliʒən]	n. 撞，冲突，抵触
ergonomic(al) [ˌəːgənɔmik(əl)]	adj. 人类工程（学）的，人机学的
infrastructure [ˈinfrəˌstrʌktʃə]	n. 基础（结构），基本设施
caterpillar [ˈkætəˌpilə]	n. 履带（式）车（辆），履带式挖土机
bulldozer [ˈbuldəzə]	n. 推土机

17.3 Complex Sentence Analysis

[1] Virtual manufacturing (VM) is an integrated, synthetic manufacturing environment exercised to enhance all levels of decision and control in a manufacturing enterprise.
Exercised：运用的：使用的，做后置定语，修饰 environment。

[2] Design-centered VM：provides designers with the tools to design products that meet design criteria such as design for X.

① to design products that meet design criteria such as design for X 动词不定式短语做定语修饰 tools。

② provide A with B 同 provide B for A：把 B 提供给 A。
e.g. Parents provide us with food and clothing.
父母亲向我们提供吃、穿所用的一切。

[3] Control-centered VM：allows the evaluation of product design, production plans, and control strategy and a means to iteratively improve all of them through the simulation of the control process.
Means：方法，手段，即可指单数，又可指复数；如果作主语，应根据意思来决

定其谓语动词用单数还是用复数。

e. g. Every means has been tried. 每一种办法都尝试过了。

All means have been tried. 所有的办法都尝试过了。

〔4〕The principal advantage of this technology is its ability to provide a multi-media environment, enhancing communication at all levels in a product's life cycle.

① to provide a multi-media environment 作定语修饰前面的 ability。

② enhancing communication at all levels in a product's life cycle 为现在分词短语做目的状语。

〔5〕Also reported were VM applications such as the virtual concurrent design and assembly of a landing gear, and simulation of side-impact collision to test vehicle safety.

该句由于副词 also 提前，采用了倒装句式。其真正主语是 VM applications，采用该句式的目的是使句子结构紧凑。

17.4　Exercise

Translate theFollowing Paragraphs

Kinematic simulation or animation can be an important CAD/CAM capability in certain settings. Through animation, users can design a product or a process that involves moving components and analyze its behavior without having to build prototypes and conduct live trial runs.

For example, mechanical linkage designs have historically been difficult because testing their actual behavior has required engineers to build models or prototypes. In such a setting, engineers frequently resort to building cardboard or wooden models, a time-consuming process. With animation, a computer model can be quickly built and displayed. By watching the computer screen, the engineer can easily see how the linkage performs.

Other useful applications of animation are in analyzing the performance of a robot in a cell or automated guided vehicles (AGV) on the shop floor. By simulating the planned behavior of a robot or an AGV, engineers and manufacturing personnel can spot and correct problems before implementing a live setting.

Lesson 18　Fluid and Hydraulic System

18.1　Text

[1] The history of hydraulic power is a long one, dating from man's prehistoric efforts to harness the energy in the world around him. The only sources readily available were the water and the wind—two free and moving streams.

The watermill, the first hydraulic motor, was an early invention. One is pictured on a mosaic at theGreat Palace in Byzantium, dating from the early fifth century. The mill had been built by the Romans. But the first record of a watermill goes back even further, to around 100 BC, and the origins may indeed have been much earlier. The domestication of grain began some 5000 years before and some enterprising farmer is bound to have become tired of pounding or grinding the grain by hand. Perhaps, in fact, the inventors were some farmer's wives. Since they often drew the heavy jobs.

【水车】

Fluid is a substance which may flow; that is, its constituent particles may continuously change their positions relative to one another. Moreover, it offers no lasting resistance to the displacement, however great, of one layer over another. This means that, if the fluid is at rest, no shear force (that is a force tangential to the surface on which it acts) can exist in it.

Fluid may be classified as Newtonian or non-Newtonian. [2] In Newtonian fluid there is a linear relation between the magnitude of applied shear stresses and the resulting rate of angular deformation. In non-Newtonian fluid there is a nonlinear relation between the magnitude of applied shear stress and the rate of angular deformation.

The flow of fluids may be classified in many ways, such as steady or non steady, rotational or irrigational, compressible or incompressible, and viscous or no viscous.

[3] All hydraulic systems depend on Pascal's law, named after Braise Pascal, who discovered the law. This law states that pressurized fluid within a closed container—such as cylinder or pipe—exerts equal force on all of the surfaces of the container.

In actual hydraulic systems, Pascal's law defines the basis of the results which are obtained from the system. Thus, a pump moves the liquid in the system. The intake of the pump is connected to a liquid source, usually called the tank or reservoir. Atmospheric pressure, pressing on the liquid in the reservoir, forces the liquid into the pump. When the pump operates, it forces liquid from the tank into the discharge pipe at a suitable pressure.

The flow of the pressurized liquid discharged by the pump is controlled by valves. Threecontrol functions are used in most hydraulic systems: (1) control of the liquid pressure, (2) control of the liquid flow rate, and (3) control of the direction of flow of the liquid.

【液压原理的实际应用】

Hydraulic drives are used in preference to mechanical systems when: (1) powers is to be transmitted between point too far apart for chains or belts; (2) high torque at low speed is required; (3) a very compact unit is needed; (4) a smooth transmission, free of vibration, is required; (5) easy control of speed and direction is necessary; (6) output speed is varied sleeplessly.

Fig. 18.1 gives a diagrammatic presentation of the components of a hydraulic installation. [4]Electrically driven oil pressure pumps establish an oil flow for energy transmission, which is fed to hydraulic motors or hydraulic cylinders, converting it into mechanical energy. The control of the oil flow is by means of valves. The pressurized oil flow produces linear or rotary mechanical motion. The kinetic energy of the oil flow is comparatively low, and therefore the term hydrostatic driver is sometimes used. There is little constructional difference between hydraulic motors and pumps. Any pump may be used as a motor. The quantity of oil flowing at any given time may be varied by means of regulating valves (as shown in Fig. 18.1) or the use of variable-delivery pumps.

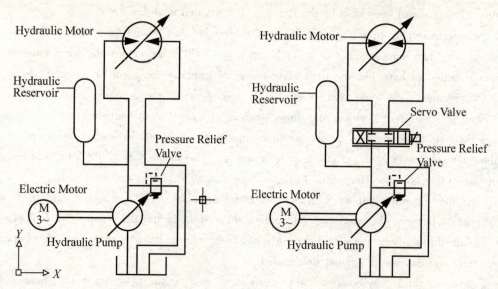

Fig. 18.1 Speed-control Methods for Hydraulic Motors

【飞行的液压助力系统】

The application of hydraulic power to the operation of machine tools is by no means new, though its adoption on such a wide scale as exists at present is comparatively recent. It was in fact the development of the modern self-contained pump unit that stimulated the growth of this form of machine tool operation.

Hydraulic machine tool drive offers a great many advantages. One of them is that it can give infinitely-variable speed control over wide ranges. In addition, they can change the direction of drive as easily as they can vary the speed. As in many other types of machine, many complex mechanical linkages can be simplified or even wholly eliminated by the use of hydraulics.

The flexibility and resilience of hydraulic power is another great virtue of this form of drive. Apart from the smoothness of operation thus obtained, a great improvement is usually found in the surface finish on the work and the tool can make heavier cuts without detriment and will last considerably longer without regrinding.

18.2 Words and Phrases

hydraulic system	液压系统
displacement [disˈpleismənt]	n. 位移，转移，置换
layer [ˈleiə]	n. 层，层次
tangential [tænˈdʒenʃ(ə)l]	adj. 切线的，切向的
Newtonian [njuːˈtəunjən, -niən]	adj. 牛顿的，牛顿学说的
nonlinear [ˈnɔnˈliniə]	adj. 非线性的，非直线的
rotational [rəuˈteiʃənəl]	adj. 旋转的，转动的，循环的
compressible [kəmˈpresəbl]	adj. 可压缩的，可压榨的
Pascal's law	帕斯卡定律
intake [ˈinteik]	n. 入口，进口，进入量
tank [tæŋk]	n. 油箱，水箱，池塘
reservoir [ˈrezəwɑː]	n. 蓄水池，水箱，蓄能器
atmospheric [ˌætməsˈferik]	adj. 大气的，空气的
discharge [disˈtʃɑːdʒ]	n. 卸货，出料，流出；vi. 卸下，放出
pressurize [ˈpreʃəraiz]	v. 增压，给……加压
prehistoric [ˈpriːhisˈtɔrik]	adj. 史前的，很久以前的
harness [ˈhɑːnis]	v. 利用（风等）作动力，治理，控制
watermill [ˈwɔːtəmil]	n. 水车，水磨
mosaic [mɔˈzeiik]	n. 镶嵌细工，马赛克
domestication [dəuˌmestiˈkeiʃən]	n. 家养，驯养
preference [ˈprefərəns]	n. 优先选择
compact [ˈkɔmpækt]	adj. 紧凑的，紧密的，简洁的
diagrammatic [ˌdaiəgrəˈmætik]	adj. 图表的，概略的
oil pressure pump	油泵
hydraulic motor	液压电机
hydraulic cylinder	油缸
kinetic energy	动能
hydrostatic driver	静压传动
variable-delivery pump	变量泵
by no means	决不……
self-contained	独立的，配套的，整体的
stimulate [ˈstimjuleit]	v. 促进，激励
hydraulics [haiˈdrɔːliks]	n. 水力学，液压系统
resilience [riˈziliəns]	n. 跳回，恢复力，回弹

virtue ['vəːtjuː]　　　　　　　n. 优点，效力，功能
detriment ['detrimənt]　　　　n. 损害，不利
regrind [riˈgraind]　　　　　　v. 重磨

18.3　Complex Sentence Analysis

［1］ The history of hydraulic power is a long one, dating from man's prehistoric efforts to harness the energy in the world around him.
① dating from：从什么时候开始。
② prehistoric efforts：很久以前的努力。

［2］ In Newtonian fluid there is a linear relation between the magnitude of applied shear stresses and the resulting rate of angular deformation.
① between：在两者之间。
② applied shear stresses：作用的剪切应力。
③ the resulting rate：总的合率（量）。

［3］ All hydraulic systems depend on Pascal's law, named after Braise Pascal, who discovered the law.
① depend on：依赖，取决于，遵循。
② named after：根据……命名的。
③ who discovered the law 是非限定性定语从句，修饰 Braise Pascal。

［4］ Electrically driven oil pressure pumps establish an oil flow for energy transmission, which is fed to hydraulic motors or hydraulic cylinders, converting it into mechanical energy.
① which is fed to hydraulic motors or hydraulic cylinders 中的 which 是指 oil flow。
② converting…into…指"转换（形式）"的意思。

18.4　Exercise

Translate the Following Paragraphs

Compressors are used in petrochemical plants to raise the static pressure of air and process gases to levels required to overcome pipe friction, effect a certain reaction at the point of final delivery, or to impart desired thermodynamic properties to the medium compressed. These compressors come in a variety of sizes, types, and models, each of which fulfill a given need and is likely to represent the optimum configuration for a given set of requirements.

Selection of compressor types must, therefore, be preceded by a comparison between service requirements and compressor capabilities. This initial comparison will generally lead to a review of the economies of space, installing cost, operating cost, and maintenance requirements of competing types. Where the superiority of one compressor type or model over a competing offer is not obvious, a more detailed analysis may be justified.

Lesson 19 Product Test and Quality Control

19.1 Text

ProductTest

Product test can be thought of as theculmination of all process control work. It can also be thought of as a quality check of the inspection process itself. If the quality plan is adequate and carried out properly, then the product's performance should have been verified and a total test is redundant. For this reason, a test of the completed product is often nothing more than a contractual requirement that must be performed before the customer accepts the product. But product test is also more than proving. And testing to whole is equal to the sum of the parts. [1] It allows for gathering data that support the design theory of the product, for interpretations to be made for further improvements in design so that future products will be better than present ones, and for evaluation of design evolution toward better performance and costs. In addition, it is a means of verifying design, since not all design parameters can be fully calculated or predicted.

【铁路系统模块元件检测】

Product test engineers work closely with design engineers to provide useful data for testing. They must also work in close harmony with engineers all other phases of manufacturing. Not infrequently, product testing will turn up deficiencies in design that requires major revisions in manufacturing processes. This is particularly true if the company produces many prototypes and has short production runs. Therefore, manufacturing engineers are as interested in product test's results as are design engineers.

For complex products, product test becomes a very important part of the total process control function. It gives the company a high degree of confidence that the product will perform as the customer expects it to, and this is a valuable marketing tool as it helps to establish the proper reputation with the customers.

GeometricErrors

Geometric errors are defined here as errors in form of individual machine components (e.g., straightness of motion of a linear bearing). Geometric errors are concerned with thequasi-static accuracy of surface, which bear upon the moving relative of the surfaces. Geometric errors can be smooth and continuous (systematic) or they can exhibit hysteresis (e.g., backlash) or random behavior. [2] Many factors affect geometric errors including: surface straightness (as shown in Fig. 19.1), surface roughness, bearing preload, kinematics versus elastic design principles and structural design philosophies.

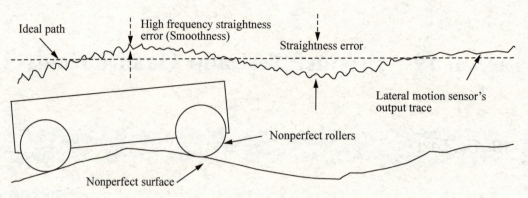

Fig. 19.1 Straightness Errors Caused by Surface Form and Finish Errors

QualityPlanning

This is the planning and strategy activity of process control, and is sometimes referred to as process planning or inspection planning. The engineers involved develop the plans for checking the adequacy of performance of shop operations to ensure that the final product performs as designed. Using plans and methods produced by measurement of productivity and work measurement (MP&WM) as a guide, quality-planning engineers determine where inspections and nondestructive tests will be specified during the manufacturing process. They also specify the type of inspection or test to be conducted and, based on design engineering requirements, determine what will constitute acceptance or rejection.

Normal manufacturing activities produce a certain percentage of deviations from drawing. Some are important, some of little consequence. It is the quality planning engineers' responsibility to evaluate these deviations and determine what the proper corrective action will be. They then ensure through MP&WM that the corrective actions are factored into manufacturing planning for rework. As the arbiter of quality via the deviation from drawing procedure, quality planning has the database to evaluate performance of the various shop and support functions. A score-keeping function is possible and desirable; in this way quality planning can report to management whether quality levels are improving or declining.

Quality status can be reported by statistically evaluating the numbers of deviations and their seriousness. This leads naturally to an evaluation of the cost of doing the repair work caused by the deviation. Repair work, which constitutes manufacturing losses, is an important measurement of organizational quality levels. Manufacturing losses are a significant measure of the adequacy of attention to detail of the operators and their foremen. High losses indicate a poorly managed operation. Quality planning engineers are responsible for setting the manufacturing losses, budgets, and measurements policy.

QualityControl

Quality control has traditionally been theliaison between manufacturing and design. This function interprets design's specifications for manufacturing and develops the quality plan to be integrated into manufacturing engineering's methods and planning instructions to operations. Quality control is also responsible for recommending to management what level of manufacturing losses (cost of mistakes in producing the product) can be tolerated. This is based on the complexity of the product design; specifically the degree of preciseness necessary in tolerances. Quality control traditionally monitors manufacturing losses by setting a negative budget that is not to be exceeded, and establishes routines for measurement and corrective action.

Within the past decade or two, quality control has become increasingly involved with marketing and customers in establishing documentation systems to ensure guaranteed levels of product quality. This new role has led to the new title quality assurance, to differentiate it from traditional in-house quality control.

Quality assurance strives through documentation of performance and characteristics at each stage of manufacture to ensure that the product will perform at the intended level. Whereas quality control is involved directly with manufacturing operations, quality assurance is involved with the customer support responsibilities generally found within the marketing function. Many industrial organizations have chosen to establish an independent quality assurance sub-function within the manufacturing function and have placed the technical responsibilities of quality control, namely process control, within the manufacturing engineering organization.

19.2 Words and Phrases

culmination [kʌlmiˈneiʃən]   n. 顶点
contractual [kənˈtræktjuəl]   adj. 契约的
deficiency [diˈfiʃənsi]   n. 缺乏，不足
quasi-static   准静态的
hysteresis [ˌhistəˈriːsis]   n. 滞后作用，[物] 磁滞现象
liaison [li(ː)ˈeizɑːn, -zən]   n. 联络，(语音) 连音

19.3 Complex Sentence Analysis

[1] It allows for gathering data that support the design theory of the product, for interpretations to be made for further improvements in design so that future products will be better than present ones, and for evaluation of design evolution toward better performance costs.
两个 for 引导的介词短语在整个句子中充当状语。

[2] Many factors affect geometric errors including: surface straightness (as shown in Fig. 18.1), surface roughness, bearing preload, kinematics versus elastic design principles and structural design philosophies.

① surface straightness 表示"平面度"。
② surface roughness 表示"表面粗糙度"。
③ versus elastic design principles（相对于弹性设计原理）介词短语修饰 kinematics（运动学）。

19.4　Exercise

Translate the Following Paragraphs

Machine parts are manufactured so they are interchangeable. In other words, each part of a machine or mechanism is made to a certain size and shape so it will fit into any other machine or mechanism of the same type. To make the part interchangeable, each individual part must be made to a size that will fit the mating part in the correct way. It is not only impossible, but also impractical to make many parts to an exact size. This is because machines are not perfect, and the tools become worn. A slight variation from the exact size is always allowed. The amount of this variation depends on the kind of part being manufactured. For example, a part might be made 6 in. long with a variation allowed of 0.003 (three-thousandths) in, above and below this size. Therefore, the part could be 5.997 in. to 6.003 in. and still be the correct size. These are known as the limits. The difference between upper and lower limits is called the tolerance. A tolerance is the total permissible variation in the size of a part. The basic size is that size from which limits of size are derived by the application of allowances and tolerances. Sometimes the limit is allowed in only one direction. This is known as unilateral tolerance. Unilateral tolerance is a system of dimensioning where the tolerance (that is variation) is shown in only one direction from the nominal size. Unilateral tolerance allows the changing of tolerance on a hole or shaft without seriously affecting the fit.

When the tolerance is in both directions from the basic size, it is known as a bilateral tolerance (plus and minus). Bilateral tolerance is a system of dimensioning where the tolerance (that is variation) is split and is shown on either side of the nominal size. Limit dimensioning is a system of dimensioning where only the maximum and minimum dimensions are shown. Thus, the tolerance is the difference between these two dimensions.

Lesson 20　Introduction of Automobile Engine

20.1　Text

It is well-known that the automobile is composed of four sections such as engine, chassis, body and electrical system. The engine which is called the "heart" of a vehicle is used to supply power for an automobile. There are various types of engines such as electric engine (motor), steam engine and internal combustion engine (ICE). Generally, an automobile is operated by internal combustion engine. It includes the fuel, lubricating, cooling, ignition and starting systems. [1]The internal combustion engine burns fuel within the cylinders and converts the expanding force of the combustion or "explosion" into rotary force used to propel the vehicle.

【两轮车上的福克斯发动机】

In general, the location relations of engine and driving wheels fall into these: (1) Engine lies in the front of automobile and driving wheels are rear drive type; (2) Engine lies in the front of automobile and driving wheels are front drive type; (3) Engine lies in the rear of automobile and driving wheels are rear drive type; (4) Engine lies in the middle of automobile and driving wheels are rear drive type; (5) full-wheel-drive, etc.

There are seven broad classifications of engines, which are introduced as follows.

(1) By the Location of the Combustion.

An internal combustion engine and an external combustion engine:

In an internal combustion engine, the combustion occurs within the engine. According to thefuel energy used, internal combustion engines are further divided into gasoline engines (spark-ignition engine), diesel engines (compression-ignition engines), other fuels engines (e.g. kerosene, alcohol, hydrogen, natural gas and liquid petroleum, etc. An external combustion engine, such as steam engine, has the combustion out of the engine. But, the internal combustion engine seems to be the one most commonly used in the automotive field.

【柴油发动机】

【燃料内部氧化发动机的优缺点】

(2) By Stroke.

Two-and four-stroke engines (the Otto cycle engine).

(3) By Cooling System.

Liquid-cooled and air-cooled engines.

(4) By the Type of Internal Motion.

【二冲程与四冲程发动机】

A reciprocating engine and rotary engine (Wankel engine):

[2] In a reciprocating engine, the motion produced from the energy within the fuel moves parts up and down. The gasoline and diesel engines are reciprocating engines. In a rotary engine (Fig. 20.1), for example, a turbine engine, the parts that are moving rotate continuously.

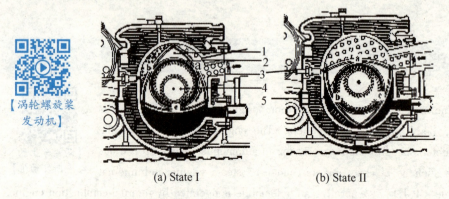

(a) State I (b) State II

Fig. 20.1 Rotary (Piston) Engine

Fig. 20.1 (a) a. intake; b. compression; c. exhaust.
Fig. 20.1 (b) a. filled fresh air-fuel mixture; b. combustion gases expand; c. exhaust.
1. rotor (rotary piston); 2. internal ring gear in the rotor; 3. spark plug; 4. stationary pinion; 5. bearing surface of the eccentric.

(5) By the Type of Ignition Systems.

Spark-ignition and compression-ignition engines.

(6) By the Type of Combustion.

Intermittent combustion and continuous combustion engines:

Intermittent combustion means that the combustion within the engine starts and stops. A standard gasoline and diesel engines are called intermittent combustion ones. Engines that use continuous combustion includeturbine engines, rocket engines, Stirling engines, and jet engines.

(7) By the Location of Cylinders.

In-line engine, V-type engine and opposed-cylinder engine.

Modern automobiles mainly install reciprocating piston four-stroke engine. When crankshaft of the engine turns (rotates) two circles, piston reciprocate four times within cylinders up and down, achieves intake air, compression, power and exhaust air four stages continually, completes a cycle.

EngineConsists of Several Systems below:

(1) Crank mechanism: cylinder block, cylinder head, piston, connecting rod, crankshaft and flywheel, etc.

(2) Valve train: valve, rocker arm, push-rod, timing gear and camshaft, etc.

(3) Fuel supply (feed) system.

① Gasoline engine fuel supply system: gasoline tank, gasoline filter, air filter, gasoline pump, carburetor, intake manifold (pipe), exhaust manifold (pipe) and muffler (silencer).

② Diesel engine fuel supply system: diesel tank, diesel filter, fuel delivery pump, fuel injection pump, fuel injection spout, governor, intake manifold (pipe), exhaust manifold (pipe) and muffler (silencer).

(4) Lubrication system: oil pump, oil filter, oil radiator and lubrication oil manifold.

(5) Cooling system: liquid (water) cooling and air cooling.

(6) Ignition system: battery, engine, ignition coil, distributor and spark plug. Battery ignition system is used mostly, and semiconductor ignition system is making a rapid progress.

(7) Starting system: starter and add-on equipment. Generally, the starter of automobiles is DC motor. The power of gasoline engine starter is commonly less than 1.5kW, and diesel engine starter power is greater (more) than 5kW.

Fig. 20.2 is a cutaway view of an in-line four-cylinder gasoline engine.

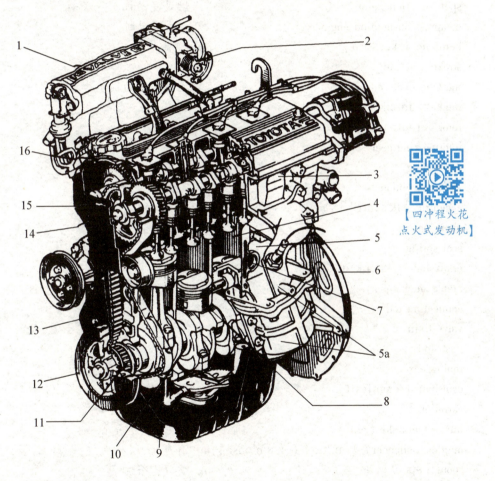

Fig. 20.2　Inline Four-Cylinder Gasoline Engine

1. intake air tank; 2. throttle valve; 3. cylinder head; 4. cylinder; 5. cylinder block; 6. flywheel; 7. cylinder jacket; 8. piston; 9. oil pan (oil sump); 10. crankshaft; 11. timing belt pulley; 12. crankshaft pulley; 13. timing belt; 14. camshaft; 15. timing belt cover; 16. spark plug; 5a. exhaust gas manifold with catalytic converter.

20.2　Words and Phrases

chassis ['ʃæsi]	n. 底盘
combustion [kəm'bʌstʃən]	n. 燃烧
internal combustion engine (ICE)	内燃机
ignition [ig'nitiʃn]	n. 点火；点燃
propel [prə'pel]	v. 推进，驱使
spark-ignitionengine	点燃式发动机
compression-ignition engines	压燃式发动机
kerosene ['kerəsiːn]	n. 煤油
stroke [strəuk]	n. 冲程
the Otto cycle engine	奥托循环发动机
intake ['inteik]	n. 进气
rotor ['rəutə]	n. 转子
internal ring gear	内齿圈
spark plug	火花塞
stationarypinion	固定齿轮
eccentric [ik'sentrik]	adj. 偏心的
apex seal	顶端密封条
seal spring	密封条弹簧
crankshaft ['kræŋkʃɑːft]	n. 曲轴
crank mechanism	曲柄连杆机构
connecting rod	连杆
valve train	配气机构
push-rod	n. 推杆
timinggear	正时齿轮
camshaft ['kæmʃɑːft]	n. 凸轮轴
carburetor	n. 化油器
intake manifold (pipe)	进气歧管，进气管
muffler (silencer) ['mʌflə] (['sailənsə])	n. 消声器
spout [spaut]	n. 喷口；喷嘴
governor ['gʌvənə]	n. 调速器
radiator ['reidieitə]	n. 散热器
distributor [dis'tribjutə]	n. 分电器
cutaway view	剖视图
four-cylinder	四缸
intake air tank	进气室
throttle valve	节气门

Introduction of Automobile Engine Lesson 20

catalytic converter 催化转化器
jacket ['dʒækit] n. [机]水套
oil pan (oil sump) 油底壳
timing belt pulley 正时齿带轮

20.3　Complex Sentence Analysis

[1] The internal combustion engine burns fuel within the cylinders and converts the expanding force of the combustion or "explosion" into rotary force used to propel the vehicle.
内燃机在气缸内燃烧燃料，并把燃料的膨胀或爆炸力转换为旋转力来驱动汽车。
① within the cylinders：作 burns 的状语。
② convert…into…：把……转换成……。
③ of the combustion or "explosion"：修饰 the expanding force。

[2] In a reciprocating engine, the motion produced from the energy within the fuel moves parts up and down.
在往复式发动机中，依靠燃料释放能量产生的动作上下推动零件。
① within the fuel moves parts up and down：修饰 energy；up and down 上下。
② produced from…：产生于……。

20.4　Exercise

Translate the Following Paragraphs

Ford's latest concept car gives shape to the ideas being explored by the New Generation Vehicle Program-the effort by a U. S. consortium to develop the so-called "super car". The goal is to create an 80-mpg, full-size affordable family sedan and make it available in the coming decade.

The car is called Synergy 2010. It's aluminum body saves some 400 pounds over a comparable-size steel body, bringing curb weight down to about 2200 pounds. The car's low profile and aerodynamic "fences" (vertical fenders) reflect the need to cut drag to about one-third that of today's sedans.

Power comes from a direct-injection diesel turbo alternator, which uses a flywheel to store energy for acceleration. Electric current produced by the system powers a separate electric motor in each wheel hub, while regenerative braking recharges the flywheel duringdeceleration. The flywheel-based hybrid drive concept has been under investigation for decades, even at Ford, but problems remain with building a production flywheel system. Likewise the wheel-in-hub motors, which are easy to package but present safety problems in the event of a single-motor failure.

The design comesup with a layered glass roof. To avoid turning the car into a hot-house, solar-powered cooling fans pull in cooler outside air and exhaust interior air. Another unusual feature is a turn-over steering column that converts to right-hand drive without modification. Many interior controls respond to a new voice-activation system that operates without initial.

Lesson 21　　The Automobile Components

21.1　Text

Engine

The engine is a power plant, which provides power to drive the automobile.

In most automobile engines, the explosive power of the mixture of air and gasoline drives the pistons. The pistons turn a crankshaft to which they are attached. The rotating force of the crankshaft makes the automobile's wheels turn.

A number of systems are necessary to make an engine work. A lubrication system is needed to reduce friction and prevent engine wear. A cooling system is required to keep the engine's temperature within safe limits. The engine must be provided with the correct amount of air and fuel by a fuel system.

The mixture of air and fuel must be ignited inside the cylinder at just the right time by an ignition system.[1] Finally, an electrical system is required to operate the cranking motor that starts the engine and to provide electrical energy to power engine accessories.

【燃料和润滑剂】

【引擎润滑】

【引擎冷却】

【汽化器和燃料添加】

Lubrication System

An engine has many moving parts which eventually develop wear, as they move against each other. The engine circulates oil between these moving parts to prevent the metal-to-metal contact that results in wear. Parts that are oiled can move more easily with less friction and hence power loss due to friction is minimized. The secondary function of lubricant is to act as acoolant and also as a sealing medium to prevent leakages. Finally, a film of lubricant on the cylinder walls helps the rings in sealing and thus improves the engine's compressions.

Cooling System

Due to the combustion of fuel with air inside the cylinder, the temperature of the engine parts increases. This increase of temperature directly affects the engine performance and the life of the engine parts. The cooling system keeps the engine operating at the efficient temperature. Whatever the driving conditions, the system is designed to prevent both overheating and overcooling.

Fuel System

The main function of the fuel supply system is to provide fuel to thecarburetor or injection system at a rate and pressure sufficient to meet engine demands under all conditions of load, speed and gradients encountered by the vehicle. The fuel system must also have enough reserve fuel for several miles of vehicle operation.

Ignition System

The purpose of the ignition system is to provide assistance for the combustion of fuel either by a high voltage spark or self-ignition in each of the engine's cylinder at the right time so that the air-fuel mixture can burn completely.

The fuel supplied to thecombustion chamber must be ignited to deliver power. In a spark-ignition engine an electric spark is used for this purpose. The compression-ignition engine does not require a separate ignition system because the ignition is affected by compression of the mixture.

Electrical System

The engine's electrical system provides energy to operate a starting motor and to power all the accessories. The main components of the electrical system are a battery, an alternator, a starting motor, ignition coil and heater.

Frame

The frame provides a foundation for the engine and the body of the vehicle. The frame is constructed from square or box-shaped steel members strong enough to support the weight of the body and other components.

The automobile frame is usually made up of a number of members welded or riveted together to give the final shape. The engine ismounted on the frame with rubber pads which absorb vibrations and also provide damping of these vibrations. Absorption and damping of vibrations protects passengers from discomfort caused by shocks.

Suspension System

The function of the suspension system is to absorb vibrations due to the up and down motion of wheels, caused by the irregularities in the road surface. The springs, connecting linkages, and shock absorber comprise the suspension system of a vehicle. The suspension system is of two types:

(1) Rigid system.

(2) Independent system.

In the rigid system, the road springs are attached to a rigid beam axle. It is mostly used in the front axle of commercial vehicles and in the car axle of all types of vehicles.

The independent system does not have a rigid axle. Each wheel is free to move vertically without any reaction on its mating wheel. The independent system is mostly used in small cars.

Power Train

The power train carries the power that the engine produces to the car wheels. It consists of the clutch (on cars with a manual transmission), transmission (a system of gears that increases the turning effort of the engine to move the automobile), drive shaft, differential and rear axle.

Clutch

A clutch is required with the manual transmission system to temporarily disconnect the engine from wheels. [2] Such disengagement of the power train from the engine is essential while changing the gear ratio or while stopping the vehicle.

Transmission

The main function of the transmission is to provide the necessary variation to the torque applied by the engine to the wheels. This is achieved by changing the gearing ratio between the engine output shaft and the drive shaft.

Drive Shaft

The drive shaft or propeller shaft connects the gearbox and the differential unit. The drive shaft has universal joints at its ends.

Differential

The function of the differential is to split the power received from the propeller shaft to the rear axle shaft. It allows the rear wheels to be driven at different speeds when the vehicle takes a bend or falls into a ditch.

Axles

Axles are the shafts on which road wheels are mounted. The road wheels are provided with the required drive through these axles.

【轮子和轮胎】

Wheels

The automobile wheels take the load of the vehicle and also producetractive force to move the vehicle. The wheels are also used for retardation and for stopping the vehicle.

【转向盘】

Steering System

Thesteering system is used for changing the direction of the vehicle. [3] The major requirements in any steering mechanism are that it should be precise and easy to handle, and that the front wheels should have a tendency to return to the straight-ahead position after a turn. A gear mechanism, which is known as steering gear, is used in this system to increase the steering effort provided by the driver. This system makes the vehicle steering very easy as the driver does not have to put in much effort. Vehicle steering is not only required on a curved road but also while maneuvering on the busy traffic roads.

The Automobile Components   Lesson 21

21.2 Words and Phrases

accessory [ækˈsesəri]	n. 附件
circulate [ˈsəːkjuleit]	v. (使) 流通, (使) 运行, (使) 循环
coolant [ˈkuːlənt]	n. 冷却剂, 冷冻剂
leakage [ˈliːkidʒ]	n. 漏, 泄漏, 渗漏
sufficient [səˈfiʃənt]	adj. 充分的, 足够的
gradient [ˈgreidiənt]	adj. 倾斜的; n. 梯度, 倾斜度, 坡
combustion chamber	燃烧室
component [kəmˈpəunənt]	n. 成分; adj. 组成的, 构成的
alternator [ˈɔːltə(ː)neitə]	n. 交流发电机
damping [ˈdæmpiŋ]	n. 阻尼, 减幅, 衰减
suspension [səsˈpenʃən]	n. 悬挂, 悬架
irregularity [iˌregjuˈlæriti]	n. 不规则, 无规律
rigid [ˈridʒid]	adj. 刚性的
beam [biːm]	n. 梁, 横梁
powertrain	动力传动系
differential [ˌdifəˈrenʃəl]	n. 差速器, 差动装置
disengagement [ˈdisinˈgeidʒmənt]	n. 脱离
tractive force	牵引力
retardation [ˌriːtɑːˈdeiʃən]	n. 延迟, 障碍物, 制动
steer	n. 驾驶, 转向

21.3 Complex Sentence Analysis

[1] Finally, an electrical system is required to operate the cranking motor that starts the engine and to provide electrical energy to power engine accessories.
   最后，电子系统用来控制启动发动机用的曲柄电动机和为发动机附件提供电能。
   ① that 引导的定语从句修饰 motor。
   ② to operate 和 to provide 并列作目的状语。

[2] Such disengagement of the power train from the engine is essential while changing or while stopping the vehicle.
   当换挡或停车时，必须断开传动系和发动机的连接。
   while 引导时间状语从句。

[3] The major requirements in any steering mechanism are that it should be precise and easy to handle, and that the front wheels should have a tendency to return to the straight-

ahead position after a turn.
① 两个 that 引导的是并列表语从句。
② steering mechanism 表示"转向机构"。

[4] As the load on the vehicle and the vehicle speed has increased according to recent trends, in modern days, the importance of the brake system has also increased and power brakes are now being preferred.
① according to 表示"按照"的意思。
② as 引导时间状语从句。

21.4 Exercise

Translate the Following Paragraphs

Brakes are required for slowing down or stopping a moving vehicle. The braking system may be operated mechanically or hydraulically. 95 percent of the braking systems in use today are of the hydraulic type.

All brakes consist of two members, one rotating and the other stationary. There are various means by which the two members can be brought in contact, thus reducing the speed of the vehicle.

The major components of the braking system are: brakepedal, master cylinder, wheel cylinder, brake drum, brake pipe, brake shoes, brake packing plant and linkages. [4] As the load on the vehicle and the vehicle speed has increased according to recent trends, in modern days, the importance of the braking system has also increased and power brakes are now being preferred. Power brakes utilize vacuum and air pressure to provide most of the brake—applying effort.

Lesson 22　Mechatronics

22.1　Text

Mechatronics was originally coined in 1970s from the integration of two engineering disciplines—mechanics and electronics. [1] More recently, with spectacular advancements in the areas of control and communications, the word mechatronics has been adapted as the synergetic integration of three disciplines: mechanics, control and electronics and is aimed at the study of mainly manufacturing machines controlled by electronics. It is also being viewed as the fusion of mechanical engineering with electronics and intelligent computer control in the design and manufacture of industrial products and processes. Of late the notion of "intelligence" or "smartness" is associated with these industrial machines and they are being called "intelligent" or "smart" machines. Mechatronics is also defined as the synergetic integration of mechanical engineering with electronics and intelligent computer control in the design and manufacture of products and processes.

[2] In engineering terms, what can be made to emerge is a new and previously unattainable set of performance characteristics. Thus mechatronics is truly an interdisciplinary subject drawn from mechanical, electrical, electronics, computer, and manufacturing engineering. The subject of mechatronics is gaining acceptance as an essential course in engineering education throughout Asia, Europe and the U.S.A and the field of mechatronics as a basis for new industrial development. The technology areas of mechatronics involve system modeling, simulation, sensors and measurement systems, drive and actuation system, analysis of the behavior of systems, control systems and microprocessor systems.

Mechatronics paradigm

[3] Mechatronics paradigm deals with benchmarking and emerging problems in engineering, science, and technologies which have not been attacked and solved. Mechatronics is an integrated comprehensive study of 【集成电路的产生】 intelligent and high performance electromechanical system (mechanisms and processes), intelligent and motion control through the use of advanced microprocessors and DSPs, power electronics and ICs, design and optimization, modeling and simulation, analysis and virtual prototyping, etc. Integrated multidisciplinary features are approaching quickly, and mechatronics, which integrates electrical, mechanical, and computer engineering areas (as shown in Fig. 22.1), takes place.

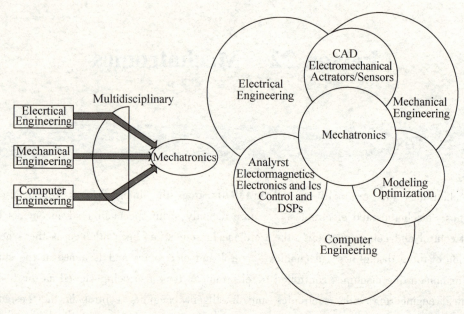

Fig. 22.1 Mechatronics Integrates Electrical, Mechanical and Computer Engineering

One of the most challenging problems in mechatronics systems design is the development of system architecture, e.g., selection of hardware (actuators, sensors, devices, power electronics, IC, microcontrollers, and DSP) and software (environment and computation algorithms to perform sensing and control, information flow and data acquisition, simulation, visualization, and virtual prototyping). [4]Attempts to design state-of-the-art man-made mechatronics systems and to guarantee the integrated design can be pursued through analysis of complex patterns and paradigms of evolutionary developed biological systems. Recent trends in engineering have increased the emphasis on integrated analysis, design and control of advanced mechanical systems. The scope of mechatronics system has continued to expand, and in addition to actuators, sensors, power electronics, IC microprocessors, DSP, as well as input/output devices. The mechatronics paradigm was introduced with the ultimate goals to:

(1) Guarantee an eventual consensus and ensure descriptive multidisciplinary features;

(2) Extend and augment the results of classical mechanics, electromechanical systems, power electronics, IC, and control theory to advanced hardware and software;

(3) Acquire and expand the engineering core integrating interdisciplinary areas;

(4) Link and place the integrated perspectives of electromechanical systems, power electronics, IC, DSP, control, signal processing. MEMS and NEMS in the engineering curriculum in favor of the common structure needed.

The study of high-performance electromechanical systems should be considered as the unified cornerstone of the engineering curriculum through mechatronics. The unified analysis of actuators and sensors (e. g. electromechanical motion devices), power electronics and ICs, microprocessors and DSP, advanced hardware and software, have barely been introduced in the engineering curriculum. Mechatronics, as a breakthrough concept in design and analysis of conventional, micro- and nano-scale electromechanical system, was introduced to attack, integrate and solve a great variety of emerging problems. Mechatronics systems, as shown in Fig. 21.2, can be classified as (1) conventional mechatronics systems, (2) microeletromechanical-micromechatronics system (MEMS), (3) nanoelectromechanical-nanomechatronics systems (NEMS). The operational principles and basic fundamentals of conventional mechatronics systems and MEMS are the same, while NEMS are studied using different concepts and theories. In particular, the designer applies the classical mechanics and electromagnetics to study conventional mechatronics systems and MEMS. Quantum theory and nanoelectromechanics are applied in NEMS. The fundamental theories used to study the effects, processes, and phenomena in conventional, micro-and nano- scale mechatronics systems are illustrated in Fig. 22.2.

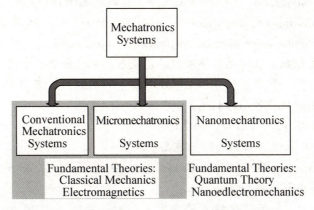

Fig. 22.2 Classification and Fundamental Theories Applied in Mechatronics Systems

22.2 Words and Phrases

mechatronics	机电一体化
coin [kɔin]	v. 造词
integration [ˌintiˈgreiʃən]	n. 集成
synergetic [ˌsinəˈdʒetik]	adj. 协同的,合作的
fusion [ˈfjuːʒən]	n. 融合
notion [ˈnəuʃən]	n. 概念,想法
unattainable [ˈʌnəˈteinəb]	a. 做不到的
interdisciplinary [ˌintəˈdisiplinəri]	adj. 学科间的

paradigm	[ˈpærədaim]	n.	范例
benchmark	[ˈbentʃmɑːk]	n.	基准，标准
entreaty	[inˈtriːti]	n.	恳求，请求
evolutionary	[ˌiːvəˈluːʃənəri]	adj.	发展的，演化的
DSP (Digital Signal Processing)			数字信号处理
IC (Integrated Circuit)			集成电路
consensus	[kənˈsensəs]	n.	一致
augment	[ɔːgˈment]	v.	增加，扩大
unify	[ˈjuːnifai]	v.	成为一体，统一
cornerstone	[ˈkɔːnəstəʊn]	n.	基石，基础

22.3　Complex Sentence Analysis

［1］ More recently, with spectacular advancements in the areas of control and communications, the word mechatronics has been adapted as the synergetic integration of three disciplines: mechanics, control and electronics and is aimed at the study of mainly manufacturing machines controlled by electronics.

最近随着控制工程和通信领域的迅猛发展，机电一体化这个术语已经用于描述机械工程学、控制工程学和电子学三大学科的集成，其目标主要是研究由电子学所控制的机械产品的制造。

① 句中的 with 表示"随着"的意思。

② is aimed at 表示"目的为"的意思。

［2］ In engineering terms, what can be made to emerge is a new and previously unattainable set of performance characteristics.

在工程上，一个新诞生的术语肯定是新的、以前不具有的一系列性能特征的组合。

① In engineering terms 表示"工程上来说"的意思。

② what can be made to emerge 是一个主语从句。

［3］ Mechatronics paradigm deals with benchmarking and emerging problems in engineering, science, and technologies which have not been attacked and solved.

机电一体化范例是处理工程、科学和技术上出现的还没有破解和解决的基准程序技术和新兴的问题。

① deals with 表示"处理"的意思。

② which have not been attacked and solved 是一个定语从句，修饰前面的 problems。

［4］ Attempts to design state-of-the-art man-made mechatronics systems and to guarantee the integrated design can be pursued through analysis of complex patterns and paradigms of evolutionary developed biological systems.

通过分析复杂的模型和高级的生物系统的范例来设计具有艺术特性的人造的机电

一体化系统，并保证这一集成设计能继续深入。

① attempts to 表示"……方面的尝试、……方面的努力"的意思。
② state-of-the-art man-made 表示"具有艺术特性的人造的"的意思。

22.4　Exercise

Translate the Following Paragraphs

Amechatronics product such as modern SLR cameras, viedo recorders, music synthesizers, automobiles with engine management systems etc. cannot be designed by a single person; it is simply too complex. Nor can it be designed by a large number of persons with different specializations unless these persons operate in a team manner.

It used to bethe case that a product containing some mechanical functionality, some electronic sensing and control would be designed sequentially. First the basic mechanical structure would be designed and made by the mechanical engineers. It would then become the job of the electronics engineers to fit it with the appropriate transducers and actuators. Finally the control engineers would be given the job of finding effective controller structures and algorithms to drive it. There are a number of striking examples of the disastrous consequences of this design philosophy when the product is of a high degree of complexity.

Instead, themechatronics design methodology demands teamwork right from the start with the team including not only the technical design experts from the various contributing disciplines, marketing, financial and other departments.

Lesson 23 Industrial Robots

23.1 Text

A robot is an automatically controlled, reprogrammable, multipurpose, manipulating machine with several reprogrammable axes, [1] which may be either fixed in place or mobile for use in industrial automation applications.

The key words are reprogrammable and multipurpose because most single-purpose machines do not meet these two requirements. The term "reprogrammable" implies two things: The robot operates according to a written program, and this program can be rewritten to accommodate a variety of manufacturing tasks. The term "multipurpose" means that the robot can perform many different functions, depending on the program and tooling currently in use.

Over the past two decades, the robot has been introduced into industry to perform manymonotonous and often unsafe operations. Because robots can perform certain basic tasks more quickly and accurately than humans, they are being increasingly used in various manufacturing industries.

Structures of Robots

The typical structure of industrial robots consists of 4 major components: the manipulator, theend effector, the power supply and the control system, as shown in Fig. 23.1.

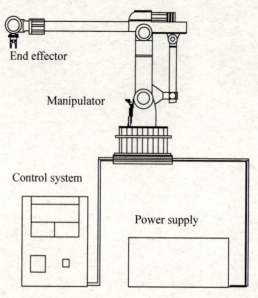

Fig. 23.1 Structures of Robots

The manipulator is a mechanical unit that provides motions similar to those of a human arm. It often has a shoulder joint, anelbow and a wrist. It can rotate or slide, stretch out and withdraw in every possible direction with certain flexibility.

The basic mechanical configurations of the robot manipulator are categorized ascartesian, cylindrical, spherical and articulated. A robot with a cartesian geometry can move its gripper to any position within the cube or rectangle defined as its working volume. Cylindrical coordinate robots can move the gripper within a volume that is described by a cylinder. The cylindrical coordinate robot is positioned in the work area by two linear movements in the X and Y directions and one angular rotation about the Z axis. Spherical arm geometry robots position the wrist through two rotations and one linear actuation. Articulated industrial robots have an irregular work envelope. This type of robot has two main variants, vertically articulated and horizontally articulated.

The endeffector attaches itself to the end of the robot wrist, also called end-of-arm tooling. [2] It is the device intended for performing the designed operations as a human hand can. End effectors are generally custom-made to meet special handling requirements. Mechanical grippers are the most commonly used and are equipped with two or more fingers. The selection of an appropriate end effector for a specific application depends on such factors as the payload, environment, reliability, and cost.

The power supply is the actuator for moving the robot arm, controlling the joints and operating the endeffector. The basic types of power sources include electrical, pneumatic, and hydraulic. Each source of energy and each type of motor has its own characteristics, advantages and limitations. An ac-powered or dc-powered motor may be used depending on the system design and applications. These motors convert electrical energy into mechanical energy to power the robot. Most new robots use electrical power supply. Pneumatic actuators have been used for high speed, nonservo robots and are often used for powering tooling such as grippers. Hydraulic actuators have been used for heavier lift systems, typically where accuracy was not also required.

The control system is the communications and information-processing system that gives commands for the movements of the robot. It is the brain of the robot; it sends signals to the power source to move the robot arm to a specific position and to actuate the endeffector. It is also the nerves of the robot; it is reprogrammable to send out sequences of instructions for all movements and actions to be taken by the robot.

An open-loop controller is the simplest form of the control system, which controls the robot only by following the predetermined step-by-step instructions. This system does not have a self-correcting capability. A close-loop control system uses feedback sensors to produce signals that reflect the current states of the controlled objects. By comparing those feedback signals with the values set by the programmer, the close-loop controller can conduct the robot to move to the precise position and assume the desired attitude, and the endeffector can perform with very high accuracy as the close-loop control system can minimize the discrepancy between the controlled object and the predetermined references.

Classification of Robots

Industrial robots vary widely in size, shape, number of axes, degrees of freedom, and design configuration. Each factor influences the dimensions of the robot's working envelope or the volume of space within which it can move and perform its designated task. A broader classification of robots can been described as below.

Fixed-and Variable-Sequence Robots. The fixed-sequence robot (also called a pick-and place robot) is programmed for a specific sequence of operations. Its movements are from point to point, and the cycle is repeated continuously. The variable-sequence robot can beprogrammed for a specific sequence of operations but can be reprogrammed to perform another sequence of operation.

Playback Robot. An operator leads or walks the playback robot and its end effector through the desired path. The robot memorizes and records the path and sequence of motions and can repeat them continually without any further action or guidance by the operator.

Numerically Controlled Robot. The numerically controlled robot is programmed and operated much like a numerically controlled machine. The robot is servo-controlled by digital data, and its sequence of movements can be changed with relative ease.

Intelligent Robot. [3] The intelligent robot is capable of performing some of the functions and tasks carried out by human beings. It is equipped with a variety of sensors with visual and tactile capabilities.

Robot Applications

The robot is a very special type of production tool; as a result, the applications in which robots are used are quite broad. These applications can be grouped into three categories: material processing, material handling and assembly.

In material processing, robots use tools to process the raw material. For example, the robot tools could include a drill and the robot would be able to perform drilling operations on raw material.

Fig. 23.2 SCARA Robot for Automatic Assembly

Material handling consists of the loading, unloading, and transferring of workpieces in manufacturing facilities. These operations can be performed reliably and repeatedly with robots, thereby improving quality and reducing scrap losses.

Assembly is another large application area for using robotics. An automatic assembly system can incorporate automatic testing, robot automation and mechanical handling for reducing labor costs, increasing output and eliminating manual handling concerns. Fig. 23.2 is SCARA Robot for automatic assembly.

【护理型机器人】

23.2　Words and Phrases

reprogrammable [ˌriːprəʊˈɡræməbl]	adj. 可重复编程的
manipulate [məˈnɪpjuleɪt]	v. （熟练地）操作，使用（机器等），操纵
accommodate [əˈkɔmədeɪt]	v. 使适应，
monotonous [məˈnɔtənəs]	adj. 单调的，无变化的
endeffector	终端操作机构
elbow [ˈelbəʊ]	n. 肘
wrist [rɪst]	n. 手腕，腕关节
stretch out	v. 伸出
Cartesian [kɑːˈtiːziən]	adj. 笛卡儿的
cylindrical [sɪˈlɪndrɪk(ə)l]	adj. 圆柱的，柱面的
spherical [ˈsferɪkəl]	adj. 球状的
articulated [ɑːˈtɪkjulɪtɪd]	adj. 铰接的，有关节的
gripper [ˈɡrɪpə]	n. 夹持器，手爪
actuation [ˌæktjuˈeɪʃən]	n. 活动，激励，动作
envelope [ˈenvɪləʊp]	n. [数] 包迹，包络线
variant [ˈvɛəriənt]	n. 变量
custom-made	adj. 定做的，订制的
payload [ˈpeɪləʊd]	n. 有效载荷
pneumatic [njuː(ː)ˈmætɪk]	adj. 气动的
discrepancy [dɪsˈkrepənsi]	n. 相差，差异，矛盾
designate [ˈdezɪɡneɪt]	v. 指明，指出
servocontrol [ˈsəːvəkənˈtrəʊl]	n. 伺服控制，随动控制
tactile [ˈtæktaɪl]	adj. 触觉的，有触觉的

23.3　Complex Sentence Analysis

[1] …which may be either fixed in place or mobile for use in industrial automation applications.

可以固定或移动的方式应用于工业自动化中。

which 引导一个定语从句，在从句中作主语，指前面的 reprogrammable axes。

[2] It is the device intended for performing the designed operations as a human hand can.
① intended for：用来，目的在于，是过去分词短语作定语，修饰 device。
② as a human hand can. 是方式状语从句。
[3] The intelligent robot is capable of performing some of the functions and tasks carried out by human beings.
① be capable of doing something：能够做某事。
② carried out："完成"，是过去分词作定语，修饰 functions and tasks。

23.4　Exercise

Translate the Following Paragraphs

Although the robot has always been a fantastic subject and produces scenes in such movies as "Star War", and even more fantastic kinds are described in science fiction books, we have found that our modern robots even seem to surpass these in reality, capacity, and development.

Humanized robots are possible if a demand for them exists. The only reason we do not have more advanced robots is not because they cannot be developed, but because there has not been a need specified for them. As that need becomes obvious, then they will appear in large number.

The future development of robotics depends mostly on the young and young-at heart scientists who are less conservative, who have active and imaginative brains and who have not learned to think in terms of "not practical" or "not possible". What robots can do around the home, office, factory and other places remains to be "seem" in their brains. These minds will create more wonderful inventions and adaptations than we have ever dreamed of. So let it be that the future of robotics belongs to the young and the young-at heart.

Lesson 24　An Army of Small Robots

24.1　Text

A group of terrorists has stormed into an office building and taken an unknown number of people hostage. They have blocked the entrances and covered the windows. No one outside can see how many they are, what weapons they carry or where they are holding their hostages. But suddenly a SWAT team bursts into the room and captures the assailants before they can even grab their weapons. How did the commandos get the information they needed to move so confidently and decisively?

The answer is a team of small, coordinated robots. They infiltrated the building through the ventilation system and methodically moved throughout the ducts. Some were equipped with microphones to monitor conversations, others with small video cameras, still others with sensors that sniffed the air for chemical or biological agents. Working together, they radioed this real-time information back to the authorities.

This is roughly the scenario that the Defense Advanced Research Projects Agency (DARPA) presented to robotics researchers in 1998. Their challenge was to develop tiny reconnaissance robots that soldiers could carry on their backs and scatter on the floor like popcorn. [1] On the home front, firefighters and search-and-rescue workers could toss these robots through windows and let them scoot around to look for trapped victims or sniff out toxic materials.

【军用机器人】

Ant mighty army

In principle, lilliputian robots have numerous advantages over their bulkier cousins. They can crawl through pipes, inspect collapsed buildings and hide in inconspicuous niches. A well-organized group of them can exchange sensor information to map objects that cannot be easily comprehended from a single vantage point. They can come to the aid of one another to scale obstacles or recover from a fall. Depending on the situation, the team leader can send in a bigger or smaller number of robots. If one robot fails, the entire mission is not lost; the rest can carry on.

【医学微型机器人与NASA（Ⅰ）】

【医学微型机器人与NASA（Ⅱ）】

But diminutive robots require a new design philosophy. They do not have the luxury of abundant power and space, as do their larger cousins, and they cannot house all the components necessary to execute a given mission. Even carrying something as compact as a video camera can nearly overwhelm a little robot. [2] Consequently, their sensors, processing power and physical strength must be distributed among several robots, which must then work in unison. Such robots are like ants in a colony: weak and vulnerable on their own but highly effective when they join forces.

Where Are We?

One vital task that requires collaboration is localization: figuring out the team's position. Larger robots have the luxury of several techniques to ascertain their position, such as Global Positioning System (GPS) receivers, fixed beacons and visual landmark recognition. Moreover, they have the processing power to match current sensor information to existing maps.

None of these techniques works reliably for midget robots. They have a limited sensor range; the millibot sonar can measure distances out to about two meters. They are too small to carry GPS units. Dead reckoning—the technique of tracking position by measuring the wheel speed—is frustrated by their low weight. [3] Something as seemingly inconsequential as the direction of the weave of a rug can dramatically influence their motion, making odometry readings inaccurate, just as a car's odometer would fail to give accurate distances if driven on an ice-covered lake.

So we have had to come up with a new technique. What we have developed is a miniaturizedversion of GPS. By alternating their transmitting and listening roles, the robots figure out the distances between them. Each measurement takes about 30 milliseconds to complete. [4] The team leader—either the home base or a larger robot, perhaps the mother bot that deployed the millibots—collects all the information and calculates robot positions using trilateration. The advantage of this localization method is that the millibots do not need fixed reference points to navigate. They can enter an unfamiliar space and survey it on their own. During mapping, a few selected millibots serve as beacons. These robots remain stationary while the others move around, mapping and avoiding objects while measuring their position relative to the beacons. When the team has fully explored the area around the beacons, the robots switch roles. The exploring robots position themselves as beacons, and the previous set begins to explore. This technique is similar to the children's game of leapfrog, and it can be executed without human intervention.

Chain of Command

Obstacles present small robots with another reason to collaborate. By virtue of its size, a little robot is susceptible to the random clutter that pervades our lives. It must deal with rocks, dirt and loose paper. The standard millibot has a clearance of about 15 millimeters, so a pencil or twig can stop it in its tracks. To get around these limitations, we have come up with a newer version of the millibots that can couple together like train cars. Each of these new millibots, about 11 centimeters long and six centimeters wide, looks like a miniature World War I-style tank. Typically they roam around independently and are versatile enough to get over small obstacles. But when they need to cross a ditch or scale a flight of stairs, they can link up to form a chain.

What gives the chain its versatility is the coupling joint between millibots. Unlike a train couple or a trailer hitch on a car, the millibot coupling joint contains a powerful motor that can rotate the joint up or down with enough torque to lift several millibots. To climb a stair, the chain first pushes up against the base of the stair. One of the millibots near the center of the chain then cantilevers up the front part of chain. Those millibots that reach the top can then pull up the lower ones. Right now this process has to be remotely controlled by humans, but eventually the chain should be able to scale stairs automatically.

Already researchers' attention has begun to turn from hardware development toward the design of better control systems. The emphasis will shift from the control of a few individuals to the management of hundreds or thousands—a fundamentally different challenge that will require expertise from related fields such as economics, military logistics and even political science.

One of the ways we envision large-scale control is through hierarchy. Much like the military, robots will be divided into smaller teams controlled by a local leader. This leader will be responsible to a higher authority. Already millibots are being directed by larger, tank like robots whose Pentium processors can handle the complex calculations of mapping and localization. These larger robots can tow a string of millibots behind them like ducklings and, when necessary, deploy them in an area of interest. They themselves report to larger all-terrain-vehicle robots in our group, which have multiple computers, video cameras, GPS units and a range of a few hundred kilometers. The idea is that the larger robots will deploy the smaller ones in areas that they cannot access themselves and then remain nearby to provide support and direction.

To be sure, small robots have a long way to go. Outside of a few laboratories, no small-robot teams are roaming the halls of buildings searching for danger. Although the potential of these robots remains vast, their current capabilities place them just above novelty—which is about where mobile phones and handheld computers were a decade ago. As the technology filters down from the military applications and others, we expect the competence of the small robot to improve significantly. Working as teams, they have a full repertoire of skills; their modular design allows them to be customized to particular missions; and, not least, they are fun to work with.

24.2 Words and Phrases

SWAT [swɔt]   n. Special Weapons and Tactics 特警队
ventilation [ˌventiˈleiʃən]   n. 通风
microphone [ˈmaikrəfəun]   n. 麦克风
diminutive [diˈminjutiv]   n, adj. 极小的，微型的
processing power   处理能力
GPS   Global Positioning System 全球位置测定系统
midget [ˈmidʒit]   adj. 小型
millibot [ˈmilisnt]   n. 毫米机器人
ultrasonic [ˌʌltrəˈsɔnik]   n. 超声的，超声波
odometry [ɔˈdɔmitə]   n. 测程法

odometer [əuˈdɔmitə]	n. 里程计
trilateration [traiˌlætəˈreiʃən]	n. 三边测量
intervention [ˌintə(ː)ˈvenʃən]	n. 干预
centimeter [ˈsentɪmiːtər(r)]	n. 厘米
cantilever [ˈkæntiliːvə]	n. 悬臂梁
military logistics	军事后勤学
political science	政治学
hierarchy [ˈhaiərɑːki]	n. 分级；等级

24.3 Complex Sentence Analysis

[1] On the home front, firefighters and search-and-rescue workers could toss these robots through windows and let them scoot around to look for trapped victims or sniff out toxic materials.

消防队员和搜救人员可以留在大后方，将这些机器人丢进窗内，让它们到处跑，寻找受困的伤者或是嗅出有毒的物质。

① home front：大后方，后方支前活动。
② search-and-rescue workers　搜救人员。

[2] Consequently, their sensors, processing power and physical strength must be distributed among several robots, which must then work in unison.

因此，传感器、处理能力及机械强度必须要分散到几个机器人身上，所以它们必须通力合作。

① physical strength：机械强度。
② in unison：共同，一起。

[3] Something as seemingly inconsequential as the direction of the weave of a rug can dramatically influence their motion, making odometry readings inaccurate, just as a car's odometer would fail to give accurate distances if driven on an ice-covered lake.

即使是地毯编织方向这种微不足道的小事，也可能大幅影响它们的移动，使得里程读数不精确，就像汽车里程计在结冰的湖面上无法显示正确的距离一样。

[4] The team leader—either the home base or a larger robot, perhaps the mother bot that deployed the millibots—collects all the information and calculates robot positions using trilateration.

团队的指挥（可能是基地或是大型机器人，也许是部署毫米机器人的母舰机器人）会收集所有的信息，并使用三边测量法来计算机器人的位置。

① home base：根据地；总部；管理中心。
② mother bot：母舰机器人。

24.4　Exercise

Translate the Following Paragraphs

Man has always used augmenters to increase the powers which nature endowed him. A simple stick, made into a lever to extend his reach and enable him to move heavy objects, may have been his first machine. Slingshots helped him kill food animals that were at greater distances. The wheel eased his movement and his burdens over the ground. But those were simple augmenters for simple tasks. Man has made his world much more complex. With the rapid development of science and technology, man's augmenters have become much more sophisticated. They are designed not only to do the work of man, but also to do it in much the same way a man would.

Some simply amplify the muscular power of their human operators. The "walking truck" being constructed, for example, is a large device that might better be called a walking horse. A man sits inside, moving his arms and legs to make the "horse" move its own four legs and carry far greater loads than the operator could. Another man, wearing a movable mechanical and electrical framework, lifts 1500 pounds six feet in six seconds.

Other machines link a man to a computer and the computer to a work device. Thanks to the computer, the man does not need to guide the device through each step. The computer "remembers" how to direct the arms of the machine by itself through many work steps.

Still other mimicry machines go where man cannot-into the ocean depths and into nuclear reactors where radiation would cause a human operator to become sick or to die.

Augmenters that extend man's mental and physical skills over long distances-but still require man's remote control-are called "tele-operators". Someday doctors may use such systems to operate on patients thousands of miles away.

With machines and robots becoming more and more sophisticated, will they someday take over the world from man? Most scientists don't think so. Instead, they say, robots will take over more of man's heavy work, giving man more time for creative work.

Lesson 25 Introduction to MEMS

25.1 Text

Development of MEMS

MEMS, which called MM (Micro Machine) inJapan, MS (Micro System) in Europe and MEMS (Micro-Electro-Mechanical systems) in USA was only the assumption of scientists 30 years ago. [1] Only when the application of manufacturing technology (semiconductor micro- processing technology) in micro-scale product field created the condition to develop MEMS, and much relative technology such as design, material, measuring, control, sensing, information processing, computer, energy and system integrating got the certain high level achievement, i. e. 1ater 80's, researchers of University Of California, Berkeley and MIT successfully researched and manufactured electrostatic micro-motor with the diameter of 100μm, did MEMS begin to be popularly studied and highly thought in worldwide and become one of the newly emerging high technology.

Since it was predicted that micrometer/nanometer technology would lead to industry revolution, many developed countries and areas looked it as the crucial technology in both economic flourishing and national defense. They took it prior project and spent huge sum of money in researching it, which made it rapidly develop and got certain achievement. For example, Stanford University researched and manufactured gemel connecting rod level mechanism with the diameter of 20μm and the length of 150μm, sliding block mechanism with the size of 210μm × 100μm, micro electrostatic motor with the diameter of 200μmand pump with the flux of 20ml/min. Tokyo University researched and manufactured micro slope climbing mechanism with the size of 1 cm. [2] Nagoya University researched and manufactured crawling wireless robot used to inspect micro pipe, which movement was controlled by magnetic field generated by circuit loop outside pipe, etc. At the same time, MEMS is also thought highly in our country. Now, the miniaturization technology on mechanical parts, integrated sensor, optics parts and actuator has been studied. Some of them has got certain achievement and turn to application studying.

Basic Characteristic

The miniaturizing of MEMS causes the scaling effect problem . i. e. the physical phenomena doesn't proportionally miniaturize with the size. When the size is certain extent small, the simulation and similarity theory of macro-mechanical is no longer adaptive. So MEMS has following characteristics:

(1) The dominant force of MEMS is surface force. We know bulk force (e. g. gravity, electromagnetic force is direct proportion to high power feature size, while surface force (friction force, surface force and electrostatic force) is direct proportion to relatively low power of feature size. MEMS has small bulk, light weight. The ratio of surface force to bulk force relatively increases. Compared with bulk force, the surface force becomes dominant force. So, after miniaturizing, compared to gravity, electrostatic force becomes dominant force (the scaling effect of mechanical miniaturization). So, MEMS often actuated by electrostatic force. Compared to gravity, effect of friction in MEMS is also larger than that in normal machine.

(2) MEMS isn't the simulative miniaturization of traditional machine. The complexity of every parts of the traditiona 1 mechanical isn't equa 1. To geometrically simulatively miniaturize them, the miniaturization of the complicated parts is very difficult, especially of highly intelligent automotive mechanical. So, to design MEMS needn't pursue complicated mechanical structure but with a view to multiple single mechanical part (include the parts with sensor and artificial intelligence) which can complete complicated work.

(3) Energy supplying. For MEMS which can move and spin, electrical cable is the obstacle of its movement. So, energy supplying usually needn't cable. Now MEMS often supplying energy by electrostatic force. Besides, often directly bestirring by vibration (piezoelectric, electromagnetic and SMA actuating).

So, the development of MEMS needs the direction of new theory and method. With the change of main resistance, new structure principle and control method are needed. With the change of the dominant element of kinematic and kinetic equation, new actuating method is needed. With the miniaturization of structure of MEMS parts, new manufacturing method is needed, etc.

Application of MEMS

The rising and development of MEMS synchronously forecasts its widely application prospect. The main field can be concluded as follows:

(1) Machine field, micro gearing, micro connecting rod level mechanism, micro sliding block mechanism etc, which are composed of micro system;

(2) Instrument, pressure sensor, acceleration sensor, etc;

(3) Hydro-control, micro pump, intelligent pump, etc;

(4) Micro optics, optical cable, optical scanner, interferometer, etc;

(5) GSI, vacuum manipulator, micro position system, gas precision control system, etc;

(6) Information machine, magnetic head, printer head, scanner, etc;

(7) Robot in next century, micro robot, multi degree of freedom manipulator, etc, which can be used in minimal environment such as micro pipe inspection and repair.

25.2　Words and Phrases

micro-processing technology	微加工技术
electrostatic [iˈlektrəuˈstætik]	adj. 静电的，静电学的

micrometer/nanometer technology	微/纳米技术
flourishing [ˈflʌriʃ]	adj. 繁茂的，繁荣的，欣欣向荣的
simulative [ˈsimjulətiv]	adj. 模拟的，假装的
miniaturize [ˈminiətʃəraiz]	vt. 使小型化，使微型化
synchronous [ˈsiŋkrənəs]	adj. 同时的，[物] 同步的，同时期的
micro gearing	微齿轮
micro connecting rod level mechanism	微连杆机构
micro sliding block mechanism	微滑块机构

25.3 Complex Sentence Analysis

［1］ Only when the application of manufacturing technology … did MEMS begin to be popularly studied and highly thought in worldwide and become one of the newly emerging high technology.

only +从句或短语提前，放在主句的前面，则主句需要倒装。试比较：

Onlywhen we broaden our views, can we realize the importance of knowledge.

Only in this way can we deal with the matter effectively.

［2］ Nagoya University researched and manufactured crawling wireless robot used to inspect micro pipe, which movement was controlled by magnetic field generated by circuit loop outside pipe, etc.

① used to inspect micro pipe 过去分词短语做定语，修饰 robot。

② which movement was controlled by magnetic field generated by circuit loop outside pipe, etc. 为非限制性定语从句，修饰 robot。

25.4 Exercise

Translate the Following Paragraphs

MIT is developing a MEMS-based gas turbine generator. Based on high speed rotating machinery, this 1 cm diameter by 3 mm thick Sic heat engine is designed to produce 10~20 W of electric power while consuming 10 grams/hr of H2. Later versions may produce up to 100 W using hydrocarbon fuels. The combustor is now operating and an 80 W micro-turbine has been fabricated and is being tested. This engine can be considered the first of a new class of MEMS device, *power MEMS*, which are heat engines operating at power densities similar to those of the best large scale devices made today.

The design of the micro-gas turbine generator presents a considerable challenge to all the disciplines involved. However, progress to date has been quite encouraging. The ability to manufacture MEMS-based high speed rotating machinery opens up a host of possibilities including various thermodynamic machines. MIT is also working on a motor-driven micro compressor and a micro-high pressure liquid rocket motor employing turbo pumps. The concept of MEMS-based, high power density heat engines appears extremely attractive and physically realizable.

Lesson 26　Dialogue—At CIMT

26.1　Text

Introduction

[1] CIMT is one of the four most important machine tool exhibitions in the world. Engineers and managers from all parts of the world flock to Beijing, where they get the abreast of the latest manufacturing technology and promote their new products.

Outside theHall

Y: You are welcome to this China International Machine Tool Show. The opening ceremony is being performed now.

E: Yes, the scene is lively.

Y: What's your name?

E: My name is Esther. Here is my card.

Y: And here is my card. Thank you for coming.

E: This seems to be a big show.

Y: Exactly. The registered visitors are already about 45000 from all parts of the world and the number is expected to increase in two or three days.

E: I'm lucky to have this opportunity.

Y: You are right. The show has been very important to China's machine tool industry. There are about 1 000 new machine tools on display. Delegations representing various countries or regions participate in CIMT'2001.

E: Fantastic! Do you have such a big show every year?

Y: Yes, it has been held in China every 2 years ever since its existence in 1989. And the show has been recognized as one of the top four marketing activities in the world's machine tool area.

E: I'm sure to come next time.

Y: You are welcome!

Inside theHall

E: Look! Aren't the exhibits spectacular?

Y: Sure. This is the exhibition hall 8A. It's composed of four sections. Here on display are some new homemade machine tools. Many of them have caught up with the technical levels of similar products made abroad. Let me show you around.

E: It's very kind of you! Oh, that's a big simultaneous five-axis CNC machine.

Y: Yes. This new machine reaches the advanced world level. It is suitable for air industry.

E: I see.

Y: This is mode SV—100 MC (Machining Center). There are 16 tools in the storage, which will make them change automatically. The working table can move forward and backward in a wide scale, which is completely fit for the processing of conventional mold.

E: Um. Is this boring-milling machine?

Y: That's right. It is highly recommended in the world because it is economical, easy to operate and outstanding in performance.

E: That sounds interesting. But the size is a bit small.

Y: It is specially designed for small works, and it is stable and efficient. The bigger one is also available. Over there, you see.

E: What's the unit price?

Y: Here is our price list and this is the catalogue.

In theNegotiation Booth

Y: How do you do? What kind of equipment are you most interested in?

E: We have studied your catalogue and we have great interest in your boring-milling machine. But your price has been found higher through repeated calculations.

Y: How many would you like to order?

E: Our quantity is surely to your satisfaction. We plan to order 15 if the price is moderate.

Y: [2] To be frank, such machine was out of stock for a while because we had too many orders. The price on the list now is the same as it was before. [3] But since your order has a size, we would like to have another new partner by reducing the unit price to ＄20000 FOB Shanghai. This is our lowest quotation, and no further concession. Actually, we won't make a profit. We will just use it as an advertisement.

E: It seems acceptable. Including freight?

Y: Um, OK.

E: When can you make the goods ready for shipment?

Y: Around August.

E: Well, we expect to use them this October, Time is too tight. We need to transit the goods at the Singapore since there is no direct steamer from Shanghai to Lagos. Could you get the goods ready for shipment in mid July?

Y: July is OK. By the way, how would you make the payment?

E: I'll pay by installment.

Y: [4] What about paying 30% upon signing the contract, and then paying the rest after delivery of the goods?

E: According to our practice, we'll pay 60% after delivery, and pay the additional 10% after three months' trial use. What about your after-sales services?

Y: We will ensure you "three warranties" (for repair replacement or compensation of faulty products) during one-year period of guarantee. Then we'll ensure you follow-up services. OK, just now Mr. Jiang said that you also want to buy NC equipment?

E: Yes, we want to buy WFC (Wire Flame Cutter), and EDM (Electric Discharge Machine).

Y: We can be your agent.

E: Mr. Yang, We'll discuss other equipment after we have done this one.

Y: Welcome!

E: When can we sign the contract?

Y: Tomorrow afternoon.

E: OK. Looking forward to mutual cooperation. See you tomorrow then.

Y: See you tomorrow.

26.2　Words and Phrases

opportunity [ˌɔpəˈtjuːniti]	n. 机会
delegation [ˌdeliˈgeiʃən]	n. 代表团
spectacular [spekˈtækjulə]	adj. 壮观的
negotiation [niˌgəuʃiˈeiʃən]	n. 谈判
booth [buːə]	n. 层位，摊位
catalogue [ˈkætəlɔg]	n. 产品样本，目录
moderate [ˈmɔdərit]	adj. 适中的
steamer [ˈstiːmə]	n. 船
contract [ˈkɔntrækt]	n. 合同
transit [ˈtrænsit]	n. & v. 运输
cooperation [kəuˌɔpəˈreiʃən]	n. 合作，协作
manufacturing technology	制造技术
opening ceremony	开幕式
participate in	参加
exhibition hall	展馆，展厅
homemade machine tool	国产机床
simultaneous five-axis CNC machine	五轴联动数控机床
boring-milling machine	镗铣床
unit price	单价
Lagos [ˈleigɔs]	n. 拉各斯，尼日利亚首都
direct steamer	直达航运

26.3　Complex Sentence Analysis

[1]　CIMT is one of the four most important machine tool exhibitions in the world. Engineers and managers from all parts of the world flock to Beijing, where they get the abreast of the latest manufacturing technology and promote their new products.
CIMT是China International Machine Tool的缩写，代表中国国际机床展览会，是世界四大机床展之一。其他国际机床展览会分别在美国、欧洲和日本举行。首届中国国际机床展览会于1989年在上海举行，以后每两年一届。第七届中国国际机床展览会CIMT'2001于2001年4月19～25日在北京举行。

[2]　To be frank, such machine was out of stock for a while because we had too many orders.
① To be frank：坦白地说，说实话。
② out of stock：脱销。
③ too many：太，过；非常。

[3]　But since your order has a size, we would like to have another new partner by reducing the unit price to ＄20000 FOB Shanghai.
① FOB是Free on Board的缩写，指离岸价，这是国际贸易术语。
② have a size：订货达一定数量。

[4]　What about paying 30% upon signing the contract, and then paying the rest after delivery of the goods?
① what about：怎么样，如何。
② sign the contract：签订合同。

26.4　Exercise

Translate the Following Paragraphs

Interview
Place：Personnel Manager's Office in a company
Characters：(Interviewer) Mike Anderson, Personnel Manager of a company
(Applicant) Chen Zhuo

I：Come in, please. Good morning, I am Mike Anderson, personnel manager of our company.
A：How do you do? My name is Chen Zhuo.
I：Sit down please and make yourself at home.

Dialogue—At CIMT Lesson 26

A: Thank you very much.

I: As I know you have applied to work in our company. Would you please introduce yourself?

A: I'm 23 years old and was born in Huangshi. I can speak and write English fluently and know how to operate the computer and NC machines. I have been an assistant engineer for half a year in a famous company one year ago. So, I am sure that I am quite efficient in technical work, like NC programming, operation, maintenance and debugging.

I: OK, I would infer that you are an excellent student in your college. Could you tell me more details about your major and English courses?

A: All right. Though I am a student in the Department of Mechanical and Electrical Engineering, I studied many English Courses including English Reading and Comprehension, Oral English, English Writing and professional English. Most of the courses are taught in English, some are even taught by foreign teachers.

I: By the way, do you have any experience as a leader at the school?

A: Yes, I was the monitor of our class. I have organized many social activities.

I: Besides all these, what do you like to do in your spare time?

A: I have a great interest in travel, reading and sports such as swimming, tennis and so on.

I: I am very glad to hear that. Travel and sports are also my hobbies. Why do you choose our company?

A: Your company is one of the largest NC machine manufacturers in East China. As you see in my resume, I specialized in CAD/CAM in college, so I expect to develop my capabilities in your company. On the other hand, the position for which I applied is quite challenging. That's the reason why I like to come to your company. I hope to display my talents fully here.

I: If I accept you, how much do you expect to be paid?

A: At least ￥2000 a month.

I: That will be no problem.

A: OK. When can I get the reply about my application?

I: I think you will know the final result within a week. It's my pleasure to have a talk with you.

A: Me too. It takes your much time. Good bye.

I: Goodbye.

Lesson 27　How to Write a Scientific Paper

27.1　Text

A scientific paper is a written and published report describing original research results. That short definition must be qualified, however, by noting that a scientific paper must be written in a certain way and it must be published in a certain way.

【论文测试写作技巧】

Title

In preparing a title for a paper, the author would do well to remember one salient fact: That title will be read by thousands of people. Perhaps few people, if any, will read the entire paper, but many people will read the title, either in the original journal or in one of the secondary (abstracting and indexing) services.

【论文写作实例】

Therefore, all words in the title should be chosen with great care, and their association with another must be carefully managed.

What is a good title? We can define it with the fewest words that adequately describe the contents of the paper.

The title of a paper is a label. It is not a sentence. Because it is not a sentence, with the usual subject, verb, object arrangement, it is really simpler than a sentence (or, at least, usually shorter), but the order of the words becomes even more important.

The meaning and order of the words in the title are of importance to the potential reader who read the title in the journal table of contents. But these considerations are equally important to all potential users of the literature, including those (probably a majority) who become aware of the paper via secondary sources. Thus, the title should be useful as a label accompanying the paper itself, and it also should be in a form suitable for the machine-indexing systems used by the Engineering Index, Science Citation Index, and others. Most of the indexing and abstracting services are geared to "key word" systems. Therefore, it is fundamentally important that the author provide the right "keys" to the paper when labeling it. That is, the terms in the title should be limited to those words that highlight the significant content of the paper in terms that are both understandable and retrievable.

Abstract

An abstract is a concise and precise summary of the paper. The role of the abstract is not to evaluate or explain, but rather to describe the paper (dissertation).[1] The abstract should include a brief but precise statement of the problem or issue, a description of the research method and design, the major findings and their significance, and the principal conclusion.[2] The abstract should contain the most important words referring to method and content of the paper: These facilitate access to the abstract by computer research, and enable readers to identify the basic content of a document quickly and accurately, to determine its relevance to their interests, and thus to decide whether they need to read the document in its entirety.

An abstract should be written in complete sentences, rather than in phrases and expressions. Generally, an abstract for a short paper is limited to a maximum of 200~250 words. The abstract should be designed to define clearly what is dealt with in the paper. Many people will read the abstract, either in the original journal or in The Engineering Index, Science Citation Index or one of the other secondary publications.

The abstract should never give any information or conclusion that is not stated in the paper. References to the literature must not be cited in the abstract (except in rare instances, such as modification of a previously published method). Because the abstract is not a part of the paper, it is neither numbered nor counted as a page.

Introduction

Now that we have the preliminaries out of the way, we come to the paper itself. I should mention that some experienced writers prepare their title and abstract after the paper is written, even though by placement these elements come first. You should, however, have in mind (if not on paper) a provisional title and an outline of the paper that you propose to write. You should also consider the level of the audience you are writing for, so that you will have a basis for determining which terms and procedures need definition or description and which do not.

The first section of the text proper should, of course, be the introduction. The purpose of the introduction should be to supply sufficient background information and the design idea to allow the reader to properly understand and evaluate the results of the present study without needing to refer to previous publication on the topic. The introduction should also provide the rationale for the present study. Above all, you should state briefly and clearly your purpose in writing the paper. Choose references carefully to provide the most important background information.

Suggested rules for a good introduction are as follows: (1) It should present first, with all possible clarity, the nature and scope of the problem investigated. (2) It should review the pertinent literature to orient the reader. (3) It should state the method of the investigation. If deemed necessary, the reasons for the choice of a particular method should be stated. (4) It should state the principal results of the investigation. (5) It should state the principal conclusion(s) suggested by the results.

Materials and Methods

Now, in Materials and Methods, you must give the full details. Most of this section should be written in the past tense. The main purpose of the Materials and Methods section is to describe the experimental design and then provide enough detail that a competent worker can repeat the experiments. Many (probably most) readers of your paper will skip this section, because they already know (from the introduction) the general methods you used and they probably have no interest in the experimental detail. However, careful writing of this section is critically important because the cornerstone of the scientific method requires that your results, to be of scientific merit, must be reproducible; and, for the results to be adjudged reproducible, you must provide the basis for repetition of the experiments by others. The experiments that are unlikely to be reproduced are beside the point; the potential for producing the same or similar results must exist, or your paper does not represent good science.

When your paper is subjected to peer review, a good reviewer will read the Materials and Methods carefully. If there is serious doubt that your experiments could, be repeated, the reviewer will recommend rejection of your manuscript no matter how awe-inspiring your results.

For materials, include the exact technique specifications and qualities and source and method of preparation. Generally, it is necessary to list pertinent chemical and physical properties of specimens (or reagents) used.

For method, the usual order of presentation is chronological. Obviously, however, related methods should be described together, a straight chronological order cannot always be followed. If your method is new (unpublished) you must provide all of the needed detail. However, if a method has been previously published in a standard journal, only the literature reference should be given.

Results

So now we come to the core of the paper, the data. This part of the paper is called the Results section.

There are usually two ingredients of the Results section. First, you should give some kind of overall description of the experiments, providing the "big picture", without, however, repeating the experimental details previously provided in Materials and Methods. Second, you should present the data.

Of course, it isn't quite easy. How do you present the data? A simple transfer of data from laboratory notebook to manuscript will hardly do. Most important, in the manuscript you should present representative data rather than endlessly repetitive data.

The Results need to be clearly and simply stated, because it is the Results that comprise the new knowledge that you are contributing to the world. The earlier parts of the paper (Introduction, Materials and Methods) are designed to tell why and how you got the Results; the later part of the paper (Discussion) is designed to tell what they mean. Obviously, therefore, the whole paper must stand or fall on the basis of the Results. Thus, the Results must be presented with clarity.

Discussion

The Discussion is harder to define than the other sections. Thus, it is usually the hardest section to write. And, whether you know it or not, many papers are rejected by journal editors because of a faulty Discussion, even though the data of the paper might be both valid and interesting. Even more likely, the true meaning of the data may be completely obscured by the interpretation presented in the Discussion, again resulting in rejection.

Whatare the essential features of a good Discussion? I believe the main components will be provided if the following injunctions are heeded:

(1) Try to present the principles, relationships, and generalizations shown by the Results. And bear in mind, in a good Discussion, you discuss—you do not recapitulate the Results.

(2) Point out any exceptions or any lack of correlation and define unsettled points. Never take the high-risk alternative of trying to cover up or fudge data that do not quite fit.

(3) Show how your results and interpretations agree (or contrast) with previously published work.

(4) Don't be shy; discuss the theoretical implications of your work, as well as any possible practical applications.

(5) State your conclusions as clearly as possible.

(6) Summarize your evidence for each conclusion.

In showing the relationships among observed facts, you do not need to reach cosmic conclusions. Seldom will you be able to illuminate the whole truth; more often, the best you can do is shine a spotlight on one area of the truth. Your one area of truth can be buttressed by your data; if you extrapolate to a bigger picture than that shown by your data, you may appear foolish to the point that even your data-supported conclusions are cast into doubt.

When you describe the meaning of your little bit of truth, do it simply. The simplest statements evoke the most wisdom; verbose language and fancy technical words are used to convey shallow thought.

27.2 Words and Phrases

salient [ˈseiljənt]   adj. 明显的
adequately [ediˈkwitli]   adj. 充分地
citation [saiˈteiʃən]   n. 引用
retrievable [riˈtriːvəbl]   adj. 可检索的
dissertation [disəteiʃ(ə)n]   n. (学位) 论文, 专题
relevance [ˈrelivəns]   n. 关联, 适用
preliminary [priliminəri; (US) -neri]   adj. 预备的, 初步的
provisional [preˈviʒənl]   adj. 暂定的, 假定的
rationale [ræʃəˈnæl]   n. 基本原理, 理论基础, 原理的阐述
above all   尤其是, 最重要的是, 首先是
pertinent [ˈpəːtinənt]   adj. 有关的, 相干的, 中肯的
cornerstone [ˈkɔːnəstən]   n. 基石; 基础; (建筑) 隅石
manuscript [mænjuskript]   n. 手稿, 原稿
awe-inspiring   令人敬畏的, 令人鼓舞的

specification [spesifi'keiʃ(ə)n]	n. 详述；[常 pl.] 规格，说明书；规范；明细表
specimen ['spesimin]	n. 试样，样品；标本
reagent [riːˈeidʒənt]	n. 反应物，反应力，试剂
chronological [krɔnəˈlɔdʒik(ə)l]	adj. 按时间顺序排列的；按年代顺序排列的
ingredient [inˈgriːdiənt]	n. 成分，要素，因素，原料
obscure [əbskjuə]	adj. 模糊的，含糊的，晦涩的，暗的，朦胧的，
	v. 使……黑暗，使不明显
injunction [inˈdʒʌkʃən]	n. 命令，指令
heed [hiːd]	v. n. 注意，留心
recapitulate [riːkəˈpitjuleit]	v. 扼要重述，概括，重现，再演
unsettled [ʌnˈset(ə)ld]	adj. 不稳定的，不安定的，未解决的，混乱的
correlation [kɔriˈleiʃən]	n. 关联，相关性，相互关系
cover up	包裹，隐藏，掩盖
fudge [fʌdʒ]	n. 捏造，梦话，胡话，空话；
	vi. 蒙混，逃避责任；
	vt. 粗制滥造，捏造推诿；
	int. 胡说八道！
implication [impliˈkeiʃən]	n. 牵连，受牵累；暗示，隐含；意义，本质
cosmic [ˈkɔzmik]	a. 宇宙的，全世界的，广大无边的
illuminate [iˈljuːmineit]	v. 照明，照亮，阐明，说明，着凉，使光辉灿烂，以灯火装饰（街道等）；vi. 照亮
spotlight [ˈspɔtlait]	n. 聚光灯，点光源，公众注意中心
buttress [ˈbʌtris]	n. 支持物，支柱；
	v. 支持，加强，扶住
extrapolate [ˈekstræpəleit]	n. 推断，外推，外插
evoke [iˈvəuk]	v. 唤起，引起，博得，移送
verbose [vəːˈbəs]	adj. 冗长的，累赘的，喋喋不休的
fancy [ˈfænsi]	adj. 奇特的，美妙的，漂亮的；
	v. n. 设想，嗜好，爱好

27.3　Complex Sentence Analysis

［1］The abstract should include a brief but precise statement of the problem or issue, a description of the research method and design, the major findings and their significance, and the principal conclusion.

摘要应该包括下列内容：论文中问题或论点的简洁而精确的陈述、研究方法及设计思路的描述、主要发现和它们的意义，以及主要的结论。

句中 a brief but precise statement of the problem or issue、a description of the research method and design、the major findings and their significance 及 the principal conclusion 均为 include 的宾语。

[2] The abstract should contain the most important words referring to method and contend of the paper: these facilitate access to the abstract by computer research, and enable readers to identify the basic content of a document quickly and accurately, to determine its relevance to their interests, and thus to decide whether they need to read the document in its entirety.

these facilitate access to…, and enable readers to…entirety 一句为并列句，facilitate 与 enable 为并列的两个谓语。句中 to identify…、to determine…及 to decide…均为 reader 的宾语补足语。

27.4　Exercise

Translate the Following Paragraphs

Ductil-Regime Machining Model for Diamond Turning of Brittle Materials

Abstract　A new machining model has been developed for single point diamond turning of brittle materials. Experiments using the interrupted cutting method allow model parameters to be determined that provide a quantitative method for determinig the machineability of a material with respect to the rake angle, tool nose radius and machining environment. The model uses two parameters, the critical depth of cut and the subsurface damage depth, to characterize the ductile-regime material removal process. Also includes in the model is a parameter used to set process limit defined as the maximum feed rate. Machining experiments have verified the model, and allow for determination of optimum machining conditions.

New Words

regime [ri'dʒim]	n. 方式，规范，范围，领域
heat treatment regime	热处理规范
critical depth of cut	临界切削深度
rake angle	（刀具的）前角
tool nose radius	刀尖半径
parameter [pə'ræmitə]	n. 参数
characterize ['kæriktəˌraiz]	v. 表……特征，以……为特征；描写，述说；分别，辨别
limit [ˈlimit]	n. 极限；极点，范围，限制；公差，极限尺寸

附录 A　关于科技英语翻译

一、翻译

翻译就是将一种语言所表达的意思用另一种语言表达出来，是一项非常复杂的语言转换活动。

翻译是一门艺术，艺术讲究美感，所以翻译需在忠实于原文（准确）的基础上发挥艺术家的灵感和创造才能。

翻译也是一门科学，是研究各种语言体系之间相互关系的新兴科学——翻译学。现代人的特征是大量吸收信息，充实自我。作为信息的载体，语言已冲破国界的限制。信息高速公路飞速发展极大地促进了信息交流。语言障碍成为首要问题，所以翻译不仅要求有追求真理的科学态度，而且本身也有逐步发展完善的理论，遵守一定的基础规律，以及长期实践总结出来的科学技巧。

二、翻译标准

科技英语的翻译标准应是准确而流畅。

科技文献的翻译，准确是第一位的，在准确的基础上再求流畅。要特别注意逻辑和术语正确，结构严谨，表达简练。

三、科技英语特点

1. 词汇

在科技英语中出现频率最高的不是专业词汇而是一些功能词：动词、介词、形容词等。

2. 语法

科技英语语法最突出的特点如下：
(1) 被动句多（因为只强调过程本身，谁做的不重要）；
(2) 形容词后置定语多；
(3) 动词非谓语形式使用率高；
(4) 祈使句，it 句型多；
(5) 复杂长句，名词化（从句套从句，介词+从句）多。

3. 翻译特点

科技文献主要论述事理，其逻辑性强，结构严谨，术语繁多，所以译文必须满足概念清晰，条理分明，逻辑正确，数据无误，文字简练，通顺易懂等要求，尤其是术语、定义、定理、公式、算式、图表、结论等更要注意准确恰当。

附录 B 怎样写科技论文的英文摘要

摘要（abstract，亦称文摘）作为对研究论文正文的精练概括，有利于读者在最短的时间内了解全文内容。随着国际检索系统的出现，摘要逐渐成为一种信息高度密集的相对独立文体，为人们在浩如烟海的文献中寻找所需要的信息提供了便利。

随着二次文献数据库的普及以及全球科学技术界对科技信息日益增长的需求和重视，论文摘要的受关注率比论文本身要大数十倍甚至数百倍。为此，一篇论文能否得到重视，能否把科研成果准确地传播出去，能否被更多重要的数据库收录，摘要的内容和质量起很大作用。

现在多数大学要求学生的毕业论文应有英文摘要（含英文题目及关键词），所以有必要了解摘要的写作。

一、定义与分类

（一）定义

abstract 即摘要、文摘之意。

"摘要"和原文献在一起，置于正文前面；"文摘"是离开正文而独立存在的，如单独出版的文摘杂志中的文摘及情报系统存储和提供的文摘。

abstract（文摘或摘要）是对文献的内容不加任何解释（interpretation）和评论（evaluation）的简要而准确地（concise and precise）表达（description）。

注：abstract、synopsis、summary 的区别

abstract 摘要，文摘，置于文前。

Synopsis 梗概，用于 movie、story、fiction 等。

Summary 概述，置于文尾。

（二）分类

摘要一般分为两类：信息性摘要和说明性、指示性摘要。目前绝大部分的科技期刊和会议论文都要求作者提供信息性摘要。

1. 信息性摘要（informative abstract）。

主要强调尽量多而完整的报道原文献中的具体内容，特别是研究目的、研究问题、研究方法和手段、主要论点和发现、得出的结论以及建议、措施等。它包括文章的主旨和数据等，适用于学位论文（dissertation）、学术刊物论文（journal paper）、学术会议论文（conference paper）、展示论文（poster）。

2. 说明性摘要（descriptive abstract or indicative）。

提供主要内容（problem or issue），但不介绍具体内容（content），适用于讨论性文章等。

二、作用及特点

1. 作用：abstract 便于搜索、查阅、浏览各种文献

摘要独立于正文，通常收录于相应学科的摘要检索类数据库或专刊内，撰写好摘要对于论文是否被数据库收录和他人引用至关重要。

摘要的目的是为读者提供关于文献内容的有用信息，即论文所包含的主要概念和所讨论的主要问题。读者从摘要中可获知作者的主要研究活动、研究方法和主要研究结果及结论。它可以帮助读者判断此论文对自己的研究工作是否有用，是否有必要获取全文，为科研人员、科技情报人员及计算机检索提供方便。

2. 特点：

（1）独立性：包括了使读者理解原文献的基本要素，可离开原文独立存在。

（2）概括性：摘要把一篇文章的精华部分以精练的文字、极短的篇幅概括出来，成为浓缩的信息。

（3）客观性：（对文章）不加评论解释的客观报道。

三、基本内容及形式

1. 完整性与准确性。

2. 基本内容：研究工作的目的、方法、结（成）果、结论及建议等。重点是结果和结论，即应突出论文的创造性成果和新见解。

3. 摘要长度：常用 100~250 个单词；学术论文、长篇报告为 500 单词以下，仅限于一页。

4. 文体：主题句开头，阐明原文主题，但注意第一句不得与原文题名（title）完全重复，以免检索系统收录后有关人员用计算机检索时出现差错。

5. 段落：一般不分段。学位论文较长时，可分段。

6. 句子：用完整的句子，不用电报式文字、短语，注意前后应连贯。

7. 用词：动词尽量用主动语态，有时亦用被动。

8. 人称：常用第三人称，如必须可用第一人称；尽量用正式的书面语用词而不用口语化的词，尽量用简单的词汇而不用复杂、生僻的词汇（详见第五部分：精炼缩短摘要的方法）。

9. 术语：避免用人们不使用的术语，首字母缩写词及缩略语符号等。

10. 顺序：摘要应在写完文章后撰写，以便将重要内容简洁地表述出来。

四、时态问题

1. 图表介绍、公式说明、实验结果、方法描述真理等——"现在时"。

2. 实验经过、试验过程、过去做的研究工作、特殊结论及推论——"过去时"。

3. 叙述从某一时间开始，对现在有直接关系并影响的——"现在完成时"。

4. 今后的研究及打算，预期的结果，数学公式推演结果等——"将来时"。

五、精炼缩短摘要的方法

1. 取消不必要的字句：如 It is reported…、Extensive investigations show that…、The author discusses…、This paper concerned with…及摘要开头的 In this paper 等。

2. 尽量简化一些措辞和重复的单元，如表 B-1 所示。

表 B-1

不　用	而　用
at a temperature of 250℃ to 300℃	at 250℃ ~ 300℃
at a high pressure of 2000 Pa	at 2000 Pa
at a high temperature of 1500℃	at 1500℃
discussed and studied in detail	discussed

3. 删除多余的文字。

例 Type B, Type A, and Type C viral hepatitis accounts for 65.2%, 20.6%, and 13.2% respectively.

正确：Type A, B, and C viral hepatitis accounts for 65.2, 20.6, and 13.2 percent, respectively.

后两个 Type 和 "%" 是不必要的重复，应删除。

4. 短语改用单词。

(1) 用正规的动词而不用短语动词。

在科技英语中，常用规范的书面语动词来代替口语中的短语动词或动词词组。因为单个动词语义明确，而短语有时多义，甚至易生歧义。如表 B-2 所示。

表 B-2

Phrasal Verb	Single Verb
take in	absorb
put together	aggregate
fall down	be precipitated
get rid of	eliminate
join together	combine
break up	decompose
spread out	diffuse
come out	emerge
make sure	ensure
get away	escape
turn … into vapor	evaporate
take out	extract
grow longer	lengthen
turn … into liquid	liquefy
make wet	moisten

（续）

Phrasal Verb	Single Verb
make neutral	neutralize
look at	observe
pour out over the top	overflow
move backwards and forwards in a straight line	reciprocate
throw back	reflect
set free	release
go up	rise
put back	replace
grow shorter	shorten
become a solid	solidify
stay alive	survive
pass on	transmit
make…weak	weaken

（2）凡能用一个单词来表达的意思就不用词组。

Robert A. Day. 认为在写作将在科技期刊发表的论文时，应多用单个词而不用啰嗦的词组，以使论文简洁明了。如表 B-3 所示。

表 B-3

Jargon	Preferred Usage
a considerable amount of	much
a considerable number of	many
a decreased amount of	less
a decreased number of	fewer
a majority of	most
a number of	many
a small number of	a few
absolutely essential	essential
accounted for by the fact	because
adjacent to	near
along the lines of	like
an adequate amount of	enough
an example of this is the fact that	for example
an order of magnitude faster	10 times faster
apprise	inform
are of the same opinion	agree
as a consequence of	because

Jargon	Preferred Usage
as a mater of fact	in fact (or leave out)
as a result of	because
as is the case	as happens
as of this date	today
as to	about (or leave out)
at the rapid rate	rapidly
at an early date	previously
at no time	never
at some future time	later
at the conclusion of	after
at the present time	now
at this point time	now
based on the fact that	because
because of fact that	because
by means of	by, with
causal fact	cause
cognizant of	aware of
completely full	full
consensus opinion	consensus
considerable amount of	much
contingent upon	dependent on
definitely proved	proved
despite the fact that	although
due to the fact that	because
during the course of	during, while
during the time that	during
effectuate	cause
employ	use
enclosed herewith	enclosed
end result	result
endeavor	try
entirely eliminate	eliminate
eventuate	happen
fabricate	make
facilitate	help
fatal outcome	death
fewer in number	fewer
finalize	end
first of all	first

（续）

Jargon	Preferred Usage
following	after
for thepurpose of	for
for the reason that	since, because
future plans	plans
give an account of	describe
give rise to	cause
has been engaged in a study	has studied
has the capability of	can
have the appearance of	look like
having regard to	about
impact	affect
implement	start, put into action
important essential	essential
in a number of case	some
in a position to	can, may
in a satisfactory manner	satisfactorily
in a situation in which	when
in a very real sense	in a sense (or leave out)
in almost all instances	nearly always
in case	if
in close proximately to	close, near
in connection with	about, concerning
in light of the fact that	because
in many case	often
in my opinion	I think
assumption that	if
in only small a number of cases	rarely
in order to	to
in relation to	toward, to
in respect to	about
in the absence of	without
in the event that	if
in the not-too-distance future	soon
in the possession of	has, have
in this day and age	today
in view of the fact that	because, since
in as much as	for, as
incline to the view	think

(续)

Jargon	Preferred Usage
initiate	begin, start
is defined as	is
is desirous of	wants
it has been reported by Smith	Smith reported
it is apparent that	apparently
it is believed that	I think
itis clear that	clearly
it is clear that much additional work will be required before a complete understanding	I don't understand it
it is crucial that	must
it is doubtful that	possibly
it is evident that a produced b	a produced b
it is generally believed	many think
it is my understanding that	I understand that
it is of interest to note that	leave out
it is often the case that	often
it is suggested that	I think
it is worth pointing out in this context that	note that
it may be that	I think
it may, however, be noted that	but
it should be noted that	note that (or leave out)
It was obeserved in the course of the experiments that	we observed
join together	join
lacked ability to	couldn't
large in size	large
let me make one thing perfectly clear	a snow job is coming
majority of	most
make reference to	refer to
meet with	meet
militate against	prohibit
more often than not	usually
needless to say	leave out
new initiatives	initiatives
no later than	by
of great theoretical and practical importance	useful
of long standing	old

(续)

Jargon	Preferred Usage
of the opinion that	think that
on a daily basis	daily
on account of	because
on behalf of	for
on no occasion	never
on the basis of	by
on the grounds that	since, because
on the part of	by, among, for
on those occasions in which	when
our attention has been called to the fact that	we belatedly discovered
owing to the fact that	since, because
perform	do
place a major emphasis on	stress
pooled together	pooled
presents a picture similar to	resembles
previous to	before
prior to	before
protein determinations were performed	proteins were determined
quantify	measure
quite a large quantity of	much
quite unique	unique
rather interesting	interesting
red in color	red
refered to as	called
regardless of the fact	even though
relative to	about
resultant effect	result
root cause	cause
serious crisis	crisis
should it prove the case that	if
smaller in size	smaller
so as to	to
subject matter	subject
subsequent to	after
sufficient	enough
take into consideration	consider
terminate	end
the great majority of	most

(续)

Jargon	Preferred Usage
the opinion is advanced that	I think
the predominate number of	most
the question is to whether	whether
the reason is because	because
the vast majority of	most
there is reason to believe	I think
they are the investigators who	they
this result would seem to indicate	this result indicates
through the use of	by, with
to the fullest possible extent	fully
transpire	happen
ultimate	last
unanimity of opinion	agreement
until such time	until
utilization	use
utilize	use
very unique	unique
was of opinion that	believed
ways and means	ways, means (not both)
we have insufficient knowledge	we don't know
we wish to thank	we thank
what is the explanation of	why
with a view to	to
with reference to	about (or leave out)
with regard to	concernssing, about (or leave out)
with respect to	about
with the possible exception	except
with the result that	so that
with in the realm of possibility	possible

六、英文摘要的常用句型

1. 本文介绍了（描述了，阐述了）……

   This paper describes…

   This paper gives an account of…

   In this paper…is introduced

   This paper treats of…

   This paper is concerned with…

e. g. This paper is concerned with the derivation（来源，推导）of optimum data of force.

本文介绍了推导出力的最优值的方法。

2. 本文提出了……

   This paper proposes/develops/extends/provides/presents…

   本文提出了一种分析公差的新方法。

e. g. This paper proposes/develops a new approach for the analysis of tolerance.

3. 本文展示了……

   This paper shows…

e. g. This paper shows results on multiple time-scale system（多时标系统）.

4. 本文分析了……

   This paper analyses（zes 英）…

5. 本文研究了……

   This paper considers/studies/deals with/makes a study of…

e. g. This paper considers the design of controllers for flexible systems（柔性系统控制器）.

6. 本文深入研究了……

eg：This paper presents a through study of the theory of temperature measurement.

7. 本文研究和分析了……

   This paper studies and analysis…

8. 本文旨在研究……

   The purpose of this article is to explore（study）…

   The main purpose of this paper is to explore（study）…

e. g The purpose of this paper is to explore the contact length between grinding wheel and workpiece in grinding.

本文旨在研究磨削时砂轮与工件的接触长度。

9. 本文讨论了……

   This paper discusses/treats of…

e. g. This paper treats of an important problem in date-base management systems.

本文讨论了数据库管理系统所涉及的重要问题。

This paper discusses the relation between the sampling period and the stability of sampled-data.

本文讨论了抽样周期与抽样数据稳定性之间的相互关系。

10. 本文论述了……

    This paper addresses…

e. g. This paper addresses problems in linear quadratic optimal control of EHT transmission line.

本文论述了超高压输电线路的线性二次优化控制问题。

11. 本文报告了……This paper reports…

12. 本文论证了……This paper establishes…

13. 本文总结了……This paper reviews…

14. 本文给出了……This paper presents…This paper gives out…
15. 本文调查了……This paper investigates…This paper makes/investigation on…
16. 本文指出了……This paper points out that…This paper indicates…
17. 本文的结论是……This paper concludes that…
18. 本文将……和……做了比较

    This paper compares…with…

    This paper makes acomparision between…and…

    e. g. This paper compares milling force with grinding force.
    本文将铣削力和磨削力进行了比较。

19. 本项研究的目的是……

    The object of this study is…

20. 本文给出了一个……新方法

    This paper gives a new approach…

21. 作者建议……（作者提出了……）

    It is suggested that…（The author puts forward…）

22. 本论文由……组成

    This paper consists of/is composed of/has…

23. 这种（液体）闻起来……smells…

    This（liquild）尝起来……tastes…

    感觉起来……feels…

    看上去像……looks…

24. 这种（现象）称为……is known as…

    叫做……is called…

    被看成……is referred to as

25. 据说；据报道，据推算……

    It is said/reported/estimated/calculated…

26. ……是最重要的/必要的/可能的/自然的/不可避免的

    It is important/necessary/possible/natural/inevitable + that（从句）或 to（不定式）…

27. （我们）认为……是重要的/可能的/必要的/自然的/理所当然的

    We think/consider it important/possible/necessary/natural that（从句）……或 to（不定式）……

    We take it for granted that…

    e. g. We think it necessary to design and build a set of machine for this kind of workpiece. 我们认为有必要设计和制造一台新的机器用于加工这种零件。

28. 因为/由于……（所以）……

    Because of…   owing to…

    Because…on account of…

    e. g. Alloys are important because of（owing to）their usefulness in industry.

因为合金在工业中用处很大，所以很重要。

29. 不管（不论怎样）……

No matter how/what/when/where/whether

However/whatever/whenever/wherever

e. g.（1）No matter what this material is composed of, it is sure to deform if subjected to such a high pressure.

不管一种材料是由什么组成的，如果处于那么高的压力下形状也会改变。

（2）No matter how elastic a material is, it will never return its original shape or size once it is stretched beyond its limit of elasticity.

不管一种材料的弹性多么好，如果被拉伸到超过其弹性极限，就永远不会恢复到原来的形状和尺寸。

30. 如果（假定，设……就……）

If…（should…Had…）

Let…; Given…; with…; without…

eg. If there were no friction (without friction), a machine would never stop operating once it is started. 如果没有摩擦，则机器启动后就不会停止运行。

2. It is impossible for this generator to wrong. If it should go out of order (should it go out of order), we could use the emergency one.

发生器是不可能出问题的。如果出现故障，我们就采取紧急措施。

31. 不但……而且……

not only… but also (as well)

32. Neither…nor… 既不……也不……

either…or… 不是……就是……

e. g. This is an alloy which will neither expand nor contract when heated or cooled.

这是一种在加热或冷却时既不膨胀也不收缩的合金。

33. as soon as ……就……（一……就……）

no sooner than…

34. 正是…… It is that…

七、英文科技论文标题的基本特点和要求

（一）特点

1. 简短扼要。美国数学学会要求不得多于12个英语单词：no more than 12 English words.

2. 标题特点。

（1）词组多，且多为名词性词组，一般为中心词+修饰语。一般不用句子。

e. g. Thermal Energy at Deep Mines

Methods to Reduce SteelWear in Grinding Mills

（2）用冒号突出题旨。

eg：Advanced Vocabulary Learning，the Problem of collocation Vocabulary：Learning to Be Imprecise.

（二）题目书写要求

1. 除冠词、连词及 5 个字母以下的介词外，其余所有实词第一个字母均应大写，当介词、冠词、连词在题目开头或最末一个词时也应大写（有些刊物规定，题目的所有字母都大写）。

2. 字数在 20 字以内。如需分解，则第二行第一字的首字母大写。

3. 标点符号：不用（或很少用），除了破折号和冒号外。

4. 每个用词要考虑到有助于编制题录、索引和关键字等。

5. 力求简、明、短，不用完整的句子，多用名词性词组。

（三）题目常用词组

1. ……的初步研究	Preliminary Study of	
2. ……的研究	A Study on…	
	A Study of the…	
	Studies on…	
	The Study of…	
3. ……的实验研究	An Experimental Study on…	
	Experimental Study for…	
	Investigation for…	
4. ……的理论和实验研究		
	A Theoretical and Experimental Study on…	
5. ……的研制及其应用		
	The Research and Application of the…	
6. ……的探讨	Exploration on… Approach on… Discussion on…	
	A study of… Study on… Investigation on…	
7. ……的新进展	Recent Advances in…	
	Recent Progress in…	
8. ……的研究报告	Research Report on…	
9. ……的方法	Methods of…	
……的计算方法	A Computational Method for…	
10. ……的分析	Analysis of…	
11. ……的测量与分析	The Measurement and Analysis of…	
12. ……方法的改进	An Improvements on the Method of	
13. ……的调查	Investigation on…	
	Survey on…	
14. ……的设计	Design of…	
15. ……的合理化设计	The Rationalized Design of…	
16. ……的优化设计	Optimization Design of…	

	Optimum Design of…
17. ……的设计准则	A Design Criteria for…
18. ……的设计与研制	Design and Development for…
19. ……的实用方案	Practical Scheme of…
20. ……的试验	Experiments on…
	Test of…

八、摘要实例

波形铣刀片的开发及其铣削力学模型

Waved-Edge Insert Development And Milling Force Model

摘　要　在铣削机理研究和实验的基础上，开发了一种新型三维槽型铣刀片—波形铣刀片，并在直线刃铣刀片（含大前角铣刀片）铣削力学模型的基础上，建立了波形刃铣刀铣削力模型，同时编制了计算机程序进行预测。

Abstract　The waved-edge insert is developed on the basis of the investigation of milling mechanism and experiments. The milling force model for the wave-edge insert (Including great rake insert), which give the theoretical secundum for developing, designing and optimizing insert groove through computer forecasting.

附录 C　课文参考译文

第 1 部分

第 1 课　机械设计导论

机械设计是一门阐述机械产品具体设计方案及解决具体机械工程问题的学科。其目的是使设计的产品满足设计要求。它涉及的学科有材料学、力学、热学、流体学、控制学、电子学和制造。

机械设计可能简单，可能复杂；可能容易，可能困难；可能要求精确，也可能不精确；有时要解决的可能是一些很平常琐碎的问题，也可能是非常重大的问题。好的设计应该是很有条理的和令人感兴趣的想法，并能提供一些成果或效用，一个好的设计产品应该是实用、高效且可靠的。这样的产品与时常出问题和经常进行修理的类似拙劣产品相比要更经济实用。

进行各种机械设计工作的人通常被称为工程师。他必须首先认真定义问题，并用工程学的方法确保所提出任何的一种方案都能解决问题。对于设计者来说，一开始就能准确判定出令人满意的设计方案，并能加以区别以便选择一个最好的，这一点很重要。工程师必须具有创造性的想象力，熟悉工程知识、生产技术、工具、机器和材料来设计、制造新产品，或者改进现有的产品。

在现代的工业化社会，一个国家的财富和生活水平与他们设计和制造工程产品的能力紧密相关，可以说机械设计和制造业的进步能显著地促进一个国家工业化整体水平的提高。我国在全球制造业大舞台上正扮演着越来越重要的角色。为了促进工业化进程，需要越来越多具有广泛知识和专门技术的高技能设计工程师。

机械零件

机器主要部分是机械系统，机械系统可以分解成机构，机构又可以进一步分解成机械零件。因此，机械零件是构成机器的基本单元。总体上来讲，机械零件可以分为通用零件和专用零件两类。螺栓、齿轮和链条是典型的通用零件，它们广泛应用在各种工业部门的不同机器上。涡轮机的叶片、曲轴和飞机的螺旋桨属于专用零件，它们具有一些特殊用途。

机械设计步骤

产品的设计需要不断探索和发展。许多方案必须经过研究、试验、完善后才能够决定是否采用。虽然每个工程学问题的内容是独特的，但是设计师可以按照类似的步骤来解决问题，完整的设计步骤如图 1.1 所示。

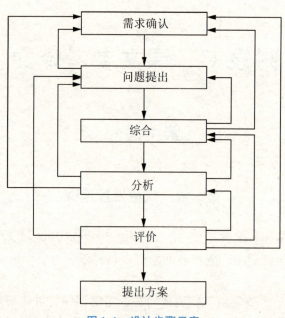

图 1.1　设计步骤示意

需求的确认

有时，设计是从设计者有了某种需求并且决定对此进行研究开始的。这种需求常常不是很明显。识别通常是由一种特殊的不利因素或一系列随机情况引起的，它们几乎同时发生，需求的确认通常是对尚不明确的问题的阐述。

问题的定义

定义问题对全面认识、理解问题非常必要，之后可以更加合理和可行的方式来重新阐述。问题的定义必须包括设计任务的所有技术条件，其中重要的要素有速度、进给量、温度限制、最大范围，以及变量、尺寸和重量的预期变化范围。

综合

综合就是对各种可供选择的设计方法进行进一步研究，这时往往不考虑这些方法的设计特点和设计质量。这有时也称为构思和发明阶段，在这个阶段中要产生尽可能多的有创意的想法。综合阶段包括材料的说明、几何特征的增加以及总体设计的更多尺寸细节介绍。

分析

分析是一种把问题分解成几部分来确定或描述事物性质的方法。在这个过程中，需要分析设计的性质和原理，以便在修改的设计目标和原始设计目标之间确定一个更加合适的方案。

评估

评估是对成功设计的最后验证，通常包括样机的实验室试验。在这个阶段我们希望发现这个设计是否真的能够满足需要。

上述描述可能会给我们一个错误印象——这个过程可能像列出来的那样以线性方式来完成。事实恰恰相反，在整个过程中都需要反复，可能会随机从任一步骤返回到以前的某个步骤。

展示

与其他人交流设计成果是设计过程最后和至关重要的阶段。基本上有三种交流方式，分别是书面表述、口头陈述和图解。一名成功的工程师除了掌握技术之外，还应该精通这三种表达方式。有能力的工程师不应该害怕在提出自己的方案时遭遇失败。实际上，失败乃成功之母。

机械设计内容

机械设计是机械工程教学中一门重要的技术基础课程。它的宗旨是提供在机械设备和系统中的机械零件设计所必需的概念、规则、数据和决定性分析技术，并培养工程类专业学生的机械设计能力，这是机械制造业至关重要，也是制造好产品的关键。

机械设计包括以下内容：
- 设计过程、计算公式及相应的安全设计指标。
- 材料特性、静态和动态载荷分析，包括梁、振动和冲击载荷。
- 应力的基本规律和失效分析。
- 静态失效理论和静态载荷下断裂力学分析。
- 疲劳失效理论并强调在压力条件下接近高周循环的疲劳设计，通常用在旋转机械的设计中。
- 机械磨损机理、表面接触应力和表面疲劳现象。
- 使用疲劳分析技术校核轴的设计。
- 润滑油膜与滚动轴承的理论和应用。
- 直齿圆柱齿轮的动力学原理、设计方法和应力分析，并简单介绍斜齿轮、锥齿轮和蜗轮等有关方面的问题。
- 弹簧设计，包括螺旋线压缩弹簧、拉伸弹簧和扭转弹簧。
- 螺钉、螺杆等紧固件的设计，包括传动螺杆和预加载紧固件。
- 盘式和鼓式离合器以及制动器的设计和技术说明。

第 2 课 机　　构

机构是两个或两个以上的构件通过活动联接以实现规定运动的构件组合，是机械的组成部分。两个有相对运动的构件间的活动连接称为运动副。其中凡为面接触的运动副称为低副，凡为点或线接触的运动副称为高副。机构的运动特性主要取决于构件间的相对尺寸、运动副的性质以及相互配置方式等。机构中用以支持运动构件的构件称为机架，并被当作研究运动的参考坐标系。具有独立运动的构件称为原动件。机构中除机架和主动件之外的被迫做强制运动的构件称为从动件。描述或确定机构的运动所必需的独立参变量（坐标数）称为机构自由度。为使机构的构件获得确定的相对运动，必须使机构的原动件数等于机构自由度数。

根据各个不同机构之间的异同点，常采用以下几种不同的分类方法。其中一种归类法是将机构分成平面、球面和空间三类。这三类机构具有许多共同点，区别分类的标准在于连杆装置的运动特性。

在平面机构中，所有的点在空间绘出的是平面曲线，且所有曲线都在平行平面上，也就是说，所有的点的轨迹都是与一个单一公共平面相平行的平面曲线。根据这一特点，就能够在单个图形或图像上以实际尺寸和形状绘出平面机构的任意选择点的轨迹。这种机构的运动变换称为"共面"。平面四连杆机构、平面盘形凸轮、从动件及曲柄滑块机构等都是平面机构的常见例子。目前应用的绝大部分机构都是平面机构。凸轮机构如图 2.1 所示。

凸轮是一个驱动从动件实现某一具体运动的机械零件。通过恰当的凸轮结构设计，可使机器零件获得任何预期的运动。这样便使凸轮广泛用于几乎所有的机械设备中，包括内燃机、各种机床、压缩机和计算机。一般来说，可按两种方式设计凸轮。

（1）设计凸轮的轮廓，将预期的运动传给从动件。
（2）选择能满足从动件运动要求的凸轮轮廓形式。

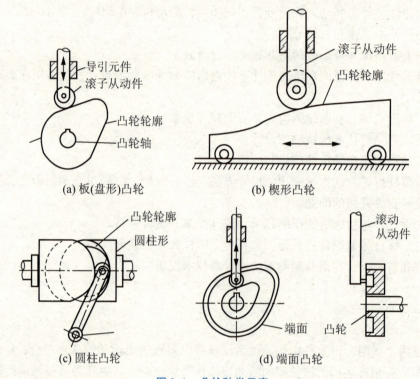

图 2.1　凸轮种类示意

一个旋转的凸轮是机器上的一个零件，可将柱面运动变为直线运动。凸轮的作用是把各种运动传输给机器的其他零件。

实际上每一个凸轮必须根据特定需要来设计和制造。虽然每一个凸轮看起来与其他的凸轮有很大的不同，但是所有的凸轮都以相似的方式工作。在每一种情况下，当凸轮旋转或转动时，与凸轮接触的另一个零件叫做从动件，也进行左右、上下或里外运动。从动件通常与机器其他零件相连接以完成预定的运动。如果从动件与凸轮不接触，则不能工作。凸轮是按照它们的基本形状来分类的。图 2.1 列出了四种不同类型的凸轮。

（1）板（盘形）凸轮。

（2）（楔形）平移凸轮。
（3）圆柱凸轮。
（4）端面凸轮。

仅采用低副的平面机构叫做"平面连杆"机构，可以只包括转动副和移动副，尽管理论上还可以包括平面副，但平面副却不能加以约束，只相当于开式运动链。平面运动要求所有移动副的轴和转动副的轴都垂直于运动平面。

第3课　机械零件（I）

齿轮

齿轮副由相互直接接触的齿轮组成，通常成对使用，在轮齿连续啮合的作用下，齿轮将运动和力从一根转轴传递到另一根转轴上，或者将运动和力从一根轴传递到滑块（齿条）上。

齿形轮廓。齿轮的接触面必须在同一方向上对齐，这样可以使得传动是正向的，也就是传递载荷不必依靠表面的摩擦作用进行。像齿轮这样直接接触的实体，垂直于表面的公法线不能经过主动轮或从动轮的轴线。

对于直接接触的实体，摆线和渐开线轮廓均提供了正向的驱动和均匀的转速比，即共轭作用。

基本关系式。一对齿轮副中较小的齿轮称为小齿轮，较大的齿轮称为大齿轮，当小齿轮安装在传动轴上时，这对齿轮用作减速；反之，若大齿轮安装在传动轴上，则这对齿轮用作加速。齿轮一般用于减速的情形要多于加速的场合。

如果齿轮有 N 个齿，并以每分钟 n 转的速度旋转，乘积 $N*n$ 表示每分钟旋转的齿数。如果每个齿都能在啮合区中与另一个齿轮的轮齿相啮合，那么这个乘积对于一对啮合齿轮的两个齿轮来说一定是相等的。

对于各种不同类型的共轭齿轮，齿轮比和速度比都可以通过大齿轮和小齿轮上的齿数比获得。如果一个大齿轮的齿数为100，小齿轮的齿数为20，齿数比为 $100/20 = 5$。这样不管大齿轮的旋转速度为多少，小齿轮的转速总是大齿轮转速的5倍。大小齿轮的接触点称为节点，由于节点位于中心线上，因此是齿形轮廓线上唯一做纯滚动的接触点。位于既不平行又不相交（交叉）的传动轴上的齿轮也有节圆，但纯滚动节圆的概念对这样的齿轮就没有意义了。

齿轮的种类一般是根据齿轮轴的排列方式来划分的，这就意味着当轴的排列布置形式决定后，齿轮的类型大致就定下来了。另一方面，如果齿轮的速度变化及类型一定的话，那么轴的排列布置形式基本上也就定下来了。

直齿轮和螺旋齿轮。轮廓为平行于其轮轴直线的齿轮称为直齿轮，直齿轮只用于轮轴平行的齿轮间的传动。

假设有一个渐开线直齿小齿轮是用橡胶制成的，并且能够均匀扭转，那么，两端就会绕着轴线做相对的转动，这样，开始是直的并平行于轴线的小齿轮上的齿，就变成了螺旋形。小齿轮就变成了螺旋齿轮。

蜗杆齿轮和锥齿轮。为了使交叉轴斜齿轮获及线接触并提高其承载能力，大齿轮可能被做成部分弯曲形状以围绕小齿轮，类似于螺母套在螺杆上，这样就形成了圆柱形的蜗轮蜗杆。蜗杆有时也做成沙漏状，而非圆柱状，目的是为了使蜗杆部分接触蜗轮，进一步提高承载力。

蜗轮蜗杆是用一对齿轮就可以提供较大速比的最简单方法，但是由于沿着齿面方向存在滑动现象，所以蜗轮蜗杆的传动总是比平行轴传动的齿轮效率低。

V形带

人造纤维和橡胶V形带广泛应用于传递动力。V形带一般做成两个系列：标准V形带和重型V形带。V形带能用于传动的中心距离较短的场合，还可以做成无缝的，避免了连接设备的麻烦。

首先，V形带成本低，通过并排增加V形带的数量可以增加传动的功率，传动中，所有V形带被拉伸相同的长度的目的是为了保持每条V形带中载荷均匀。当一条V形带断裂时，通常所有V形带都被调换。带轮可以是从上到下以一个任意角度传动。由于V形带工作在一个相对较小的带轮中，因此采用一个带轮就可以达到较大的减速。

其次，带轮槽的倾斜角度通常为34°~38°。V形带在槽中的嵌入作用可以大大增加V形带的牵引力。

第三，带轮可以用铸铁、钢、锻压等材料制成。在带轮槽的底部需要留有足够的间隙，以保证V形带不接触带轮槽的底部，因为那样容易磨损。有时较大的带轮没有轮槽，这时靠带的内表面来获得牵引力，从而可以省下在带轮上加工槽的成本。厂家供应出售的带轮可据用户要求调节槽宽。带轮的节距是会变化的，通过适当的调整可以满足速度比的要求。

链传动

第一条链传动即"安全"自行车出现在1874年，那时，链用于驱动早期自行车的后轮。如今，随着现代设计和制造方法的改进，链传动的应用越来越广泛，已经极大地提高了农业机械、钻探设备、矿业和建筑机械的效率，大约从1930年以来，链传动已经变得日益普遍，尤其是在动力锯子、摩托车和自动扶梯等设备上。

目前至少有6种类型的动力传送链，本文介绍其中的3种，分别名为滚子链条、齿型链条或低噪声（无声）链条、滚珠链条。滚柱链条传动的基本组成部分有链板、销轴、套筒、滚子、两个或多个链轮，每个链轮上有类似齿轮形状的齿。滚子链条是用销轴和滚柱等进行装配而成的，用两个销轴插入两个链板中的孔，可以连接内、外链板，销轴紧紧地插入孔中，形成压紧连接。滚子由内、外链板和两个压紧的套筒组成，硬的钢质滚柱可以自由转动。装配好后，销轴与套筒之间为自由配合，随着链条在链轮上传动，销轴可相对于套筒作轻微的转动。

标准滚子链条可以是单排的，也可以是多排的。如果是多排的，那么两条或多条链条一起连接在同一个销轴上，这时要使滚子以一定的排列方式对齐，单个驱动的速度比一般控制在10:1范围内，较合适的轴中心距离一般为30~35倍滚柱与滚柱之间的距离。链条速度一般不要超过每分钟2500英尺（每分钟800米）。当同时驱动几个平行轴时，滚子链条传动尤为合适。

齿型链条或低噪声链条基本上就是齿轮齿条的组合件，每个齿条有两个齿，轴向连接形成一个封闭的、内面有齿的链条，链轮上有共轭齿。链条连接采用销子连接平钢板，平钢板上通常是倾角为60°的直齿，便于许多链条同时传递动力。相对于滚子链条来说，这种类型的链条噪声较低，能在较高速度下工作，同样的宽度能传递更大的载荷。有时汽车就采用这种低噪声的凸轮轴驱动的链条。

滚珠链条用于连接平行或非平行轴之间的运动，连接的方式灵活，且价格便宜，通常用在传动速度和动力较低的场合。链轮含有球形或锥形凹槽，小滚珠可以在凹槽内活动。链条看上去像一串串钥匙链子一样，把用普通碳钢、不锈钢或实心塑料做成的滚珠安在链条上。滚珠链条用于计算机、空调、电视调谐器、百叶窗帘等场合，链轮可以用钢、压铸成形的锌或铝以及浇注成形的单件尼龙等制成。

第4课　机械零件（Ⅱ）

紧固件

紧固件可以将一个零件与另一个零件相连接。因此，几乎在所有的设计中都要用到紧固件。

紧固件可以分为以下3类。

（1）可拆式。采用这种紧固方式连接的零件很容易被拆开，而且不会对紧固件造成损伤。例如普通的螺栓螺母连接。

（2）半永久式。采用此类紧固件连接的零件虽然能被拆开，但通常会对所用的紧固件造成损伤，如开口销。

（3）永久式。采用这种紧固件表明所连接的零件不能拆卸，例如铆接和焊接。

对于任何复杂产品来说，紧固件都非常重要。以汽车为例，它是由数千个零件装配而成。一个紧固件的失效或松动可能会带来车门嘎嘎响这类小麻烦，也可能造成车轮脱落这种严重后果。因此，在为一个特定用途选择紧固件时，应该考虑到上述各种可能性。

由于紧固件应用非常广泛，所以对它们来说，价格低，功效高是非常必要的。

当激振力大于摩擦力时，普通螺母就会松开。在螺母与锁紧垫圈组件中，锁紧垫圈具有独立的锁紧特性以防止螺母松动。锁紧垫圈仅在螺栓与装配件间长度相对变化而松动时才起作用。这种螺栓长度的变化可由多种因素引起——螺栓内部蠕变、弹性丧失、螺栓与被连接件间的热膨胀差异或磨损。在上述静态情况下，膨胀的锁紧垫圈在轴向载荷的作用下固定螺母并确保紧固。当振动相对改变时，锁紧垫圈将失去作用。

铆钉是不可拆连接件。它们依赖于结构的变形来固定。铆钉通常比螺纹连接件牢固，而且生产成本低。铆钉既可热铆也可冷铆，取决于铆钉材料的机械特性，例如铝铆钉是冷铆，因为冷却可以提高铝的强度。但是大多数大型铆钉是热铆的。

轴

实际上，几乎所有的机器中都装有轴。轴最常见的形状是圆形，其截面可以是实心的，也可以是空心的（空心轴可以减轻重量）。

轴安装在轴承中，通过齿轮、皮带轮、凸轮和离合器等传递动力。通过这些零件传递的力可能会使轴发生弯曲变形，因此，轴应该有足够的刚度以防止支承轴承受力过大。总而言之，在两个轴承支承之间，轴在每英尺长度上的弯曲变形不应该超过0.01英寸。

直径小于3英寸的轴可以采用含碳量大约为0.4%的冷轧钢，直径在3~5英寸之间的轴可以采用冷轧钢或锻造毛坯。当直径大于5英寸时，则要采用锻造毛坯，然后切削加工到所要求的尺寸。轻载时，广泛采用塑料轴。由于塑料是电的不良导体，在电气工程应用中用塑料轴比较安全。

在轴的设计中，轴与轴之间的连接方法是要重点考虑的，可由刚性或者弹性联轴器来实现。

轴承

轴承是一种经过特定设计并用于支承机器上运动部件的零件。轴承最常用的应用是支撑传递运动的转动轴。由于轴承和配合表面间存在相对运动，因而会产生摩擦。在许多场合，例如设计皮带轮、制动器和离合器时，摩擦是有益的。然而，设计轴承时，减小摩擦是要考虑的基本因素之一，因为摩擦会导致功率下降、发热和配合表面的磨损。

对于球轴承和滚子轴承，一个机器设计人员应该考虑下面5个方面：(1) 寿命与载荷的关系；(2) 刚度，也就是在载荷作用下的变形；(3) 摩擦；(4) 磨损；(5) 噪声。对于中等载荷和转速，根据额定负荷选择一个标准轴承，通常都可以保证良好的工作性能。当载荷较大时，轴承零件会发生变形，尽管变形的程度远小于轴或其他与轴承相连的零部件，但仍然会有很大的影响。在转速高的场合需要有专门的冷却装置，这可能会增大摩擦阻力。磨损主要由污染物的进入引起，必须选用密封装置以防止周围环境的不良影响。

尽管球轴承和滚子轴承的设计由轴承制造厂负责，但是，机器设计人员必须对轴承的使用有一个正确估计，不仅要考虑轴承的选择，而且还要考虑轴承的正确安装条件。

轴承套圈与轴或轴承座的配合非常重要，它们之间的配合不仅应该保证所需要的过盈量，而且也应该保证轴承的内部间隙。不正确的过盈量会产生微振腐蚀磨损，导致严重的故障。内圈通常是通过紧靠在轴肩上进行轴向定位的。轴肩处的圆弧半径主要是为了避免应力集中。在轴承内圈上加工出圆弧或者倒角，可用来提供容纳轴肩处圆弧半径的空间。

滑动轴承最简单的形式是由合适的材料和合适的加工尺寸制成的衬套。轴颈通常是旋转在轴承内的轴的一部分，如图4.1所示。

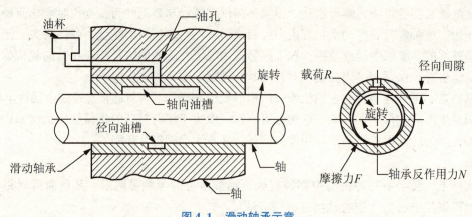

图4.1 滑动轴承示意

滑动轴承工作中伴随着滑动接触，为了减小由于滑动摩擦所引起的问题，应当使用与配合材料相对应的润滑油。在选择润滑油和配合材料时，通常要考虑轴承压力、温度和滑动速度等因素。在滑动轴承中，润滑油的基本作用是阻止摩擦表面直接接触，因此，在不同载荷、速度和温度下，油膜的维护是在滑动接触中首要考虑的问题。

第5课 第三角投影画法工程图学

前言

图学一词来源于希腊语 grapho，其延伸意义为"绘图"或"图样"。图样是开发和交流技术思想的主要工具。工程图样可为零件提供准确而完整的描绘。除了物体的形状外，工程图样还给出制造所需的全部资料，如尺寸、公差等。人们常说工程图样是工程界的通用语言，每一位工程技术人员都必须掌握这门语言。工程图学的主要任务有：

学习投影知识；

培养绘图和读图的能力；

培养和开发空间分析能力和空间想象能力。

作为工程界的共同语言，图样是用来指导生产和交流技术的。因此，必须对制图的各个方面，如图样格式、图样画法、尺寸标注等，做出统一规定。

三视图的形成

三面投影体系：仅用一个投影无法确定空间点的位置，因此需要添加多个投影面。通常，三个互相垂直的投影面构成正投影面体系，分别是水平投影面、正投影面、侧投影面，记作 H、V、W 面。

第三角投影：三投影面将空间分为八个部分或者 1~8 象限，如图 5.1 所示。依据中国机械制图国家标准，制图采用第一角投影，而其他一些国家像美国和加拿大则采用第三角投影。在本篇中，我们采用第三角投影法。

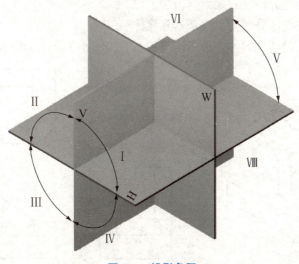

图 5.1 投影象限

三视图的形成：在第一角投影中，物体放在第一象限，观察者透过物体看投影面，而在第三角投影中，物体放在第三象限，观察者透过投影面看物体，投影面被假想为透明的，从而形成视图。

第一角投影和第三角投影的识别符号如图 5.2 所示：

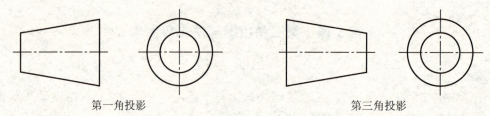

第一角投影　　　　　　　　　　第三角投影

图 5.2　第一角投影和第三角投影的识别符号

组合体

物体的投影规律：主视图和俯视图长对正；主视图和右视图高平齐；俯视图和右视图宽相等。

画组合体三视图：

（1）形体分析法：任何一个组合体都可以看作由一些简单的基本体组成。这些基本体都易于确定，可分为叠加式和切割式。

（2）视图选择：主视图是表达组合体的一组视图中最主要的视图，确定主视图时，应选择最能反映组合体形状特征的方向作为主视图的投影方向。

（3）画图步骤：定轴线，对称中心线和基线；用 H 铅笔画底稿；检查全图，并加深图线。

组合体视图阅读：

读图要点：将物体分解为一个个单独的基本形体；读图时至少要把两个视图联系起来分析；明确视图中线和面的含义。

读图的方法：形体分析法、线面分析法。

形体分析法：将物体分解为一些基本几何体。

线面分析法：将物体分解为各种不同线和面。如图 5.3 所示为组合体及其三视图。

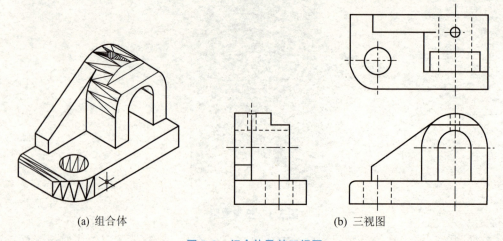

(a) 组合体　　　　　　　　　(b) 三视图

图 5.3　组合体及其三视图

零件图

零件图：表示零件结构、大小及技术要求的图样。零件图描绘零件的形状、给出零件尺寸，并提供生产该零件所需要的全部资料。

零件图的内容：

足够的视图，以完整地表达零件内、外结构的形状；

制造零件所需要的全部尺寸；

技术要求，包括公差、形位公差、表面粗糙度、材料规格和热处理要求等。

视图选择：为了满足完整、清晰地表达物体形状的要求，在开始画图之前，首先要决定需要哪些视图和零件的最佳投影方案。

主视图选择：形状特征原则、功能位置原则、加工位置原则。

其他视图选择：用最少的视图表达最完整信息原则；避免使用虚线原则；避免细节的不必要重复原则。

装配图

装配图：表示机器或部件的各个零件按其工作位置装配在一起的图样称为装配图。

装配图的内容：

一组视图：表示在装配中的各个零件的位置关系和相互作用。

少数尺寸：这是表示重要零件间的位置关系和产品的安装定位等所必需的。

技术要求：包括装配、检验和维修机器所需信息。

各个零件的件号、明细栏和标题栏。

装配图的规定画法：

一般规定：在装配图中，两接触表面或配合表面之间无任何间隙可画，反之，在非接触表面或非配合表面间应画出间隙；邻接零件的剖面线应从不同的方向或以不用的间隙画出；在装配图中，实心件沿着其轴线被剖时不画剖面线，如转轴、心轴、杆件、手柄、销和键等，螺钉、螺栓、螺母及垫圈也保持不剖的状态。

特殊规定：沿结合面剖切或把某些零件拆开的画法；单独表示零件画法；使用假想线画法；夸大画法；简化画法。

第 6 课　CAD/CAM/CAPP 导论

在工业社会发展的进程中，人们已经开发出了许多新技术和新产品。与以前出现的任何科学技术相比，对工程制造业冲击最快，影响更大的是数字计算机。如今计算机已被广泛应用在工程产品的设计中。

计算机辅助设计（CAD）就是在产品设计过程中，利用计算机和图形软件，对产品进行辅助设计以提高产品设计效率的一种技术。在计算机辅助设计过程中，通常要用到一个交互式的计算机图形系统，该系统称为计算机辅助设计系统。计算机辅助设计系统是功能强大工具，可用于产品及零部件的机械设计和几何建模。

使用 CAD 系统进行产品辅助设计的优点如下：

• 提高了产品的生产率；

- 提高了产品的设计质量；
- 统一了产品的设计标准；
- 建立了产品的制造加工数据库；

减少了手工绘图（描图）中出现的错误和图样间标准不统一的问题。

CAD 中的几何模型可以分为二维模型、二维半模型和三维模型。二维模型表示的是平面图形；三维模型一般能突显出机械零部件的形状特点（如图 6.1 所示）；二维半模型则可以表示出零件单侧连续截面的形状细节，它的主要优点在于不需要建立完整的三维模型就可以表达出零部件必要的形状特点。

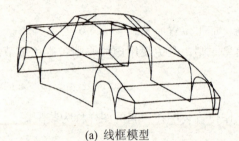

(a) 线框模型　　　　　　　　　　　　(b) 曲面模型

图 6.1　三维模型

在完成零部件详细的结构设计之后，接下来需要对其进行功能性分析，这也是零部件设计过程的一个环节。功能性分析涉及零部件（或机构）的应力—应变分析、传热分析以及动力学仿真分析等。在 CAD 系统中通常有一些机械零部件功能性分析的应用实例，如零部件的质量特性分析和有限元分析。质量特性分析包括计算几何体的体积、表面积、重量和重心等。在大多数 CAD 系统中可以进行有限元分析，主要分析内容包括对零部件进行传热状况分析、应力—应变分析、动力学特性分析等。目前大多数 CAD 系统都能够自动生成用于有限元分析的二维或三维网格形式。

CAM 定义为计算机辅助制造，它包括制造决策、生产过程和操作规划、程序设计、人工智能、自动化控制制造设备（如数控机床、数控加工中心、数控加工单元、数控柔性制造系统）及相应的技术（如数控单元技术，直接数控成组技术）。

计算机辅助制造涵盖了成组技术、制造数据库、自动化和公差检测等技术。图 6.2 所示的是 CAM 的总体框架图。

产品设计好之后，接下来就是对其进行制造。如今在机械产品制造中的许多环节里，计算机都扮演着重要的角色，例如，现代造船业中建造的结构都是由大型钢板上裁剪下来的钢板焊接成的。这时人们常使用计算机控制的火焰切割机；同时，人们还利用计算机对船体部件的结构布局方式进行优化，以达到将材料的浪费量降到最低的目的。

计算机辅助工艺设计（CAPP）就是工艺员借助计算机制定产品工艺流程的过程，利用的程度取决于制定流程的方法。低层次的辅助工艺设计是指工艺员利用计算机对手工完成的工艺数据进行存储和修改，同时为编制新的工艺流程提供数据。与上述应用相对比，高层次的计算机辅助工艺设计是指工艺员借助计算机自动完成一些形状简单工件的工艺流程。这个时候，工艺员有时需要输入一些必要的数据，有时需要对不符合特定生产要求的工艺流程进行修改。最高层次的计算机辅助工艺设计也是 CAPP 的最终实现目标，它将工艺流程编制的理论、技术以及经验编成程序输入计算机，由计算机自动完成工艺流程的编制，不需要工艺员的参与。此外，它的数据库可直接与其他系统集成，如 CAD 系统和 CAM 系统，因此，CAPP 被认为是计算机集成制造系统中的一个重要组成部分。

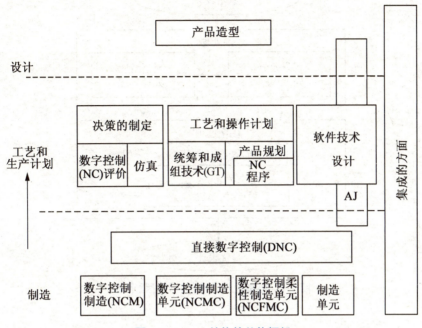

图 6.2　CAM 结构的总体框架

第 7 课　现代设计优化方法基础

如今，综合运用机械优化设计方法、有限元分析方法和计算机辅助设计技术进行产品设计对设计过程产生了深远影响。这种综合运用的手段将工程师身上的设计重担交由计算机完成，因而降低了产品的设计成本。此外，正确运用优化设计中严谨的数学推理也可以提高产品设计的可靠性。优化方法决定了产品设计过程中的精度问题，包括 CAD 软件建模的准确度，有限元分析中网格划分的正确度以及分析处理器的计算精度等，这种方法能够在考虑机械，热等许多实际情况的影响下，对 CAD 系统构建的零部件、装配体的结构进行优化。

现代优化设计技术能够对 CAD 软件构建的零件结构进行优化。从优化设计理论的角度上说，CAD 格式的文件和 FEA 格式的文件之间不需要任何的格式转换，就可以实现数据的无缝交换。这时，只要这两个文件之间存在关联性，对 CAD 文件所做的任何修改在相应的 FEA 文件中都能反映出来。例如，在使用有限元分析软件 ALGOR 对某零部件或装配体计算时，根本不需要建立其有限元模型就可以进行优化设计。用户只要挑选出零部件或装配体 CAD 模型中需要优化的几何尺寸，确定相应的设计准则（如最大应力、最高温度和最大频率），然后运行相应的分析计算过程，该软件通过计算、比较，就可以完成 CAD 模型的结构优化，并且整个过程通常不需要使用者参与。需要注意的是，CAD 与 FEA 格式文件之间的关联性使得 FEA 模型更新了，但约束和施加的载荷保持不变，因此需要对更新过后的有限元模型进行计算,对整个过程不断重复迭代,直到最终的计算结果满足设计要求为止。图7.1 所示的是零部件形状优化流程图。

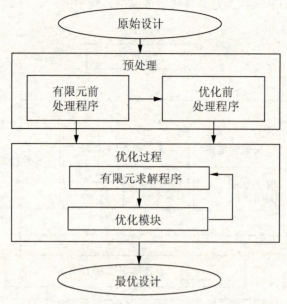

图7.1　零部件形状优化设计过程示意

引言

零部件结构的优化设计过程往往需要进行多步迭代计算,在整个计算过程中,零部件的几何外形不断变化、优化。在每一步迭代计算中要进行一定的分析,以便得到与工程实际较为相符的设计结果。优化设计一般需要很多步这样的迭代计算,每一步计算都较为费时。所以,在进行机械结构优化设计过程中使用优化设计软件的主要目的是自动运行上述的迭代计算,减少工程师的工作负担。乍看上去,优化设计技术是一种能够替代工程师进行工程设计的工具,但事实上不是这样,因为任何优化设计软件都不能确定应该优化什么对象,哪些是设计变量,需要改变哪些量或参数,所以,优化设计软件只是工程师进行设计的一种工具,其用途由其优化计算的能力来决定。

优化设计软件常常要进行零部件几何外形的优化计算,一般要具有较强的数值计算能力。庆幸的是,大多数零部件结构优化设计的问题都可以看成是数学中的极值问题。求极值的有效方法很多,但方法太多也不好,因为对于一个特定的问题,其最佳的解法只有一种。利用优化设计软件可以很好地解决这个问题,因为优化设计软件不仅可以帮助工程师选择解决问题的方法,而且还能够帮助工程师找到最佳解决方法。

本文重点阐述机械零部件或装配体结构的优化设计。我们经常需要优化零部件或装配体在实际工作过程中承受的最大应力,所涉及的设计变量一般是零部件或装配体的几何尺寸,比如一个指定零件的厚度。我们一般先用 CAD 软件构建零部件或装配体的几何外形,如果设计结构正确,那么工程师会选择相应的有限元分析软件,对上述结构的机械性能进行数值模拟;然后根据计算结果,比如最大应力的分布状况,来判断设计是否有效。在设计过程中,工程师可能需要改变 CAD 或 FEA 模型的一些参数或特征属性,如零部件或装配体的几何尺寸、材料参数以及约束和加载的状况。CAD 和 FEA 软件之间的关联性使得工程师只需要修改其中任何一个模型即可，例如，在 CAD 软件中改变了某个零件的厚度或增加了一个孔，它的有限元模型会也自动做相应修改。大多数情况下，工程师采用线性静力学的方法来分析应力状况，这种方法的优点在于能用较少的耗时，较多的有限元分析单元得到需要的有限元分析结果。但该方法也存在缺点，例如，在估算处于运动状态的零部件或装配体的载荷大小或方向时，往往需要较丰富的专业知识（这种方法无法满足要求）。

基础知识和理论

本部分着重讨论优化设计的一些数学理论方法，首先介绍利用有限元方法进行优化设计的过程，该过程一般有 3 个步骤：

（1）在 CAD 软件中构造出某一零部件或装配体的几何模型；
（2）建立相应的有限元分析模型；
（3）对有限元分析的计算结果进行分析和判断。

现在只讨论线性静力学有限元分析方法，需要计算的是零部件/装配体在外载荷作用下的应变和应力分布状况。一般人工优化设计过程都要涉及上述 3 个步骤，也需要根据计算结果来判断设计的合理性；如果设计结果不合理，就要对步骤（1）或（2）做修改，也可能步骤（1）、（2）都要改。可以清楚地看出，有限元分析的结果就是优化的结果，由于每个输入到 CAD 或 FEA 模型中的参数或特征属性都可以看成是设计变量。优化设计算法对许多有限元分析都有指导作用，它的每一种算法对不同的设计变量会产生不同的数据组，所以，CAD 软件和 FEA 软件之间必须具有关联性，才能将人工设计方法转化成优化设计算法。可以通过例子来说明上述问题，例如，在刚开始对某一零部件或装配体进行有限元分析时，工程师一般要对其有限元分析模型上的某一平面施加约束。假定这个平面就是零部件或装配体 CAD 模型上的平面。现在需要优化这个平面的结构，由于 CAD 软件和 FEA 软件之间的关联性，其 FEA 模型上的平面会随着 CAD 模型的变化而变化，这样，上述约束就会施加在改变了的平面模型上。为了实现 CAD 模型与 FEA 模型之间的自动数据交换，CAD 软件和 FEA 软件之间必须具备这种关联性。下面要讨论的问题是使用什么样的数学方法来解决这些问题。

大多数优化设计都要涉及以下 3 个基本问题：

（1）目标函数的最小值（或最大值）：例如，在设计汽车的仪表板时，往往需要它在某一指定区域上受到应力最小。
（2）影响目标函数值的设计变量组：例如，在汽车仪表板设计中用来确定仪表板几何外形和材料的变量。
（3）约束条件：这些约束条件使得优化设计中的变量只能在某一范围内取值。例如，在设计汽车的仪表板时，常常需要限制它的质量。

实际上，建立一个无约束的优化问题也是非常可能的。也许有人会认为几乎所有的问题都应具有一定的约束条件。例如，汽车仪表板的厚度不能为负值，不过实际上无须对一些设计变量施加约束条件，常常也可以获得与基本常识相符的结果，如上述的仪表板厚度为正值的问题即是如此。

优化设计的优点和缺点

目前许多应用软件都以解除或减少人的重复工作为目的。基于计算机的优化设计技术属于一种最新的应用设计技术,其目的就是增加计算机的计算量,减少人的工作时间。实际上在进行优化设计计算时,使用计算机需要的计算量甚至比人工设计方法还要少,这是因为优化设计技术采用了严谨的数学计算方法,所以它的设计效率要比人工设计方法高。当然基于计算机的优化设计技术取代不了人的思维,因为人的思想有时可以大大缩短设计过程。基于计算机的优化设计方法与人工设计方法相比,其明显的优点是,如果优化设计软件使用正确,它能够考虑到所有的设计方案,也就是说,会考虑到各种可行的设计参数,因此利用优化设计软件进行计算的结果应该是最精确的。

第8课　建筑机械开发中的动态仿真技术应用

引言

所有的工程师可能都了解虚拟样机技术的应用目的。现在出台的一些严格的法律制度(如关于废气排放和噪声)和较高的用户指标(如有关设备性能和操作方面)均需要更为先进、复杂的技术来完成产品设计。如果采用传统设计方法,将需要更多的研制费用和较长的研制时间,但竞争激烈的市场则要求降低产品的研制费用和缩短产品的研制周期。

目前汽车行业已经广泛采用了虚拟样机技术,目的是解决行业中出现的上述矛盾。人们已经能够对整台车的各个子系统进行仿真计算,但现在需要研究如何对车辆的整体性能进行数值计算,这是虚拟样机技术的发展趋势,如图8.1所示。对整个车辆系统进行数值计算的目的是评估车辆的控制性能、舒适程度和稳定性;测试车辆的碰撞性能。

图8.1　VolvoL220型装载机的多系统模型

在汽车工业的设计领域中,越野行业相对滞后的原因主要体现在以下几个方面。

第一、行业的规模较小;第二、在购买最新 CAE 软件和培训上的费用太多;第三,制造的产品在外形和所使用的子系统上也各不相同,这可能是最重要的因素。

最近公布了一些对整台车辆进行仿真计算的应用实例,涉及仿真技术、车辆子系统、舒适度和稳定性。本文讨论的是整台车辆的动态仿真问题,目的是分析、优化车辆的整体工作性能。虽然研究的对象是液压驱动式挖掘机,但得到的结果也适用于其他越野机械设备。

设计过程与可视化

在越野机械设计领域,人们研究的课题是如何变革现在使用的产品研制方法和设计过程，主要研究的问题是如何利用动态仿真技术，改变现在使用的设计理念。因此本文重点讨论如何利用动态仿真技术分析、优化越野机械设备的整体工作性能，这在前面已经提到过。

变革现在设计方法的目标是：将节约的资源（如时间、资金和人力）投入到优化产品的研制过程、方法以及性能上。设计产品的具体目标如下：
- 较高的工作性能、生产率和操作性；
- 较好的越野性；
- 较短的研制周期；
- 较低的研制费用。

在越野汽车设计的早期阶段，人们已经有了一些有价值的设计经验，即在越野汽车的反复改进设计阶段，尤其在其概念设计时期，汽车速度的设计非常重要。Volvo 公司使用较先进的设计计算程序替代以前使用的程序，使得设计工作可以由专门的仿真计算程序完成。该程序是在多体动力学和现代数据库的基础上研制的。现在人们已经证明：对用户来说这种新研制的计算程序适应性、精度和效率都比较高，但新研制的数值仿真系统车对于那些从事预测性研究的工程师来说，其优越性并不明显，原因是这种程序利用的是多体动力学仿真技术，而不是深奥的数学程序，所以每次运行的时间比以往的程序都要慢上两秒。但使用以往程序，优化越野汽车的受力状况非常耗时。所以，在使用新的仿真程序时，如果事先了解了车辆的受力情况，并在设计时加以考虑，人们完全可以研制出一个结构更为紧凑的程序来解决上述问题，该程序虽然计算精度低，但速度比以前提高了。引进这个新计算程序的主要目的是让那些从事预测性研究的工程师们放弃使用那些计算时间虽短，但精度不高的程序。

在课题进行过程中还发现了其他类似问题：目前进行静载荷计算的程序速度较快，所得到精度也较高（如图 8.2 所示）；但缺点是，在研究整台车辆的动态特性时，常常先需要进行概念样机测试，然后对真正的样机进行试验，最后再改进设计。

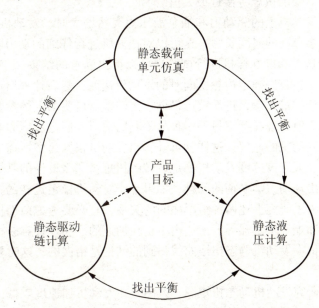

图 8.2　初始静态计算循环示意

和实际设计过程一样，在利用动力学仿真程序进行越野车辆设计时，首先，将产品的设计目标函数值输入到初始计算静载荷的程序中，如果对计算结果不满意，则修改目标值；接着进行所谓的"动态增加，静态计算"（见下面的解释）。同样，只有当计算误差在允许的范围内，程序才会对目标值进行迭代循环计算。由于进行迭代的目标值不可能包括设计对象的所有条件（包括动态特性），所以循环计算中的误差检验准则需要在一定范围之内进行设置。只有当计算误差过高时，才会使用新的静态计算循环程序（这时需重新输入产品目标值）。如果计算结果仍不合理，那么就应该对目标值进行修改。由于整台车辆的仿真计算需要的时间较长，所以快速检验初始循环计算结果非常必要。通常，检验过程在循环计算的第二步完成，但具体方法仍需要进一步改进。比如，在一个"挖掘机性能的循环计算中"就存在着这么一个临界阶段，让一个装满货物的机械设备（该设备带有一个装满货物的大桶，如挖掘机）改变其运送货物的方向，这时车辆的各个子系统之间就存在着相互协调的关系。

（1）为了挖掘机转向，操作人员往往要降低发动机的速度（否则齿轮换挡速度较快，传动联合器可能提前失效、损坏）。发动机转速降低了，其转动所需要的扭矩也会相应变小，但由于涡轮增压器的转动惯性，发动机的启动变得非常迟缓。

（2）当换向齿轮由反转变为正转时，由于此时的挖掘机仍在后退，这样发动机的涡轮旋转方向发生突变，涡轮齿轮的轮齿间发生了相对滑动，造成发动机需要的扭矩急剧增大。

（3）有些操作人员在挖掘机转向的时候并不停止装载货物，这样就需要更多的油液提供动力。通常发动机需要的油液量和液压泵的排液量、发动机机轴的转速成一定比例关系。假定液压泵与发动机机轴直接相连，当发动机转速降低、需油量增加时，液压泵的排液量也接近最大值。发动机油泵运转需要的扭矩大小与该泵的排液量、液压成一定比例关系，这是因为挖掘机装满货物时（包括装载货物的大小），其液压泵的液压变高，排液量趋于最大值，因而需要的扭矩将接近最大值。

当工效降低的发动机上的驱动力和油泵液压力突然增大时，发动机是否能安全运行，取决于上述3种因素存在的时间长短，这可以对挖掘机进行仔细的动力学计算，得出满意的结果（对实际制造的功能性样机进行试验也可以得出满意的结果）。然而，最近似、耗时最少的计算方法是：首先确定齿轮换向时的发动机速度，然后计算出油泵轮和扭矩转换器涡轮之间相对滑移的最大量，进而就可借助扭矩转换器说明书上的参数求出发动机正常运转需要的最大扭矩值。现在考虑另外一种最不利的情形，假定液压力和油泵的排液量均达到最大值，已知发动机的速度，这样就可计算出发动机正常运转所需要的扭矩。如果这两次计算的扭矩的和大于该速度发动机稳定运转的扭矩，那么设计的系统方案在实际运行过程中，就可能会出现动力学平衡的问题；如果小于发动机稳定运转的扭矩值，则方案能够按照要求运行。为了研究上述两种情况之间的关系，有必要考虑前面提到的发动机涡轮增压器的转动惯量和烟雾限制器等因素。由于正在加速的发动机很难获得低速稳定转动的扭矩值，所以，只依据发动机静态扭矩曲线得到的结论是错误的，这时发动机运转状态不安全。

现在我们需要研究发动机动态扭矩图。该图是在发动机加速度较低，且其静态扭矩和动态扭矩差别不太大时测量出来的（如图8.3中所示的虚曲线）。

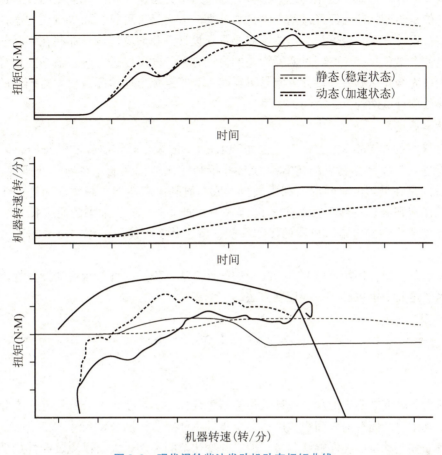

图 8.3 现代涡轮柴油发动机动态扭矩曲线

由于快速增加发动机的内部压力会提高发动机的加速度。假定车辆倒车时，发动机空转，那么，此时发动机的加速度可以从其最大扭矩时的速度和空转时的速度差值中求出。利用带有电磁装置的试验台对发动机加速状况进行测试，测出的扭矩就是制动需要的扭矩（见图 8.3）。

在图 8.3 中，虚曲线代表的是发动机加速较小时测量出来的结果。从理论上说，这种情况下的扭矩值应该更大一些，原因是：（1）发动机旋转部件在加速时需要的扭矩较小；（2）发动机用于增压的时间较长。正如第一个曲线图描述的那样，发动机加速度增幅不大时，其扭矩的增幅也不大。现在理论上已经证明，发动机扭矩的增加幅度是与其速度大小密切相关的。这可以从发动机加速度增幅不大时的静、动扭矩仿真曲线的差别中看出来。即如果发动机的加速度增幅较小，其动态扭矩曲线（粗实线）会向静态扭矩曲线（细实线）的方向延伸。

为了尽快找出有动力学问题的设计方案，需要研究更多的检验方法，同时还需要改进目前使用的一些方法和规律。

现在仔细研究这些经过改进的设计方法，即使这些方法在本文一开始被称为"一种在原有基础上进行发展的设计方法，不是一种创新的设计方法"，仍可以清楚地看出该设计方法与以往的方法相比，变化的地方很多。通过对该方法的介绍，我们明白，建造功能性样机的目的是验证那些已经经过动力学仿真计算的方案是否可行，而进行动力学计算是为了确定某一设计方案是否可行，需要不需要重新设计。我们应该摒弃那些在实际使用中不可行的设计方案，只有那些经过实验检验的设计方案，才可以进一步建造功能性样机，所以没有人事先会知道哪一种设计方案是可行的。为了避免上述情况，树立对产品的设计信心，应该处理好这两种方法之间的关系。

总结和展望

本文介绍的是 Volvo 挖掘机制造公司和 Linköping 大学合作研究的科研项目。该项目的目的是通过对整个挖掘机的仿真设计来分析和优化整机性能。在项目的研究过程中，企业的目的是在最短的时间内，利用最少的成本研制出高性能、高效率和高操作性的产品。目前已经研究出一些经过改进的设计方法，同时也制定了未来的研究计划。将来的研究重点将集中在确定整台机器的操作性能，解决其实际使用过程中出现的动力学仿真问题。

从长远角度看，仍需要研究更为复杂的设计方法，仍要进行整台机器操作性能优化的研究，当然这其中也包含了一些控制方法的问题。

第 9 课　工 程 公 差

引言

物体由其轮廓来确定形状。设计人员会给零件标注满足要求的公称尺寸。实际上，由于表面不规则以及固有的表面粗糙度，各个零件不能完全按照公称尺寸加工出来。必须允许尺寸有一些变动量以确保能够制造，但尺寸变化范围不能太大，以免装配性能变差。单个零件所允许的尺寸变化量范围称为公差。

零件公差

为了确保零件的装配和互换性，有必要控制尺寸，对于影响间隙和过盈配合的关键尺寸应指定公差。指定公差的一种方法是在公称尺寸后标出容许偏差，如尺寸可以标注为 40.000 ± 0.003mm。这意味着加工的尺寸必须在 39.997 mm 和 40.003mm 之间。误差可以在公称尺寸两侧变化的公差叫做双向公差。对于单向公差，一个公差为零，如 $40_0^{+0.006}$。

当图中没有明确给出尺寸公差时，可以采用通用的尺寸公差。对于加工尺寸，通用公差可能是 ±0.5mm。因此，被指定为 15.0 mm 的尺寸范围可以是 14.5 mm ~ 15.5 mm。其他通用公差可以适用于如角度、钻削的孔和冲裁出的孔、铸件、锻件、焊缝以及焊角等情形。

在确定零件的公差时，可以参考以前的图纸或普遍的工程惯例。公差通常以英式或 ISO 标准来定义范围。表 9-1 给出了通用公差应用指南。对于给定的公差，比如 H7/s6，为零件尺寸提供一组与图表对应的数值。下面给出关于装入孔内的轴或圆柱形零件配合的具体例子。

表9-1 公差带及其典型应用的实例

分类	说明	特性	ISO码	装配	应用
	自由转动	对大的温度变化、高转速或大的轴颈压力有益	H9/d9	显著间隙	多轴承轴、液压缸内的活塞、活动杠杆、滚筒轴承
	紧动配合	适用于在精密机械上转动及在中等速度和轴颈压力下精确定位	H8/f7	间隙	机床主轴承、曲柄轴和连杆轴承、轴套、离合器套、导向块
	滑动配合	当部件不用自由转动但必须精确移动、转动和定位时	H7/g6	压配合,没有显著间隙	推进齿轮和离合器、连杆轴承、指标活塞
	定位间隙配合	为固定件的定位提供密配合,但可以自由装配	H7/h6	手的压力、带润滑	齿轮、尾架套筒、调整环、活塞螺栓
过渡配合	定位过渡配合	适用于精确定位(位于间隙配合与过盈配合之间)	H7/k6	容易用锤子敲	滑轮、离合器、齿轮、飞轮
	定位过渡配合	适用于更精确定位	H7/n6	需要压力	电动机轴衔铁、轮子上带齿的轴环
过盈配合	定位过盈配合	适用于需要有定位精度的刚性和对正的部件	H7/p6	需要压力	开式滑动轴承
	中等驱动配合	适用于普通钢机件或小截面上的紧缩配合	H7/s6	需要压力及温度差	离合器从动盘毂,滑块、轮子和连杆内的轴承轴瓦

孔和轴的标准配合

制造工程中常要求确定圆柱形零件的公差,比如安装在相应的圆柱形零件或孔内的,或者是在其内部旋转的轴。配合的松紧取决于应用场合。例如,定位在轴上的齿轮需要"紧"配合,这里轴的直径实际上比齿轮轮毂的内径稍微大一些,以便能传递所需的扭矩。另外,滑动轴承的直径必须大于轴的直径以使其旋转。假定从经济上讲不能把零件制造成精确的尺寸,则必须确定轴和孔尺寸上的大小变化量,但是变化的范围不应太大,以免装配时受损。为了不至于有太多的公差尺寸,已经制定了国家和国际标准公差带,实例列在表9-1中,比如H11/c11。为了使用这一资料,表9-1和图9.1给出了常规的公差规定。通常使用的是基孔制,因为这会减少所需的钻头、铰刀、拉刀和计量工具的种类。

尺寸:以专用单位表示的尺寸数值。

实际尺寸:通过测量得到的部件尺寸。

尺寸极限:零件允许的最大和最小尺寸。

最大尺寸极限:两个尺寸极限中较大的。

最小尺寸极限:两个尺寸极限中较小的。

基本尺寸：用以确定尺寸极限的参考尺寸。
偏差：尺寸与其对应的基本尺寸的差值。
上偏差：最大尺寸极限与其对应的基本尺寸的差值。
下偏差：最小尺寸极限与其对应的基本尺寸的差值。
公差：最大尺寸极限与最小尺寸极限的差值。
轴：用于常规设计一个零件所有外部特征的术语。
孔：用于常规设计一个零件所有内部特征的术语。

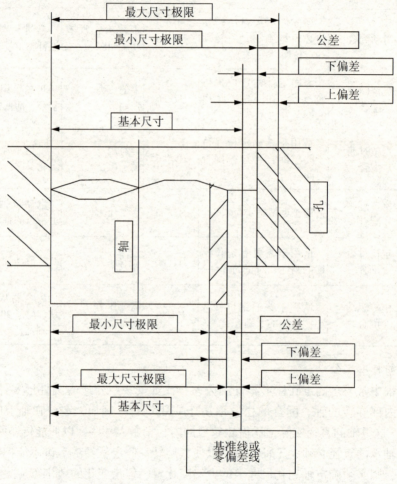

图 9.1　传统公差制定中使用的术语的定义

第 10 课　数 控 技 术

数控技术是一种利用程序实现自动控制的技术，加工制造设备采用数控技术后能由数字、字符和符号等进行控制。这些数字、字符和符号等被编码成按一定格式定义的指令程序，用于特定的加工或工作。这些指令可以采用两种二进制编码的数字系统中的任意一种进行定义，这两种二进制编码数字系统分别为电工协会代码（EIA）和美国标准信息交换代码（ASCII）。一般来说，ASCII 编码的机床控制系统不能接受 EIA 编码的指令，反之亦然。当然，这样的问题已经逐渐得到解决。数控加工制造目前已经广泛地应用于几乎所有的金属加工机床：车床、铣床、钻床、镗床、磨床、回转冲床、电火花或线切割机床以及焊接机床，甚至弯管机也可采用数控加工技术。

数控技术的基本组成

一个数控系统主要由以下 3 部分组成：

（1）程序指令

（2）加工控制单元

（3）制造装备

程序指令由一条一条的详细指令组成，制造装备按要求执行这些指令。最常用的指令形式可以按要求使机床刀具主轴位于工作台上的具体位置，工作台是用于固定加工零件的。许多更高级的指令还包括主轴速度选择、刀具选择及其他一些功能。

加工控制单元（MCU）包括一些用于阅读和解释程序指令并将其转换为机床刀具或其他制造装备的机械动作的电子和控制硬件。

制造装备是一种进行金属加工的数控技术装备，在常用的数控技术领域中，制造装备用于进行机械制造。制造装备包括工作台、主轴、电机及控制驱动单元。

数控技术的类型

数控技术系统主要有两种类型：点对点数控系统和轮廓线数控系统。

点对点数控系统也称为位置数控系统，比轮廓线数控系统简单，其主要的原理是移动刀具或工件从一个程序控制点到另一个控制点，通常像钻床这样的加工功能，每个点都可以通过 NC 程序中的指令进行控制。点对点数控系统适用于钻孔、沉孔加工、沉孔镗孔、铰孔和攻螺纹等。其他冲孔机床、点焊机和装配机床等也都采用点对点数控系统。

轮廓线数控系统也称为轮廓线路径数控系统，定位和切割操作都是以不同的速度沿着控制的路径进行的。由于刀具沿路径进行切削，因此刀具的运动和速度的精确控制和同步性能是非常重要的。轮廓线数控系统经常应用于车床、铣床、磨床、焊接机床和加工中心中。刀具沿着路径的运动可称为插补，逐渐出现了几个不同的方法。有多种插补方法用于处理在轮廓线数控系统中生成光滑的轮廓线时遇到的各种问题，几种比较常用的方法有线性插补、圆形插补、螺旋形插补、抛物线插补和立方插补等。在所有的插补方法中，路径控制是以刀具的旋转中心为标准，在数控程序中对类型不同，直径不同的刀具以及在加工过程中的不同刀具磨损量给予不同的补偿。

数控系统的编程

一个数控系统（NC）的程序包括使数控（NC）机床进行操作和加工的一系列指令。数控程序可以由数控机床内部的程序库开发生成，也可以从外面采购获得。另外，程序可以通过手工编写，也可以进行计算机辅助编程。

数控程序包括一系列指令系统和命令系统。几何类指令用于定义刀具和工件之间的相对位置和运动；加工类指令用于定义主轴转速、进给、刀具转速等；传送类指令用于定义刀具或工作台的运动速度和插补的类型等；开关类指令用于冷却液供给、主轴旋转、主轴旋转方向选择、换刀、工件进给、夹具开关等。第一个用于数控编程的数控编程语言是 20

（2）麻花钻内的热管离钻头的尖部距离越近，其传热的效率越高。尽管麻花钻上的热应力并不随热管的长度增长而变大，但实际的加工条件限制了麻花钻内热管的长度，如图11.3所示。

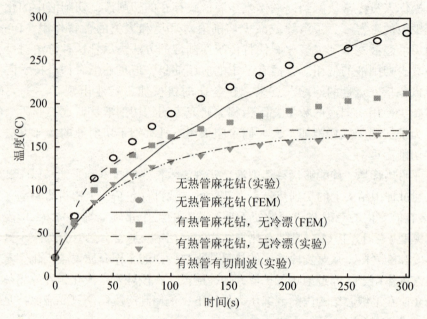

图11.2　麻花钻上的钻削温度

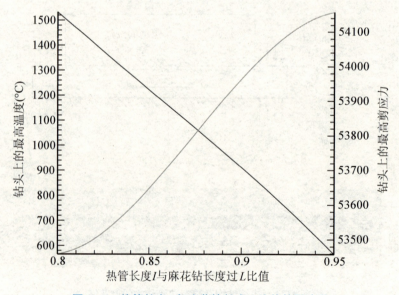

图11.3　热管长度 l 与麻花钻长度 L 比值的影响图

（3）热管直径的大小对麻花钻钻头上热应力的影响程度超过对温度的影响。虽然热管直径对钻头上最高钻削温度值影响不大，但它对其上温度场分布状况的影响较大，如图11.4所示。

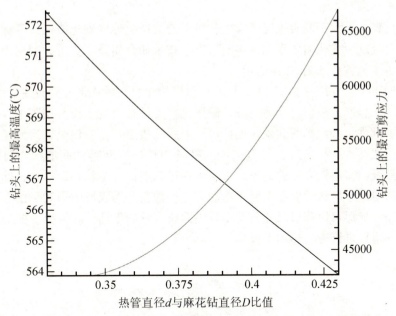

图11.4 热管直径 d 与麻花钻直径 D 比值的影响示意

第12课 材料成形导论

材料成形工艺体系

材料成形指的是将固体材料工件的原有形状变成另外一种形状而不改变工件材料的质量和化学成分的一系列制造工艺方法的总称。

制造工艺的分类：材料"成形"常常与下面的制造工艺分类的第Ⅱ组方法中的"变形"通用。机械制造工艺可以分为下面6大主要类别。

第Ⅰ类——最初的成形：即将材料由熔融态、气态或未定型的固态颗粒制成一定的形状，也就是将材料的粒子牢固地聚合起来。

第Ⅱ类——变形：将固体材料由一种给定的形状转变为另外的一种形状而不改变原来的成分和质量，即保持聚合状态。

第Ⅲ类——分离：切削加工或材料的去除，即分离。

第Ⅳ类——连接：将单个的工件连接到一起以形成大的零部件、工件等，即使分散的工件连接起来，增加工件间的聚合力。

第Ⅴ类—涂覆：在工件表面涂覆薄层，如电镀、刷油漆、喷塑等，即要使材料的基体与涂覆层间产生聚合力。

第Ⅵ类—材料属性的变化：有目的地改变材料的性能以在加工处理过程中获得某些方面的最优性能。这些方法包括改变微粒的取向，以及通过扩散产生或消除这些微粒，即重排、增加或减少微粒。

在制造工艺特别是Ⅰ至Ⅳ类工艺中，我们总是要面对在兼顾保证满足公差、表面构造及材料性能的前提下如何最经济地制造好一个特定的科技产品的问题。

冷成形及热成形

通过对材料施加大于屈服强度的应力，可以使其产生形变硬化或进行冷却加工的同时产生变形。完成这一变化需要采用许多制造工艺技术如金属丝拉拔等。利用冷加工及热加工的几种制造工艺方法如图 12.1 所示。

许多冷加工工艺方法（如图 12.1 所示）可以用于材料的成形并同时使金属得以强化。例如，轧制用于生产金属板材及薄板等。锻压是将工件材料置于模具型腔中，以获得形状相对复杂的零部件，如汽车的曲轴、连杆等。采用拉拔工艺，一根金属棒料经过拉拔模拉拔可变成线材或纤维。挤压时，材料被推入模具中挤压以获得截面形状均匀的产品如棒类、管类产品及门窗用铝合金镶边等。拉深可用于制造铝合金饮料罐等。拉伸、弯曲及其他工艺方法都可用于材料的成形。所以冷加工是一种在金属成形的同时又使金属强化的好方法。用冷加工成形可以获得尺寸公差小且表面质量好的零部件。值得一提的是许多工艺方法如轧制等可以进行冷、热加工成形。

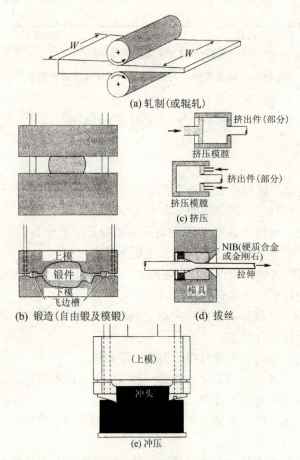

图 12.1 几种材料成形工艺方法（冷加工及热加工）

我们可以采用热加工而不是冷加工方法使金属产生变形以获得所需的形状。如前所述，热变形被定义为金属材料在再结晶温度以上的塑性变形。热变形加工很适于较大零件的成形，因为金属在高温时屈服强度降低而塑性很好。另外，具有密排六方晶体结构的金属如镁等在高温时滑移系会增多。高塑性使热成形有比冷成形允许更大的变形量。如一块厚板可以经过一系列的连续热加工变为薄片（板）。

热加工的优点是通过加工能消除材料中的缺陷：可以消除原材料中的一些缺陷或使其不良影响减至最小；气孔能被压合或熔合，材料中的成分偏析会减少；通过结晶再可以很好地细化及控制金属的显微组织。因此，金属的机械性能及物理性能都得到明显的改善。

塑性成形原理

塑性理论是金属成形工艺方法数学处理的基础。材料科学及冶金学可以解释金属固体塑性状态的本质及其各影响参数，如成形速度、前期工艺历史及温度等。但早期的塑性理论主要进行应力、力及变形的计算。

塑性理论是基于宏观上所观察到的现象建立起来的，换句话说，就是以材料在变形过程中如拉伸及压缩试验中所能观察到或测试出的性能为基础的。这就引出了下面关于塑性状态的简单定义。

塑性是材料在外力（当应力状态达到了该材料的临界值，即屈服强度或初始流变应力时）作用下永久地改变其形状的能力。正如我们在拉伸试验中可看到的那样，当应力低于屈服强度时，载荷去除后变形将自行回复：此时，材料的变形为弹性行为。如果应力增加到高于屈服极限，则会产生永久变形，卸载后，工件变成了与原来不同的新的形状。此时，我们就说材料发生了塑性变形或永久变形，或者最终变成了一定的形状，就可以说材料成形了。具有弹塑性行为的材料在产生了永久变形后再次承载时，在达到流变应力前不会再发生塑性变形。这种由于前面的变形导致流变应力增大的现象称为形变硬化或加工硬化。

加工硬化现象可以通过回复和再结晶的动态软化过程消除。

产生了加工硬化的显微结构由含有大量复杂的位错变形的晶粒组成，当将这种金属加热时，热能会促使位错运动并形成多边形亚晶粒的边界。但是位错密度不会变小。这种在较低温度下加硬化以消除残余应力而没有改变位错密度的过程称为回复。

当把产生了加工硬化的金属材料加热到某一温度（再结晶温度）以上时，快速的回复将进一步消除残余应力并形成多边形的位错结构。新的细小的晶粒在多边形晶粒的晶界处形成核，同时大多数位错被消除。由于位错数量大大减少，所以再结晶金属的强度下降而塑性增大。这种通过加热产生加工硬化的材料以形成新晶粒的过程叫做再结晶。再结晶时如加热温度太高，将会引起晶粒变大。

材料成形方法

下面将变形方法分成 5 大类别，主要是根据实际有效的应力的显著不同来分类的。根据工艺的种类，将同时有不同的应力状态存在，或者在变形的过程中应力状态可能改变，所以将应力状态简单描述为某种形式是不可能的。因此，只能选择最主要的应力状态作为分类依据。如此就可以将材料成形工艺方法分类如下：

（1）压缩（压制）成形（在压应力作用下成形）：德国标准定义这种固态形变为其塑性状态主要是由于单向或多向压缩载荷的作用而获得的；

（2）拉压成形（在拉、压应力结合的载荷作用下成形）；

（3）拉伸成形（在拉应力下成形）；

（4）弯曲成形（借助于弯曲应力的作用成形）；
（5）剪切成形（在剪应力作用下成形）。

第13课 材料成形工艺

本文通过一些实例简单介绍几种材料成形的工艺方法，但不包括装配和连接工艺。

锻造

锻造是对固态金属材料进行的最基本的机械塑性成形加工工艺方法，整个加工过程满足质量守恒定律。从工艺学上来说，锻造可定义为在冲击力或压力的作用下，经过一定的塑性变形使金属通过成形、精锻及力学性能的改善而提高其使用性能的工艺方法。锻造有很多类型，图13.1（a）表示的是最普通的落锤锻造工艺：金属加热到适当的温度后，将其放入到型腔内；上型腔与下型腔合拢，迫使金属充满型腔；多余的材料挤入型腔周边的飞边槽内，由后续的切边精整工艺进行清除。提到锻造，通常是指热锻，因为冷锻有其专门的名称。锻造工艺中损失的材料一般很少。由于锻造的公差和表面粗糙度通常不能满足产品的设计需要，因此需要对锻造的零件进一步加工。锻造机械包括落锤、机械或液压驱动的锻压机。这些机械设备一般只做简单的平动。

轧制

轧制是对固态金属材料进行的最基本的机械塑性成形加工工艺方法，整个加工过程满足质量守恒定律。轧制广泛应用在板材、薄板和结构桁条等制造中。图13.1（b）所示的是板材或薄板的轧制。铸造生产出的铁锭加热后，经过加工，其厚度变薄。但由于工件的宽度保持不变，所以其长度将随着厚度的变薄而变长。热轧的最终阶段是冷却，这样可以提高工件的表面质量、公差和强度。在轧制工艺中，根据需要，常常将轧辊的外形设计成所期望的几何形状。

粉末（压制）成形

粉末（压制）成形也属于对固态金属材料进行的最基本的机械塑性成形加工工艺方法的范畴，整个加工过程满足质量守恒定律。这里仅介绍金属粉末压制成形工艺，但一般成形砂、陶瓷材料的挤压等也属于此类加工工艺。金属粉末压制时，型腔内充满了标称体积粉末，如图13.1（c）所示，图中施加了大约500 N/mm^{2}的压力压紧粉末。在压制过程中，粉末颗粒充满型腔并发生塑性变形。挤压后的密度通常是固态材料密度的80%。塑性变形后，粉末颗粒"焊合"到一起，其强度足以满足一般的操作过程要求。挤压后，零件一般要进行烧结热处理，该温度是材料熔化温度的70%~80%。烧结时的空气一定要控制好，以防止出现氧化现象。根据材料和工艺参数，烧结过程的时间是30分钟~2小时，烧结后的零件强度非常接近相应固体材料的强度。

闭合的型腔形状与最后得到的零件几何形状相对应。粉末成形压机包括机械式压机和液压式压机两种。生产率为每分钟6~100个零件。

铸造

铸造是将液态材料充满型腔的最基本的机械塑性成形加工工艺方法，整个加工过程满足质量守恒定律。铸造不但是最古老的加工方法之一，同时也是人们最熟悉的加工工艺。

材料被熔化并浇注到与铸件形状尺寸相应的铸型型腔内（见图13.1（d））。液态材料充满型腔，随后冷却凝固，最终得到所需要的零件几何形状。

铸造工艺的流程包括制作适当的铸型、熔化材料、将材料充满或灌注进型腔内及冷却凝固。采用不同的铸型材料可以得到不同特性和尺寸精度的铸件。铸造工艺中使用的设备有熔炉、铸型制作机械和铸造机械。

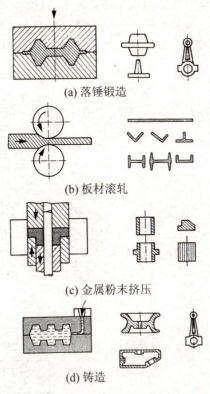

(a) 落锤锻造

(b) 板材滚轧

(c) 金属粉末挤压

(d) 铸造

图 13.1　固态下的工件材料质量不变的成形工艺

车削

车削是对固态金属材料进行切除的最基本的机械加工工艺方法。车削工艺广为人知，使用最为普遍。在车削工艺中，人们使用切削刀具从工件上切除材料，形成切屑碎片。如图13.2（a）所示的是一般用于加工的各种类型的圆柱形工件。车削时，工件旋转，切削刀具纵向进给。与工件材料相比，切削刀具材料具有很高的硬度和耐磨性。车削时，可以根据需要采用不同类型的车床。车床通常由电动机驱动，通过不同的齿轮系统向工件提供必要的扭矩，使刀具完成进给运动。

利用相同的金属切削原理，也可以得到其他完全不同的加工操作方法或加工工艺，磨削和钻削就是其中最常用的两种工艺方法。由于使用了不同的加工刀具，因而采用的操作方法也完全不同。使用不同的形状的刀具并使刀具相对于工件进行各种形式的运动可加工出许多不同形状的零件，如图13.2（b）和13.2（c）所示。

电火花加工

电火花加工（EDM）是通过熔化和蒸发，对固态金属材料进行以热变化为主要方式的加工工艺方法，如图13.2（d）所示。电火花加工时，工件和工具（电极）之间产生了许多电火花，这些电火花对工件材料有侵蚀作用，这种侵蚀作用可以达到去除材料的目的。这时工具上常常留有工件外形的反转形状。当工件和工具之间的电压差足够大时，其间的流体介质被击穿，在电压作用下，流体介质进入到工具和工件之间的缝隙内，形成了传导火花的通道，出现放电现象。流体介质一般是矿物油或煤油，它的作用是作为绝缘的流体和散热剂，保持均匀的电阻并带走从工件上蚀除的材料。电火花通常以每秒成千上万次的速度出现，一般积聚在工具和工件之间最小缝隙的点上，因而产生了大量的热量，这些热量将工件的材料侵蚀并散入液体中。电火花加工的材料表面特点是其上有许多小蚀坑。

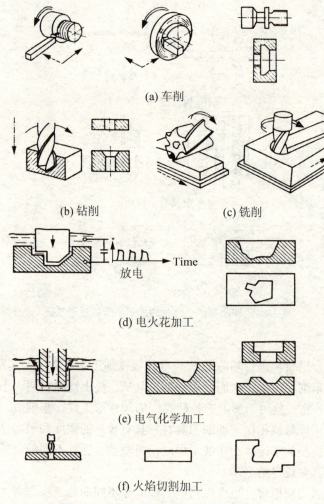

(a) 车削

(b) 钻削　　　　(c) 铣削

(d) 电火花加工

(e) 电气化学加工

(f) 火焰切割加工

图13.2　固态下的工件材料质量减少工艺

电气化学加工

电气化学加工（ECM）是通过电解分解，对固态金属材料进行以热变化为主要方式的加工工艺方法，如图13.2（d）所示。工件的电解是通过电路来实现的，工件为阳极，工具为阴极，工具上留有工件外形的反转形状。电解液通常使用水基盐（氯化钠10%和硝酸钠30%），电压一般为5V~20V，可维持的电流密度为0.5~2A/mm²，移动速度为0.5~6 cm³/min·1000A，但上述的这些参数通常需要根据具体的工件材料确定。

火焰切割

火焰切割是通过燃烧对固态金属材料进行以化学变化为主的加工工艺方法，如图13.2 (f) 所示。火焰切割前，一般需要将材料（含铁金属）加热到可以与氧气发生燃烧反应的温度。理论上，燃烧释放出的热量足够维持上述反应，但是由于有一部分热量散失到空气或传递到材料中，因此要持续地提供热量。人们目前使用喷枪来提供上述反应所需的热量，使用最广泛的是乙炔切削喷枪，它通过燃烧乙炔和氧气发生的化学反应产生热量。切削用的氧气通常由喷枪顶端中心的孔提供。

火焰切割工艺仅适用于易燃材料。对于其他材料，可采用以热变化为基础的切削工艺（如切削、等离子切削等）。这是人们利用热化学方法进行金属材料切割的道理。

精密冲裁

精（密）冲（裁）是一种用来生产冲裁件的工艺。冲裁件往往表面很平整，且有光洁的切边，其精度可以和精加工后的零件相媲美。当需要加工大批零件，费用合理，且省去刮削、修整等工序时，应该采用这种快捷、简便的工艺方法。

有一种精冲工艺方法是使用圆形刃口模具和小间隙进行冲裁。这种工艺很适于落料，但冲孔效果不太理想。在这种工艺中，模具的刃口半径需要根据加工材料的硬度、厚度及零件的具体形状来选定。精冲的基本特点是，在实际加工过程中，模具的刃口半径往往取最小值，这样可以得到质量较高的零部件，根据情况，最小半径一般的取值范围是0.3 mm~2 mm。

在设计精冲模时，冲头与下模之间的间隙总是比一般冲裁模具的间隙更小。通常认为，模具的总间隙在0.01 mm~0.03 mm范围时，可以获得质量较好的精冲件，但需要强调的是这里的总间隙不是孔或者落料件的单边间隙。

第14课 模具导论

模具是工业生产的一个基本技术装备。人们借助模具完成工业产品的成形过程，而这些模具是为产品特别设计和制造的。模具是零件生产过程的核心，因为它的型腔形成了零件的形状。模具类型很多，例如铸模、锻造模、陶瓷模、压铸模、拉丝模、玻璃模、磁铁成形模、金属挤压成形模、塑料模、橡胶模、塑料挤压模、粉末冶金模、冲压模等。

下面介绍一些模具成形的工艺过程以及在该过程中使用的模具。

压制成形

压制成形是最不复杂的模具成形工艺，适用于大型零件或小批量生产。对于小批量的生产需求，制造一个冲压模具要比制造一个注塑模具经济得多。冲压模具常用作初始制模，所制作的试样用于组合件的试装配和组装。这样可以在制造用于大批量生产的注塑模具之前对冲压模具做进一步改进。冲压成形最适合用于对公差要求不高的设计中。

冲压模具结构简单，可以由两块带有型腔的模板构成，也可以由一块带有型腔的模板，另一块不带有型腔的模板构成。此外，还可以在上下两块模板之间再加一块板子，以便在成形部件内形成孔穴。图 14.1 所示的是一款最基本的两模板单型腔模具，该模具不需要加热元器件和温度控制器，它的成形温度完全由成形压力控制。

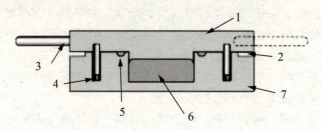

图 14.1　冲压模具示意
1. 顶板；2. 开式条形槽；3. 手柄；4. 定位销及衬套；5. 溢料和裂缝修整浇口；6. 零件型腔；7. 底板

由于冲压模具结构简单，所以它是市场上价格最便宜的模具，目前被广泛地应用在小批量的产品制造中。

注塑成形

注塑成形是最复杂的成形工艺。由于注塑模具结构设计复杂，所以购买注塑模具的费用比铸造模具和冲压模具高。尽管注塑模具成本较高，但其循环期要比其他工艺短，零件的费用也比较低，尤其是工艺过程实现自动化时。注塑成形最适合用于外形精致的零件的成形，在成形时，它可以在材料上产生高达 29 000 帕的压力，将材料填充到模具型腔的各个角落。

注塑成形中采用的模具由两部分对半组成：一半是静止的，另一半是移动的。静止的一半直接固定在固定模板上，在操作时与注塑装置的喷嘴直接接触。移动的一半固定在活动模板上，通常装有脱模装置。采用这种平衡流道系统的模具可以将塑料从浇口送到各个型腔。

注塑模具可以是由两块板组成的结构简单的模具，这种模具带有一个浇道系统，可以将橡胶复合物从合模线处注入到各个型腔中；也可以是由许多板块组成的结构复杂的模具，这种模具的模芯内带有一个脱模销和附加的加热元件。

图 14.2 所示为三板和两板多型腔注塑模具的基本结构型式。这些模具不要求有加热元件或温度控制器，其成形温度完全由所施加的注塑压力所控制。

铸造成形

铸造成形有两种方法：开式铸造成形法和压力铸造成形法。采用开式铸造成形法时，将液体混合物倒入到敞开的模具型腔中，然后使其固化；而采用压力铸造成形法时，则将液体混合物倒入敞开的模具型腔中，然后将盖子盖好，对型腔加压。压力铸造常用于结构复杂的零件或泡沫材料的成形。

压力铸造成形与注塑成形原理相同，但成形的材料不同。事实上铸造成形可产生与注塑成形具有相同几何形状的零件。在许多场合，由于零件的成本低，所以通常用注塑成形替代铸造成形，但对于结构较为特殊的零件，尤其是那些壁厚较薄的零件，铸造成形常常是更好的选择。

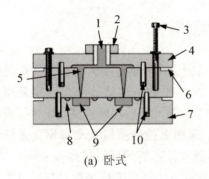 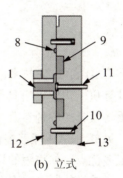

(a) 卧式 (b) 立式

图 14.2 注塑模具的结构

1. 注塑浇道；2. 喷嘴套筒；3. 脱模螺栓；4. 顶板；5. 浇口；6. 开式条形槽；7. 底板；8. 溢料和裂缝修整浇口；9. 零件型腔；10. 定位销及衬套；11. 脱模销；12. 固定板；13. 移动板

由于模具的材料通常是以低压液体形式流动的材料，所以，其制造费用往往并不是很高，适合用在小批量生产和样模制作，不适用于中等批量生产。用聚氨酯化合物制作的液体印模有极强的抗磨蚀、抗冲击和抗弯曲疲劳的能力，且可用于制造较复杂的零件形状和较厚的零件截面。但与其他成形工艺相比，这种工艺的循环周期和固化时间都比较长，并且材料一旦成形，就不能对其重新研磨和使用了。

铸造成形模具的结构与注塑成形模具的结构几乎完全相同。它主要由脱模部分和顶盖部分两部分组成，两者在合模线处汇合。通常型腔和模芯均加工在上述两部分内的嵌件上。模具的顶盖部分固定在静止的模板上，脱模部分则固定在活动模板上，型腔和加工模芯的设计必须方便模具从铸件的位置脱开。当模具打开时，要求用脱模销将零件从模具中移出，同时为了防止零件和模具之间粘结太牢，还必须在型腔内喷射润滑剂。

模具通常由工具钢、模具钢或马氏时效钢等材料制成。由于模具材料上没有天然的透气孔，并且融化的金属在注入时会快速流入到模具内，因此在合模线处必须开设排气孔和通道，以方便型腔内空气和气体排出。

挤压成形

虽然挤压模具的结构相当简单，但是挤压成形工艺在制定、制造和最后的加工过程中要非常仔细，目的是保证产品的设计与制造相一致。压力是通过有一定外形的模板施加的，但需要控制进给速率、温度及压力的变化幅度。

与冲压或注塑成形不同的地方是，橡胶从挤压模具中脱落时尚未固化。未加工的橡胶只有放置在圆盘或长盘（取决于其外形）上，且装入到高压釜中以后，在一定的热量和压力的作用下才能固化。

对于较长的橡胶，可采用一个盐浴固化系统成形，而对于硅橡胶挤压则采用连续加热的装置，所采用的固化工艺方法取决于要求挤压模具的数量和外形。

大多数挤压模具其实就是一个简单的圆形钢件，但其内部需要有起挤压作用的轮廓外形，同时必须留有一定的余量，以便于成形复合物的收缩/膨胀。挤压模具是最不复杂的模具。

这些模具建造起来相对简单，但是由于涉及的工艺不同，所以，哪怕是最少的浇注过程，其外形都可能会有所变化。

第 15 课　模具设计与制造

目前 CAD 和 CAM 技术已经广泛地应用在模具的设计和制造中。例如，首先利用 CAD 软件在计算机上构建出模具的模型，然后采用三维动画的方法从各个角度察看模具的结构，最后将模具的各种参数（压力、温度、冲力等）导入到数字模拟模型中进行模拟试验与分析。另外，CAM 能够控制模具的制造质量。采用上述计算机技术对模具进行设计和制造有很多优点：如较短的设计时间（该时间可随着计算机的运行速度而变化）、较低的制造成本和较高的制造效率等。这种新的设计、制造方法可以进行小批量的模具生产，可以在最后时刻对某个特定的模具零件进行修改。此外，这些新的工艺过程还可以用来制造复杂的模具零件。

模具的计算机辅助设计

通常手工绘制模具结构图是一项费时的任务，虽然它不属于创造性工艺过程的一部分，但对工艺过程来说必不可少。

计算机辅助设计（CAD）是指采用计算机及其辅助装置来简化设计任务和提高设计质量的过程。CAD 系统提供了一套高效的设计方法，它可以和坐标测量等其他检验设备一起使用，组成模具设计的检验程序。在选择工艺顺序时，CAD 数据常常能够发挥十分重要的作用。

一个 CAD 系统由 3 个基本部分组成：硬件、软件、用户。典型 CAD 系统的硬件部分包括处理器、系统显示器、键盘、数字转换器和绘图仪；其软件部分由能够完成设计和画图功能的程序组成；用户是模具的设计者，他采用 CAD 系统的硬件和软件来完成模具的设计过程。

根据产品的三维数据，首先需进行模芯和型腔的设计。通常设计人员可以对模芯和型腔的相关零件进行预设计，这说明，现在对模芯和型腔进行设计的方法改变了。目前 CAD 系统可以进行如下设计过程：首先计算出一条分模线，将零件分成模芯和型腔两侧，生成出流表面和截流表面，根据计算出的最佳零件草图确定出型腔、滑道和嵌件的位置和方向；然后在概念设计阶段，粗略地定出模具部件的位置和几何形状，如滑动装置、喷出系统等。这时可根据上述设计数据确定出模芯和型腔板的大小和厚度，并从产品标准目录中选取出标准模具。如果没有一个标准模具与上述设计要求相符合，则可以选择离要求最接近的标准模具，并做相应修改，如通过调整约束条件和结构参数的方法，使得某尺寸的板子可以用在设计中。最后，对功能部件进行细化设计，并添加一些标准部件，完成整个模具的结构设计（图 15.1），整个过程是在三维空间中完成的。此外，模具系统还提供了对零件进行检查、修改和细化的功能，因此，在模具设计的早期阶段就可以自动生成图纸和材料的清单。

通过运用模具设计系统的三维结构设计方法和智能化功能，可以在模具开始设计阶段就能够避免二维设计中出现的典型错误，例如冷却系统和部件/型腔结构之间的干涉以及孔的定位错误等；可以在设计的任何阶段生成零件的图样和材料清单，从而可以准时定购模具材料，可以利用模具零部件的实际设计数据材料向用户推销产品，或对模具制造企业进行报价。

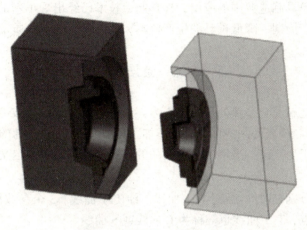

图 15.1　模具的三维立体模型

使用专门的三维模具设计系统能够缩短模具的研发周期、提高模具的设计质量、增进团队合作精神以及使设计人员从单调乏味的日常工作中解脱出来。然而经济上的成功主要取决于合理规划的工作流程。只有采取了适当的组织方法和人员考核制度，才能缩短产品的研发周期。因此，零件设计、模具设计、电气设计以及模具制造等部门必须紧密合作，协同工作。

模具的计算机辅助制造

一个较为有效地减少制造费用，缩短研发周期的方法是建立能够充分发挥设备和人员潜能的制造系统。这类制造系统的基础是 CAD 系统设计模具的数据。通过这些数据，可以帮助我们对主要工艺过程做出决策，提高模具制造的精度，减少非生产的时间，这个过程称为计算机辅助制造（CAM）。CAM 的目的是在可能的条件下，利用计算工作站的计算机，直接生产出模具的断面而不需要任何中间步骤。

一个好的 CAM 系统自动化程度的好坏不仅体现在一个零件的某个特征的制造上，而且还体现在这个零件所有细节特征的制造上，且最终实现制造路径的最优化。当需要制造多种特征时，CAM 系统会为制造者制定一个工艺规划，相关的操作都要依据这个规划，目的是为了减少加工过程中变换刀具的次数和所使用的刀具数目。

目前 CAM 的发展趋势是研制一些计算机辅助制造方面的新技术和新工艺，例如微研磨技术。该技术采用复杂的三维结构设计方法和表面制造精度高的技术制造出精度较高的注塑模具。CAM 软件将继续在智能化加工的深度和广度上发展，直至计算机数控（CNC）编程工艺过程实现完全自动化。这种需求对于那些能够实现柔性化、组合机械加工的先进多功能机床来说更是如此。CAM 软件将在机械工的操作下，使冗余的制造过程逐渐实现自动化，使其在计算机的帮助下，更快、更精确地制造出产品。

在保证模具生产质量，强调高效的今天，模具制造商们需要利用最新的软件制造技术快速地制定出生产规划，制造出复杂的模具产品，并减少相应的生产时间。总之，模具制造业正朝着提高 CAD、CAM、CNC 数据交换质量的方向发展，同时 CAM 软件在加工过程方面也变得越来越智能化，这大大减少了产品的生产周期和总的加工时间。此外，五轴联动加工模式也应该应用在模具制造方面，尤其在进行深型腔加工的场合。随着电子数据处理（EDP）技术在模具制造业中的应用，模具制造技术已经出现了新的发展时机，这将极大地缩短模具的生产周期、降低模具的生产成本，提高模具的生产质量。

第16课　金属热处理

普遍认同的对金属及合金热处理的定义为：以一定的方式加热或冷却固态金属或合金以达到一定的条件和/或获得某些性能。以热加工（如锻造）为目的的加热不在此定义之列。同样，有时用于生产诸如玻璃或塑料制品的热处理也不属于该定义的范畴。

相变曲线

热处理的基础分别是时间-温度-相变曲线，即 TTT 曲线，3 个参数都绘制在一个图中。根据曲线的形状特点，TTT 曲线也被称为 C 曲线或 S 曲线。

为了绘制 TTT 曲线，将特定的钢置于给定温度下，以预先确定的时间间隔检查其结构，记录发生相变的量。知道共析钢（T8）在平衡条件下，在 727℃ 以上时全为奥氏体，低于此温度则为珠光体。为了形成珠光体，碳原子将扩散形成渗碳体。扩散是一种渐进过程，需要足够的时间完成奥氏体向珠光体的转变。对于不同的样品，可以记录下在任一温度时产生相变的量。然后把这些点绘制在一条以时间和温度为坐标轴的曲线上。通过这些点就可以得到如图 16.1 所示的共析钢的相变曲线。左边的曲线表示任一给定温度下奥氏体开始转变为珠光体所需的时间。类似地，右边的曲线表示相变完成所需的时间。两条曲线之间是表示部分相变的点。两条水平线 M_s 和 M_f 表示马氏体转变的开始和结束。

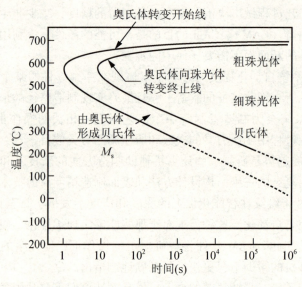

图 16.1　共析钢（T8）的等温转变曲线

热处理工艺的分类

在某些场合，热处理过程可以根据其工艺和应用明确地区分开来。而在另一些场合，因为同样的工艺常常可以用来达到不同的目的，因此对该术语的说明和简单的解释是不够的。例如，消除应力的热处理和回火处理常常使用同样的设备、同样的时间和温度循环来实现，但这两种工艺的目的是不同的。

下面对主要热处理工艺的描述大体上是按其相互关系来安排的。

正火：把铁类合金加热到指定的相变温度上限以上的合适温度，接下来在不流动的空气中冷却到至少比相变温度低得多的某一温度。对于低碳钢，得到的结构和性能与完全退火相同。而对于大多数铁类合金，正火和退火意义不同。

正火一般作为起调节作用的热处理工艺，特别是用于细化在锻造或其他热加工工艺中经受了高温的钢的晶粒。正火处理之后通常还要接着进行下一个热处理操作，如为了后续淬火、退火、回火而进行的奥氏体化。

退火：热处理的一个通用术语，指的是加热到一定温度并保温，然后以合适的速度冷却，主要用于降低金属材料的硬度，同时在其他性能或显微组织方面产生一些理想的变化。这种变化的目的是改善机械加工性，便于冷加工（被称为中间退火），改善机械或电性能，或增加工件的尺寸稳定性，但也不仅局限于此。如果仅用于消除应力，就叫做去应力退火，与应力消除热处理是同义词。

当"退火"这个术语用于铁类合金而又无其他限制条件时，指的是完全退火。这种处理是把合金加热到其相变温度以上，再进行循环冷却以使硬度下降最大。冷却过程的变化范围较大，要看具体合金的成分和特性。

淬火：把钢或合金浸没在液体或气体介质中，从奥氏体化温度下快速冷却。常用的淬火介质有水、5%的盐水、5%的碱性水溶液、油、聚合物溶液或气体（常为空气或氮气）。

对淬火介质的选择主要取决于材料的淬透性以及被处理材料的质量（主要是淬火部分的厚度）。

上面列出的各种淬火介质的冷却能力有很大的区别。在选择淬火介质时，最好避免选择比达到预期效果所需的冷却能力更强的溶液，从而尽量降低处理零件开裂或变形的可能性。淬火包括直接淬火、喷雾淬火、高温淬火、分级淬火、局部淬火、喷射淬火和等温淬火。

回火：在铁类合金的热处理中，回火指的是把奥氏体化和淬硬的钢或铁再加热到预先设定的相变温度下限以下的某一温度（通常低于1300°F或705℃）。回火提供了获得各种综合机械性能的方法。用于淬硬钢的回火温度通常为150～200℃。不要把回火与中间退火或去应力退火混淆。即使三种处理方法的时间和温度循环可能相同，但是被处理的材料的状态和目的可能是不同的。

去应力退火：与回火相似，去应力退火总是把钢和铁加热到相变温度下限以下的某一温度。对于有色金属，这个温度可以稍高于室温，也可以达到几百度，取决于合金的种类和期望去除的应力大小。

去应力退火的主要目的是消除在模铸、轧制、机加工、焊接等过程中在工件中产生的应力。通常这一过程是把工件加热到预先设定的温度并保持足够长的时间来降低残留的应力（这是一个与时间和温度有关的工序），接下来以较慢的速度冷却，以避免产生新的应力。

第 17 课 虚拟制造技术

什么是虚拟制造技术

虚拟制造是一种高度集成化的、虚拟的制造环境，其作用是为了增强生产企业的决策和控制能力。人们把虚拟制造定义成一个实际生产组织的虚拟模型，这个实际的生产组织在现实生活中可能存在，也可能不存在。虚拟制造包括了所有与生产过程、生产过程控制与管理以及产品数据有关的信息；也包含部分实际上存在或不存在的，与生产企业有关的信息。虚拟制造技术借助计算机模型模拟产品的生产制造过程，以达到辅助产品设计与制造的目的。

1996 年 Lawrence Associate 把提供完整生产制造环境的虚拟制造技术分成以下 3 种不同的模式。

（1）以设计为中心的虚拟制造：向设计师提供能够设计出满足产品设计要求的必备工具。

（2）以生产为中心的虚拟制造：提供研制、分析产品生产制造过程的方法。

（3）以控制为中心的虚拟制造：借助产品生产过程的数字仿真技术，对产品的设计、制造及管理过程进行分析、评估，并进行优化、改进。

虚拟制造技术的意义

虚拟制造技术为许多相对孤立的产品制造技术，如计算机辅助设计技术，计算机辅助制造技术以及计算机辅助工艺技术提供了一个综合运用的生产制造环境，使不同需求的用户无需自己集成上述各个制造技术，就可以完成产品的部分，甚至所有的加工制造任务。例如，通过虚拟制造技术，产品工艺师和制造工程师能够对产品的生产、制造过程进行评估，并将评估的结果反馈给异地的产品设计师，由他根据反馈结果对产品进行改进设计。

虚拟制造技术的另一个重要的贡献是促使了虚拟企业的诞生。1995 年 Lin et al 把虚拟企业定义为为了完成某种产品的设计和生产，快速组建的，多学科联合的，有特定目的的小型网络化公司。许多个人和公司通过虚拟制造技术提供的虚拟环境中的信息共享彼此之间的技术、资源，对市场中有利的时机进行投资。虚拟制造技术的主要优点在于给用户营造了一个信息非常丰富的环境，加强了产品生命周期各个阶段的信息交流。

虚拟制造技术的应用

在实际应用过程中，虚拟制造技术往往贯穿于产品的整个生命周期。例如，近期的研究报告提到了一种基于虚拟环境的产品决策系统，该系统是由日本 Matsushita 公司的 Imamura 和 Nomura 于 1994 年研制成功的。这个系统目前主要应用在厨具销售行业中，它可以使用户体验到厨房环境，能够使他们根据自己的亲身感受对厨具进行比较，并挑选出自己喜欢的厨具组合。同时，顾客喜欢的厨具会以图样形式保存在系统中，并反馈给公司的生产部门。

Owen 在 1994 年向公众介绍了由 John Deere 公司生产部门完成的一项工作，他们利用虚拟制造技术实现了电弧焊生产系统的安装过程。该工作在虚拟三维环境下，对机器人生产系统进行设计、性能评估和测试。一部分工作中由 John Deere 公司完成，而另一部分由 Genesis System 公司和 Technomatrix Technologies 公司共同完成。由于使用了虚拟制造技术，因而缩短了该产品的设计—生产制造周期。

1994 年 DuPont 对虚拟现实技术的应用做了总结，同时他也介绍了英国 Coventry 艺术与设计学院研制的轿车虚拟样机。这些虚拟样机在轿车设计的初始阶段就已经在计算机里完成了，它可以使设计人员提前对轿车的性能，舒适程度及视野状况等方面进行测试。此外，该报告也提到了虚拟制造技术应用的其他实例，例如，飞机起落架的虚拟并行设计方法和虚拟装配过程、汽车侧面安全性碰撞试验的过程模拟等。

Kim et al 在 1994 年也介绍了一些虚拟现实技术运用的实例，例如，波音飞机公司的设计师们利用虚拟制造技术对产品的操作性能和可维护性，进行了环境方面的评估。另一个有关虚拟现实技术的运用实例是利用虚拟制造技术的环境训练机器人，即在虚拟现实环境里训练机器人对操作者的动作进行识别、理解，并最终以运动指令形式进行储存的能力。Shenai 描述了虚拟胶片构造技术的应用实例，该技术可以对在研的半导体器件进行主要工艺参数和设计变量方面的优化。1994 年 Larijani 还介绍了虚拟制造技术在其他领域应用的例子，包括机器的故障诊断和检测、安全、维护培训及环境分析设计等。例如，Caterpillar 公司生产的每一辆汽车和每一台推土机都要经过实际驾驶人员的检测，目的是检测它们在实际使用过程中是否出现运动不平衡的问题，而这种检测通常就是利用虚拟制造技术在计算机中完成的。

第 18 课　流体和液压系统

水力的历史由来已久，其历史可以从人类开始利用能源时算起。世界上最容易利用的能源是两种可自由流动的流体—水和风。

水车是第一台液力装置，属于水力领域中最早的发明物。从 15 世纪早期，水车图画就出现在拜占庭华丽宫殿的马赛克上。磨粉机由罗马人发明，而水磨机的历史更早，可以追溯到大约公元前 100 年。当时谷物的种植已经有 5000 多年的历史了，当时一些颇具事业心的农场主厌烦了手工碾碎、研磨谷物的工作方式。但实际上，真正的水磨机发明家应该是那些农场主的妻子，因为她们经常要干一些繁重的农活。

流体是可以流动的物体，也就是说，构成流体的粒子可以连续地改变它们之间的相对位置，而且，随着流体层之间位置的改变（不论这个改变有多大），其流层之间的流动阻力也将发生变化。

流体可以分为牛顿流体或非牛顿流体。在牛顿流体中，流体层间作用的剪切力和角度变形的大小呈线性关系；而在非牛顿流体中，流体层间作用的剪切力和角度变形的大小呈非线性关系。

流体流动方式有很多种分类方式，如定常流或非定常流、有旋流或无旋流、可压缩流或不可压缩流以及黏性流或无黏性流。

所有的液压系统都遵守帕斯卡定律，该定律是用其发明者 Braise Pascal 的名字来命名的。帕斯卡定律指出，在密封的容积内，如圆柱筒或管子内，压缩的液体在容积的各个不同的曲面上作用着大小相等的力。

在实际液压系统中，帕斯卡定律是解释系统内各种现象的依据。泵驱使液体在液压系统中流动，泵的进口连接到被称为油槽或油箱的液流源上，作用在油箱液面上的气压驱动流体进入油泵。油泵工作时，流体在适当泵压的作用下，从油箱流动到出口。

油泵泵出的压缩液体由各种阀门进行控制。在大多数液压系统中，通常采用以下3种控制形式：（1）液体压力控制；（2）液体流速控制；（3）液体流动方向控制。

下列几种情况通常优先使用液压驱动：（1）动力传递的位置太远，但链传动和皮带传动除外；（2）低速高转矩的场合；（3）需要紧凑结构的场合；（4）要求传动平稳、避免振动的场合；（5）速度和方向容易调节的场合；（6）需要输出无级可调速度的场合。

图18.1给出了液压元件安装的示意图。电力驱动的油泵驱使油液流动，进行能量传递，将能量传递给液压电动机或油缸，从而将液压能转换成机械能。在阀门的控制下，压力油液产生了线性或旋转的机械运动。油液流动的动能相对较低，因此有时采用静压传动。液压电动机和液压油缸之间几乎不存在构造上的差异，因此任何一个油泵都可以当做液压电动机使用。可以通过调节阀门或变量泵控制在任一时间里的油液流量，如图18.1所示。

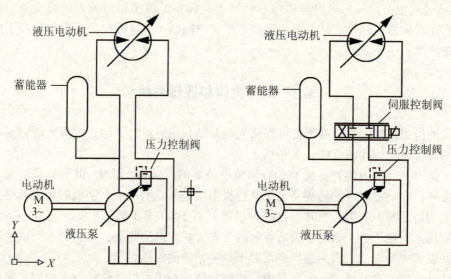

图18.1　液压电动机的速度控制方法示意

尽管目前很多机床上采用了液压传动，但这并不是一种新的应用。实际上，现代独立油泵技术的发展已促使液压传动技术广泛地应用在机床上。

液压驱动机床有许多优点，例如，采用液压驱动可以在较大的速度范围内向机床提供无极变速。此外，它还能像变速一样非常方便地改变驱动方向。在其他许多类型的机床上，采用液压传动可以简化，甚至完全不使用结构复杂的机械装置。

液压驱动的另一个优点是柔性和缓冲性能较好。除了能使机床运行平稳之外，液压驱动在机床上还有许多其他优越之处。例如，可以改善工件表面的光洁度；可以在不损坏刀具的前提下增大刀具上的作用载荷；可以进行长时间的切削加工，而无需再次刃磨刀具等。

第 19 课　产品测试与质量控制

产品测试

产品测试不但是所有工艺控制过程中至关重要的部分,也是整个工艺过程监控中的质量检验部分。如果产品质量控制计划制定合理,执行情况良好,那么其性能就会有保障,不需要对其进行总体性能测试。因此,产品质量的总体测试只不过是客户取货之前必须履行的合同要求。但产品测试不仅仅是一个验证过程,从整体上说是所有部分检验的总和。通过产品检验能收集数据,这些数据可支持、验证产品设计理论;能为以后产品的改进设计提供依据,使产品的性能更加优越;能对产品的更新换代进行性能和成本评估。此外,在产品的实际设计过程中,并不是所有的设计参数都能被计算和预测的,所以,产品测试也是检查设计方法是否合理的一种方法。

产品测试工程师应与产品设计工程师密切合作,为产品的测试提供有用的数据,同时他们也必须与各个工序的制造工程师的协同工作。在产品的测试过程中,经常会发现设计工作中的一些错误,这些错误是产品制造过程中需要重点修改的地方。因此,制造工程师和设计工程师一样,都关心产品的测试结果。

对于复杂的产品来说,产品测试已经成为产品整个工艺控制过程中的一个重要组成部分。它为公司提供了较高的可信度,使产品达到了客户所希望的性能。由于产品测试能帮助公司在客户中建立良好的声誉,因此,它是一个极有价值的市场调控工具。

几何误差

几何误差被定义为单个机械零件的误差(如线性轴承运动的直线度)。与几何误差相关的是准静态时的表面精度,这与零件表面的相对运动有关。零件的几何误差可以减小,也可以保持不变(系统误差),可能滞后出现(如齿轮隙),也可以随机产生。影响零件几何误差的因素很多,如表面直线度(图 19.1)、表面粗糙度、轴承的预加载荷、弹性运动设计方法和结构设计原理等。

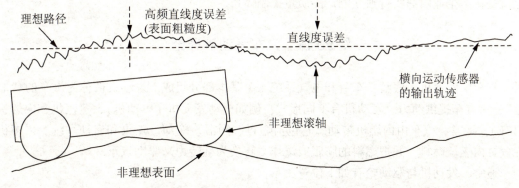

图 19.1　表面形状和粗糙度引起的直线度误差

质量规划

这是工艺控制中的规划和决策行为,有时指工艺规划或检测规划。工程师提出充分的执行计划是为了保证产品的性能能够达到设计要求。质量规划工程师则以产品的实际生产效率和检测结果为指导原则，确定在制造过程中何处应该进行检测和非破坏性测试，同时还要确定进行检查和测试的内容，并且依据产品的设计要求决定产品是否合格。

通常产品的制造与设计会存在一定的偏差。有些偏差对产品的质量影响较大，有些则没有什么影响。质量规划工程师的主要职责是对产品制造和设计过程中的偏差进行评估，并对影响产品质量较大的偏差找出恰当的修改办法。作为产品设计与制造偏差的评判者，质量规划部门可以通过数据库对产品的各个加工工序及制造情况进行评估，因此，稳定的产品质量是能够达到的。通过这种方法，产品质量规划部门可以向管理部门汇报产品的质量状况。

利用统计的方法对上述偏差进行评估，可以了解产品的质量状况，也可以估算出改进这些偏差需要多少成本。维修作为产品制造耗材的一个组成部分，也是产品质量水平控制的一个重要度量方式。产品制造过程中的浪费状况是对操作工及以前工序的操作员工作态度的一个衡量指标。浪费多了说明管理差，因此，质量规划工程师的责任就是减少产品制造过程中的浪费，做好预算和制定检测方案。

质量控制

从传统意义上讲，质量控制是制造和设计之间的联系纽带。它的功能就是对产品的制造进行设计规范，同时制定用于产品制造、操作的质量规划。此外，质量控制还负责向管理部门建议容许损耗的范围。这个范围是根据产品设计的复杂程度，尤其是误差范围内精度的级别确定的。传统的质量控制方法是通过设置不允许超出的负预算来控制产品的制造损耗，并以此建立产品检测和维修的准则。

在过去的一二十年里，人们为了保证产品的质量，建立了与市场和顾客有关的质量控制文件系统。这一做法给产品的质量控制赋予了新的使命，与传统意义上的产品质量控制方法是有区别的。

质量控制的目的是借助产品各个阶段的制造规范，确保制造出符合要求的产品。尽管质量控制与制造过程直接相关，但它通常还和市场调控功能中的用户职责有关。许多工厂企业已经有选择地建立了独立的产品质量控制功能，也设置了相应的质量控制技术职责，也就是在本企业内部实行独立的产品质量控制体系。

第 20 课　汽车发动机导论

汽车由发动机、底盘、车身和电气系统 4 个基本部分组成。发动机被称为汽车的"心脏"，为汽车提供动力。发动机有不同形式，例如电动发动机（电动机），蒸汽机和内燃机（ICE）。通常，汽车由内燃机带动。它包括燃料、润滑、冷却、点火和启动系统。内燃机在气缸内燃烧燃料，并把燃料的膨胀或爆炸力转换为旋转力来驱动汽车。

通常，发动机与驱动轮有如下位置关系：

（1）发动机前置后轮驱动；

（2）发动机前置前轮驱动；

（3）发动机后置后轮驱动；

（4）发动机中置后轮驱动；

（5）全轮驱动等。

发动机主要有7个类别，介绍如下：

（1）根据燃烧位置

内燃机和外燃机。

在内燃机中，燃烧发生在发动机内部。按照使用的燃料不同，内燃机进一步分为汽油发动机（点燃式发动机）、柴油发动机（压燃式发动机）、其他燃料发动机（煤油、乙醇、氢、天然气和液化石油等）。外燃机，例如蒸汽机，燃烧在发动机外进行。但是，在汽车领域，内燃机看上去应用最多。

（2）根据冲程

两冲程和四冲程发动机（奥托循环发动机）。

（3）根据冷却系统

水冷式和风冷式发动机。

（4）根据内部运动形式

往复式发动机和旋转发动机（汪克尔发动机）。

在往复式发动机中，依靠燃料释放能量产生的动作上下推动零件。汽油机和柴油机是往复式发动机。在一个旋转的发动机中，其运动的零部件连续旋转，如图20.1所示。

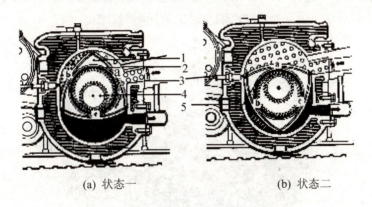

(a) 状态一　　　　　　　(b) 状态二

图 20.1　旋转（活塞）式发动机

图（a）　a. 进气；b. 压缩；c. 排气

图（b）　a. 充满新鲜混合气；b. 燃烧气体膨胀；c. 排气

1. 转子；2. 转子内齿圈；3. 火花塞；4. 固定齿轮；5. 偏心轴承座面

（5）根据点火系统形式

点燃式发动机和压燃式发动机。

（6）根据燃烧形式

间断燃烧和连续燃烧发动机。

间断燃烧意味着燃烧在发动机启动和停止间进行。标准的汽油机和柴油机是间断燃烧发动机。连续燃烧发动机有汽轮机（涡轮机）、火箭发动机、斯特灵（林）发动机和喷射（喷气）发动机。

（7）按气缸布置分

直列式发动机、V型发动机和对置式发动机。

现代汽车主要安装往复活塞式四冲程发动机。在这种发动机中，曲轴每转动两周，活塞在气缸内上下往复运动四次，连续实现进气、压缩、做功和排气四个过程，完成一个循环。

发动机由下面几个系统组成。

（1）曲柄连杆机构：缸体、缸盖、活塞、连杆、曲轴和飞轮等。

（2）配气机构：气门、摇臂、推杆、正时齿轮和凸轮轴等。

（3）燃料供给系统

① 汽油机燃料供给系统：汽油箱、汽油过滤器、空气过滤器、汽油泵、化油器、进气管、排气管和消声器。

② 柴油机燃料供给系统：柴油箱、柴油过滤器、输油泵、喷油泵、喷油嘴、调速器、进气管、排气管和消声器。

（4）润滑系统：包括机油泵、机油过滤器、机油散热器和润滑油管路。

（5）冷却系统：有水冷式和风冷式。

（6）点火系统：蓄电池、发动机、点火线圈、分电器和火花塞。使用较多的是蓄电池点火系统，半导体点火系统正在迅速发展。

（7）启动系统：它包括启动机及其附属装置。汽车用启动机一般为直流电动机。汽油机用的启动机的功率一般在 1.5kW 以下，柴油机用启动机的功率则在 5kW 以上。

如图 20.2 所示是一个直列四缸汽油发动机的局部剖视图。

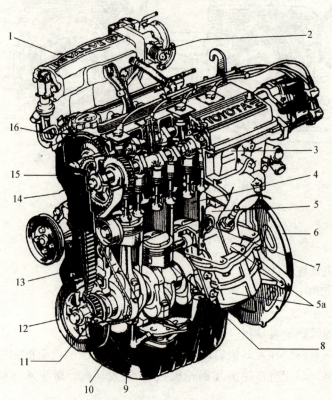

图 20.2　直列四缸汽油发动机

1. 进气室；2. 节气门；3. 气缸盖；4. 气缸；5. 气缸体；6. 飞轮；7. 气缸水套；8. 活塞；9. 油底壳；10. 曲轴；
11. 正时齿带轮；12. 曲轴带轮；13. 正时齿带；14. 凸轮轴；15. 正时齿带罩；16. 火花塞；5a. 带催化转化器的排气总管

第 21 课　汽车部件

发动机

发动机是一种动力设备，它为汽车提供动力。

在大部分汽车发动机中，空气和汽油的混合气体产生的爆炸力驱动活塞运动。活塞使它们所连接的曲轴转动。曲轴的旋转力带动车轮转动。

发动机工作时有很多系统都是必要的。润滑系统可以减少摩擦并减轻发动机磨损。冷却系统用来保持发动机的温度在安全范围内。发动机必须有燃油系统保证适当数量的空气和燃料供给。

空气和燃油混合物必须由点火系统在适当的时间在气缸内被点燃。最后，电子系统用来控制启动发动机用的曲柄电动机和为发动机附件提供电能。

润滑系统

发动机有许多相互接触运动的部件最终会被磨损。发动机润滑油在这些运动的部件间循环，以避免因金属与金属之间的接触而导致磨损。润滑的部件因摩擦减少而易于运动，并减少摩擦导致的能量损失。润滑油的第二个功能是作为冷却液和防止泄漏。最后，气缸壁上的润滑油薄膜有助于活塞环密封并因此提高发动机的压缩性。

冷却系统

由于燃料与空气在气缸内燃烧，从而使发动机部件温度升高。温度升高直接影响发动机的性能和发动机部件的寿命。冷却系统使发动机在安全的温度下工作。不管驾驶条件如何，该系统既能阻止过热又能防止过冷。

燃料供给系统

燃料供给系统的主要功能是以一定的比例和压力给化油器或喷射系统提供燃料，并在汽车遇到的任何情况下，满足发动机对负载、速度和坡度的需要。燃料系统也必须为汽车行驶几英里保留足够的燃料。

点火系统

点火系统的作用是在适当的时间使燃料燃烧，不管是高压电火花还是在每个发动机气缸中的自燃，以便于气体混合物的完全燃烧。

提供给燃料室的燃料必须被点燃以提供能量。在火花点火发动机中，电火花就是用于这个目的。因为点火会受混合气压影响，压缩点火发动机不需要独立的点火系统。

电气系统

发动机的电气系统提供能量给启动电动机并给所有附件提供电能。电气系统的主要构件是蓄电池、交流发电机、启动电动机、点火线圈和加热器。

车架

车架为汽车发动机和车身提供了一个安装基础。车架用方钢或盒形钢铁制造，有足够的强度支撑车身和其他构件的重量。汽车车架通常由一些焊接或铆接在一起的零件构成，从而形成最后的形状。发动机和橡胶垫被固定在车架上，橡胶垫可以吸收振动，也可以使这些振动衰减，以减轻乘客由于振动产生的不适。

悬架系统

悬架系统的功能是吸收由于路面不平使车轮上下运动所产生的振动。弹性元件、连接装置和减振器组成了汽车的悬架系统。悬架系统有两种类型：

（1）刚性悬架系统

（2）独立悬架系统

在刚性悬架系统中，弹簧装在刚性横梁上，这种系统主要用在商用车辆的前轴和所有类型车辆的车轴上。

独立悬架系统没有一根刚性轴。每个车轮可以纵向自由运动而不会对另一侧车轮产生影响。独立悬架系统主要用在小汽车上。

传动系

传动系把发动机产生的能量传递给车轮。它包括离合器（汽车上用手动变速器）、传动系（一系列的齿轮，把发动机产生的转矩增强，推动汽车）、驱动轴、差速器和后桥。

离合器

离合器用于手动变速的传动系统。用它暂时把发动机和车轮之间的动力传递分开。当换挡或停车时，断开传动系和发动机的连接。

变速箱

变速箱的主要功能是通过发动机把各种必需的扭矩提供给车轮，这是通过改变发动机输出轴和驱动轴两者之间的传动比来实现的。

驱动轴

驱动轴或叫传动轴，与齿轮箱和差动器相连。驱动轴通常在末端具有万向节。

差速器

差速器的功能是把来自传动轴的动力分给后桥。当汽车转弯或掉进沟里时，它允许后轮以不同的速度驱动。

车桥

车桥是指用来安装车轮的轴，通过车桥给车轮提供驱动力。

车轮

车轮支撑着整辆车，并产生牵引力来驱动车辆。车轮也用于减速和停车。

转向系

转向系是用来改变汽车方向的，转向机构要求转向精确且容易控制，同时前轮在转向后又能自动回正。齿轮机构即转向齿轮，在系统中用来增强由驾驶员提供的转向力，使驾驶员不用费很大的力就可以轻松转向。不仅在弯路上需要汽车转向，在交通拥挤的路上也需要灵活控制转向。

第22课　机电一体化

机电一体化这个术语一开始是在20世纪70年代由两个工程类学科——机械学和电工电子学结合而形成的，但是最近随着控制工程和通信领域的快速发展，机电一体化这个术语已经用于描述机械工程学、控制工程学和电子学三大学科的集成,其目标主要是研究由电子学所控制的机械产品的制造,同时也被认为是机械工程学、电子学和智能计算机控制学在工业产品设计制造和加工过程上的集成。随后由于这些工业产品具有"智能"和"灵巧"的特征,因此人们经常将这些工业产品称之为"智能化"或"灵巧型"的产品,因此,机电一体化也可以定义为在工业产品的设计和制造加工过程中,应用了电子学技术、智能计算机控制技术与机械工程学等的集成学科。

在工程上,一个新诞生的术语肯定是新的、以前不具有的一系列性能特征的组合,因此,机电一体化真正是从机械学、电子学、计算机科学和制造工程学等学科中产生的一个交叉学科。机电一体化课程在亚洲、欧洲和美洲等地区的工程教学中已经作为一门必修课程,机电一体化领域已经作为新的工业产品开发基础日益被人们所接受。机电一体化技术主要包括机电一体化的系统建模、仿真、传感和评估系统、驱动和执行系统、系统行为分析、控制系统及微处理系统。

机电一体化系统范例

机电一体化范例处理工程、科学和技术上出现的还没有破解和解决的基准程序技术和新兴的问题。机电一体化使用高性能的微处理器和 DSP 芯片、驱动电子元件和 IC 集成电路来进行系统设计、优化、建模、仿真、分析和建立有效的模型等工作,是一种可以获得智能化、高性能机电系统(包括机械和加工),实现智能化和运动控制的综合性研究。它具有多学科交叉的特点,集成了电子学、机械工程学和计算机工程学等学科,如图 22.1 所示。

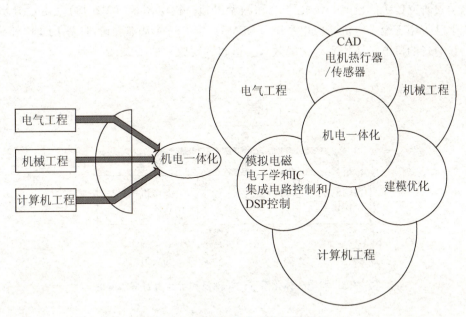

图 22.1 机电一体化系统分类示意

在机电一体化系统设计中,具有重要意义的问题是系统结构的开发设计,包括硬件(执行器、传感器、装备、电子产品、集成电路、微控制器和 DSP 等)和软件(实现传感与控制、信息流与数据采集、模拟仿真、可视化处理和建立有效模型等的软件环境和计算机算法）的选择。通过分析复杂的模型和高级的生物系统的范例来设计具有艺术特性的人造的机电一体化系统，并保证这一集成设计能继续深入。

现在的工程设计趋于高级的机械系统的集成分析、设计和控制。目前机电一体化系统的范围已经得到了扩展，除了执行器、传感器、驱动电子元件、IC 集成电路、微处理器、DSP 外，还集成了输入/输出设备及其他许多子系统。机电一体化系统范例最终目标如下：

（1）保证最终结果的一致性及具有学科交叉的特征；

（2）拓宽和增加传统的机械、电机系统、驱动电子元件、IC 集成电路和控制理论，以满足高级的硬件和软件需求；

（3）获取和拓展多学科的工程核心集成领域；

（4）将电机系统、驱动电子元件、IC 集成电路、DSP、控制、信号处理、微型机电系统和纳米电子系统技术相融合，以便于构成机电一体化的综合体系。

高性能电机系统的研究被认为是机电一体化系统范例课程的重要基础。执行器和传感器（例如电机驱动装置）、驱动电子元件和 IC 集成电路、微处理器和 DSP、高级硬件和软件系统的统一分析基本上没有被引入到工程课程教学中。机电一体化在传统的微型和纳米规模的电机系统中是一个突破性的概念，已经被用于破译、集成和解决大量的工程问题。机电一体化系统如图 22.2 所示，可分类为：（1）传统的机电一体化系统；（2）微型电机—机电系统（MEMS）；（3）纳米电机—机电系统（NEMS）。传统的机电一体化系统和微型电机—机电系统（MEMS）在工作原理和基础理论上是相同的，而纳米电机—机电系统（NEMS）研究使用的是不同的概念和理论。特别值得一提的是工程设计人员应用经典力学和电磁学去研究传统的机电一体化系统和微型电机—机电系统（MEMS）。定量分析和纳米电机学已应用于纳米电机—机电系统（NEMS）中。一些基本理论可以用于研究传统的、微观的和纳米的机电一体化系统中的效果、过程和现象，如图 22.2 所示。

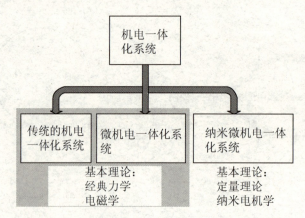

图 22.2　机电一体化系统的类别及其所运用的基本理论

第 23 课　工业机器人

机器人是一种自动控制，可编程，多功能的，由几个可重复编程的坐标系来操纵的机器装置，可以固定或移动的方式应用于工业自动化中。

机器人的主要优点在于可重复编程和多功能性，因为大多数功能单一的机器不能满足这两种要求。"可重复编程"包含两层含义：机器人根据已设定的程序工作，并且这个程序可以被重写以适应多种任务。"多功能"意味着机器人可以有多种不同的功能，以适应通用的不同程序和工具。

经过20年的发展，机器人已经进入工厂来完成许多单调的和不安全的操作任务。因为机器人可以比人更快更准确地完成某些基本任务，所以广泛地用于制造业。

机器人的结构

工业机器人的典型结构包含4个主要部分：操纵器、终端执行机构、动力供给和控制系统，如图23.1所示。

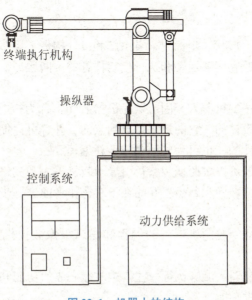

图 23.1 机器人的结构

操纵器是机械系统，进行类似于人的手臂的运动。它通常有肩关节、肘和腕部。它能旋转或平动，以一定的灵活性在各方向上伸缩。

机器人操纵器的基本机械构造可以分为笛卡儿形、圆柱形、球形和铰接形。笛卡儿坐标式机器人可以在立方体或矩形范围内把手爪移到各个位置，这可界定为它的工作范围。圆柱坐标式机器人可以在定义的柱体范围内移动手爪，可以通过在 X 和 Y 方向的线性运动和相对于 Z 轴的一定角度的旋转来定位工作范围。球形手臂机器人通过两个旋转和一个线性运动定位腕部。铰接形工业机器人具有一种不规律的工作范围，这种类型的机器人具有两个重要变量：垂直铰接和水平铰接。

终端执行机构与手腕相连，也称为手臂夹持器，是类似于手的操作装置。终端执行机构一般根据特殊需要设计。机械手是最常用的，一般装有两个或多个手指。终端执行机构的选择取决于有效载荷、环境可靠性和价格等因素。

动力源是移动机械手，控制关节，操作终端执行机构的驱动器。基本的动力源包括电力、气动、液压三种。每种动力源和发动机都具有自身的特性、优点和局限性。根据系统的设计和用途选择交流或直流电动机。发动机把电能转化为机械能为机器人提供能量。大多数新型机器人采用电力驱动。气动应用于高速、非伺服机器人，也应用于驱动工具，如手爪。液压驱动用于较重的提升系统，尤其是精确度要求不高的场合。

控制系统是通信和信息处理系统，由它发出指令驱动机器人动作。它是机器人的大脑，向动力源发出信号，把机器人手臂移到特定位置，并驱动终端执行机构。它也是机器人的神经系统，对机器人的所有运动及动作所发送的指令序列是可重复编程的。

开环控制器是控制系统的最简单形式，它通过预定的指令逐步控制机器人。这样的系统没有自我纠错能力。闭环控制系统由反馈传感器产生信号，信号反映被控目标的当前状态。通过将反馈信号与程序设定值相对比，闭环控制器能引导机器人向准确的位置运动并实现期望的状态。闭环控制系统可以使被控目标与预定值间的误差达到最小，终端执行机构可以高度精确地运作。

机器人的分类

工业机器人在尺寸、形状、坐标数、自由度和设计构造上都多种多样。每个因素都影响着机器人的工作范围或它能够运动和执行指定任务的空间区域。广义的机器人分类如下所述。

固定顺序和可变顺序的机器人。固定顺序机器人（也称为拾取和定位机器人）是为完成一系列特定的操作而设计的。它的运动是点到点的，并且可以循环。可变顺序机器人是为完成特定顺序进行设计的，也可为其他操作重新编程。

示教机器人。操作者可以按照期望路径引导示教机器人和其终端执行机构运动。机器人可以记忆和记录运动的顺序和路径，并能在没有操作者的进一步引导和示范的情况下连续重复这些动作。

数字控制机器人。数字控制机器人的编程和操纵很像数控机床，由数字数据伺服控制，运动顺序易于改变。

智能机器人。智能机器人能够执行一些人类才能完成的功能和任务。它可以配备各种传感器以具备视觉和触觉功能。

机器人的应用

机器人是一种很特别的生产工具，因此，机器人的应用范围十分广泛。这些应用可以被划分为三类：材料处理、材料搬运和装配。

在材料处理中，机器人用工具来加工和处理原材料。例如，机器人工具可包括钻头，可以在原材料上钻孔。

材料搬运包括装载、卸载和转移制造设备上的加工零件。这些操作可以由机器人可靠地重复执行，因此提高了质量，减少了废料损失。

装配是机器人技术的另一个广泛应用。自动装配系统能合并自动测试、机器人自动控制和机械处理，以减少劳动成本，提高产量，消除人工操作的危险性。如图23.2所示是应用于自动装配的SCARA机器人。

图23.2　自动装配的SCARA机器人

第 24 课　小小机器人兵团

一群恐怖分子强行闯入一栋办公大楼，劫持了不知多少名的人质，他们封锁了各个入口，也遮住了窗户。外面的人完全看不到他们有多少人，携带什么样的武器，或是将人质关在哪里。但突然间，特警队闯了进去，将来不及拿起武器的匪徒一网打尽。自信与果断的行动需要确切的信息，这些突击队员是怎么得到的呢？

答案就是一组合作无间的小型机器人。它们经由通风系统偷偷溜进大楼，从输送管井然有序地到处移动。它们有些配备监听对话的麦克风，有些配备小型摄影机，还有一些则配备传感器，可嗅到空气中是否有化学或生物药剂。它们采用合作的方式，将这类实时信息以无线电传回有关当局。

这近乎是美国国防高等研究计划署在 1998 年呈现给机器人研究者的情节。他们的挑战就是要开发出微小的侦察机器人，以便士兵随身携带，像爆米花那样撒在适当的地点。消防队员和搜救人员可以留在大后方，将这些机器人丢进窗内，让它们到处跑，寻找受困的伤者或是嗅出有毒的物质。

蚂蚁雄兵

原则上，比起笨重的大机器人，具体而微小的小机器人有许多优势。它们可以爬进管道，探查倒塌的大楼，也可以藏身在不明显的隙缝里。一群组织良好的机器人可以互相交换传感器信息，给一个从单个角度无法全面理解的物体给出全图。它们可以互相支持，共同攀越障碍物，或是在跌倒后爬起来。团队指挥官可以评估状况，决定送出数量多寡的机器人。如果一个机器人有故障，也不会因此拖垮整个群体，其余的成员还可以是继续行动。

但是，微小的机器人需要一种全新的设计观。不像体积较大的机器人，它们没有充裕的电源和空间，也无法容纳执行特定任务所需的全部组件，即使只是携带摄影机之类的小东西，也可能压垮小小的机器人。因此，传感器、处理能力及机械强度要分散到几个机器人身上，而它们必须通力合作。这类机器人就像群体里的蚂蚁：单独的时候很脆弱，但联合起来却极有战斗力。

团队定位

有一项非合作不可的事就是定位，即算出团队的位置。大型机器人有近于奢侈的好几种确定位置的方法，例如全球定位系统（GPS）接收器、固定信标及视觉地标辨识。此外，它们的处理能力也足以将目前传感器的信息与原有的地图进行比对。

方法虽多，却没有一样能确实用在小不点机器人身上。毫米机器人的声纳范围有限，只能测出大约两公尺内的距离。它的体型也太小，携带不动 GPS 装置。至于推算航法（利用测量车轮速度来记录位置的方法），也会因为重量太轻而行不通。即使是地毯编织方向这种微不足道的小事，也可能大幅影响它们的移动，使得里程读数不精确，就像汽车里程计在结冰的湖面上无法显示正确的距离一样。

因此，必须想出新的技术，我们开发出来的是一种小型化的 GPS。这种技术不使用卫星，而是利用音波来测量同组机器人之间的距离。利用交替传输与听取的方式，机器人会算出彼此之间的距离。每次测量需要大约 30 毫秒来完成。团队的指挥（可能是基地或是大型机器人，也许是部署毫米机器人的母舰机器人）会收集所有的信息，并使用三边测量法来计算机器人的位置。这种定位方法的优点在于毫米机器人不需要固定的导航参考点。它们可以进入一个不熟悉的空间，然后自行勘测。在绘图的过程中，有几只特定的毫米机器人会把自己当做信标，暂时保持不动，而其他几只就在附近走动，绘出地图并避开物体，同时测量自己相对于信标的位置。彻底探勘信标周围的区域之后，它们的角色就会互换。原来在探勘的机器人会移到适当位置，变成信标，先前的信标组就会开始探勘。这种方法很像儿童玩的跳马背游戏，而且不需人类介入就能执行。

连成一串的战车

路上的障碍是小型机器人必须合作的另一个理由。由于体积的关系，小机器人容易受制于随处可见的杂物，它必须应付石块、污泥或碎纸片。标准的毫米机器人可跨越的高度大约是 15 毫米，所以，一支铅笔或小树枝就可能挡住它的去路。为了避开这些限制，我们设计出一种新型的毫米机器人，它们可以像火车车厢那样联结起来。这种新型的毫米机器人，每只大约 11 厘米长、6 厘米宽，看起来就像是缩小版的第一次世界大战用的坦克车。它们通常会独立行进，能够灵活绕过小型障碍，但在需要跨过沟渠或爬楼梯的时候，就可以连接起来，形成一串锁链。

这串锁链的灵活功能来自毫米机器人之间的联结接头。毫米机器人的联结接头可不像火车的车厢联结或是汽车后面的拖车挂钩，它含有一个强力的马达，可以上下转动接头，转矩的力量足以举起几只毫米机器人。要爬楼梯的时候，这串机器人会先用力挤向楼梯的底部，比较靠中间的几只毫米机器人会以悬臂方式举起前面的机器人，而到达顶端的毫米机器人可以把底下几只拉上来。目前，这个程序还必须由人类遥控，但假以时日，这一串机器人应该就能自动爬楼梯了。

研究人员原本比较注重硬件的开发，但现已开始转向控制系统设计的改良。研究的重点会从控制少许的个体转移到管理几百或几千只个体，这是一种截然不同的挑战，需要相关领域的专门技术，例如经济学、军事后勤学甚至政治学。

我们设想的大规模控制方法之一，就是透过阶层式的管理，采用类似军队的方式，将机器人分成几个较小的团队，各小队有其控制指挥的队长，队长上头还有层级更高的指挥官。毫米机器人已经可以接受大型机器的人指示，这些长得像坦克车的大机器人的 Pentium 处理器足以完成绘图与定位的复杂计算。这种比较大的机器人可以拖着一串毫米机器人，就像母鸭带小鸭一样，在必要的时候将小机器人部署到适当的区域。管理大机器人还有更大的全地形车辆机器人，这些全地形车辆机器人拥有几台计算机、摄影机、GPS 装置，行程可达几百千米。这个想法就是让大机器人部署小机器人，进入大机器人进不去的地方，然后留在附近提供支持与指示。

小型机器人还有很长一段路要走，还没有任何小型机器人团队能走出那少数的几个实验室，在大楼的走廊漫游，四处寻找危险物品。虽然这类机器人有很大的潜力，但是，它们目前的功能有限，只能算是新奇的小玩意儿，差不多就像 10 年前的移动电话和掌上型计算机那样。随着科技从军事应用慢慢扩大到其他用途，我们可以预见，小型机器人的能力将会大幅提升。由于团队合作，它们可以做到各式各样的技能，模块化的设计也便于针对特殊任务而进行修改。而且，再怎么说，和它们一起工作实在有趣极了。

第25课 微机械技术导论

微机械技术的发展

微机械（日本称 MM：Micro-Machine，欧洲称 MS：Micro-System，美国称 MEMS：Micro-Electro-Mechanical Systems）在30年前仅仅是科学家提出的一种设想。然而当微制造技术（如半导体微细加工技术）及其他相关技术（如设计、材料、测量、控制、传感技术、信息处理、计算机、能源及系统集成等）发展到一定程度后，美国加州大学伯克利分校和麻省理工学院的研究小组在80年代后半期就利用了半导体制造技术，成功地研制出直径约 100μm 的静电微型电动机。这在国际上掀起了微机械研究的热潮，受到了各国专家的极大重视，因此，微机械也成为本世纪出现的一项高新技术。

人们预测微/纳米技术将会给工业领域的发展带来一场大的变革，所以许多发达国家和地区都把它看成是"对繁荣经济和国防安全至关重要的技术"，成为优先支持的项目，投入巨额资金进行研究开发。这促使微机械技术得到了迅猛的发展，也取得了一定的成绩。在美国，斯坦福大学已分别成功地研制出直径为 20μm，长度为 150μm 的铰链连杆机构，210μm×100μm 的滑块机构，转子直径为 200μm 的静电电动机以及流量为 20ml/min 的液体泵。在日本，东京大学研制出了 1cm 大小的爬坡微型机械装置，名古屋大学研制出一种不需要电缆，用于微小管道检测的爬行机器人，它是通过管外的电磁线圈产生的磁场来控制其运动的。在我国，微机械也开始引起了广大学者的普遍重视。目前研究集中在机械零件、集成传感器、光学元件、驱动器等方面，已取得一定得成效，现在正进行相关应用方面的研究。

微机械技术的基本特征

微机械尺寸的小型化带来了尺度效应的问题。随着机构的尺寸减小，其物理量并非成比例的缩小；当尺寸缩小到一定程度时，宏观机械常使用的计算方法和理论将不再适用，所以，微机械技术有以下基本特征：

（1）表面力起主导作用。我们知道体积力（如重力、电磁力）与特征尺寸的高次方（L^3）成正比，而表面力与特征尺寸的较低次幂成比例，如摩擦力（L^2）、表面力（L^1）、静电力（L^1）。微型机械体积小，重量轻，其表面力与体积力的比值较大，因此与体积力相比，表面力成了主要载荷。同样与重力相比，静电力也成了主要载荷，这叫做机械微型化的尺度效应。所以，在微机械中经常使用静电力驱动。此外，与重力相比，摩擦力对微机械的影响程度也比宏观机械大得多。

（2）微型机械并不是宏观机械原型的缩小。传统机械各部件的复杂程度一般各不相同。因此，用几何方式缩小这样的机械结构，对复杂部件很难做到，对高智能自动设备更是如此。所以，设计微型机电系统不必追求复杂的机械结构，而应该着眼于用多个结构简单的机械元件（包括带有传感器和人工智能的器件）来完成复杂的工作。

（3）不同的能量供给方式。对于具有移动和转动功能的微型机械系统来说，电缆常常会限制其运动范围，所以一般不采用电缆供电。目前微机械一般采用静电力提供能量。有时也使用振动激励的方式提供能量（如利用压电特性、电磁特性以及形状记忆合金进行驱动）。

因此，微机械的研制需要一些新的理论和新的方法。如微机械在运行过程中，受到的阻力形式发生了变化，需要一些新的机构设计原理和控制方式；运动及动力的形式发生了变化，需要一些新的驱动方式；器件的结构微型化了，需要一些新的制造技术和加工方法，等等。

微机械技术的应用

微机械技术的兴起和发展表明它有较广泛的应用前景，主要应用的领域如：

（1）在机械设计领域，用于设计微系统中的各种微型机械结构，如微齿轮、微连杆机构、微滑块机构等；

（2）在仪器仪表领域，用于设计压力传感器、加速度传感器等；

（3）在流体控制领域，用于设计微泵、智能泵等；

（4）在微光学领域，用于设计光纤、光扫描仪和干涉仪等；

（5）在超大规模集成电路制造领域，用于制造真空机械手、微小定位系统和气体精密控制系统等；

（6）在信息机械领域，用于设计磁头、打字机头和扫描器等；

（7）用来设计下个世纪的微机器人，如可用于微型管道检测与修复等极限工作环境的微机器人和多自由度手等。

第26课　对　　话

介绍

中国国际机床展览会是四大国际机床展之一。世界各国的工程师和经理云集北京，以了解世界制造技术新动态，推销最先进的机床制造产品。

展馆外

杨：欢迎来到本届中国国际机床展览会。现在正在举行开幕仪式。

艾：没错，场面很热烈。

杨：能知道您的尊姓大名吗？

艾：我叫艾丝特，这是我的名片。

杨：这是我的名片，谢谢您的光临。

艾：看起来是一个大展会。

杨：一点也不错。已经登记的参观者已达45000人，来自于世界各地，这个数目在未来两三天会继续增加。

艾：能有这次机会，我感到很荣幸。

杨：你说得对。本次展览会对中国的机床工业非常重要。有将近1000种新机床参展，各个国家和地区的展团代表参加了CIMT2001。

艾：太棒了！你们每年都有这样的展会吗？

杨：是的。自从1989年第一届中国国际机床展览会以来，每两年在中国举行一次。该机床展览会被公认为世界机床领域四大展销活动之一。

艾：下次我肯定会来的。

杨：欢迎，欢迎！

展馆内

艾：看！这些展品真的很壮观！

杨：当然了！这是 8A 展馆，由 4 部分组成。这里展出的是一些国产新机床，其中很多已经赶上国外同类产品的技术水平。我带你转转。

艾：你真是太好了！哟，那儿是一台大型 5 轴联动数控机床。

杨：是的。这台新机床达到了世界先进水平，适用于航空工业。

艾：哦，是这样。

杨：这是 SV-100 加工中心，刀库有 16 把刀，能快速自动换刀；工作台行程范围较大，完全可以胜任常规模具加工。

艾：哦。这是镗铣床吗？

杨：对，由于它经济实用、操作简便、性能优良，世界上都推荐使用该机床。

艾：有意思，但是机床尺寸小了点。

杨：它专为小工件设计，稳定性好，效率高。大一点的也有，你看，在那儿！

艾：单价多少？

杨：这是我们的价格表，这是产品目录。

在谈判厅

杨：您好，您对哪台设备最感兴趣？

艾：我们已经看过你们的目录，对你们的镗铣床很感兴趣。但通过反复计算发现价格高了一点。

杨：你们要订多少？

艾：我们的数量肯定让你满意。如果价格合适，我们计划订 15 台。

杨：说实话，由于我们订单太多，这种机床已销售一空了。现在价格表上的价格和以前是一样的。但是，由于你们的订单有一定的数量，我们把单价降到上海离岸价 20000 美元，这样我们可以成为新的合作伙伴。这数是我们的底价。不能再让了。其实，已无利可言了。就算是做个广告吧！

艾：看起来可以接受。包括运费！怎么样？

杨：唔，好吧。

艾：什么时候交货？

杨：8 月份左右。

艾：我们希望在今年 10 月份使用这些机床。时间非常紧迫，由于从上海到拉各斯没有直达航运，我们要把机床运到新加坡中转，7 月中旬能交货吗？

杨：7 月可以。顺便问一下，你们怎样付款？

艾：我们将分期付款。

杨：签约首付 30%，提货时付清怎样？

艾：按我们的惯例，提货时付 60% 还有 10% 余款待试用 3 个月后付清。另外你们的售后服务怎么样？

杨：一年保修期内实行三包，过后跟踪服务。噢，刚才听蒋先生说，好像你们还要买什么数控设备？

艾：是的，我们还要买线切割、电火花等。

杨：对啊，线切割、电火花，我们也可以代理啊。

艾：杨先生，等这笔生意做好后再谈别的设备吧。

杨：好啊！

艾：我们什么时候签订合同？

杨：明天下午。

艾：好，祝我们合作愉快！明天见！

杨：明天见！

第27课　如何撰写科技论文

科技论文是为了描述最新研究成果而写作并出版的论文报告。但这一简短的定义必须有一前提条件限制，即科技论文必须以一定的形式写作并以一定的方式出版。

题目

在拟订论文题目时，作者应牢记：论文的题目将被成千上万的读者阅读，但会阅读整篇论文的人只是少数几个人，而多数读者或通过原始期刊，或通过二次文献（文摘或索引）来阅读论文的题目。因此，题目中的每一个词都应该经过仔细推敲，词与词之间的逻辑关系也应该认真处理好。

一个好的题目应该是怎样的呢？我们可以将好的题目定义为：用精炼的文字确切表达文章的内容。

论文的题目是个"标记"，而不是一个句子，所以，它不必像通常的句子那样具有主语、谓语动词和宾语结构。它确实比句子简单（或者，至少通常比较短），但是也正因如此，词的排列顺序显得更为重要。

题目中每个词的含义和词序对于阅读期刊目录中的标题来说是非常重要的。而这一点对于所有可能使用文献的人，包括通过二次文献查找论文的人（可能大多数读者如此）也同样重要。因此，不仅题目本身应与论文相符，它的形式还应该适合于工程索引（EI）、科学引文索引（SCI）等自动检索系统。大部分索引和摘要服务系统都采用"关键词"分类法，因此，作者在确定论文题目时，最重要的是能够提供确切表达论文内容的"关键词"，也就是说论文的题目用词应该容易理解、便于检索、又能突出论文的重要内容。

摘要

摘要是一篇论文（学位论文）的简明而精确的概要。摘要的作用不是去评价或解释论文，而是对论文进行描述。摘要包括下列内容：论文中问题或论点的简洁而精确的陈述、研究方法及设计思路的描述、主要发现及其意义、结论。摘要应当包含能表达论文方法和内容的最重要的词汇（关键词），这样就可方便计算机对摘要进行检索，并能使读者迅速而准确地了解论文的基本内容，据此确定是否与所需论文相关，进而决定他们是否要阅读全文。

摘要应写成完整的句子形式，而不能写成短语或电报式的文字。一般来说，一篇短文的摘要应限制在 200～250 字以内，清楚地反映论文的内容。许多人将阅读原始期刊上或者工程索引、科学引文索引或者其他的二次出版物上刊登的摘要。

摘要切忌提及论文中没有涉及的内容或结论。在摘要中不要引用与该文有关的参考文献（在极少数情况下除外，例如对以前发表过的方法的改进）。摘要不是论文的一部分，所以摘要不作为论文的一页与论文一起计数和统计。

引言

我们已经结束了对正文前面的内容的讨论，现在就开始研究如何写正文了。应该指出，尽管题目和摘要都放在论文的前面，但是一些有经验的作者往往是在写好论文后再写题目和摘要。但在写论文时，心里必须要有（如未写在纸上的话）一个暂定的论文题目和论文的提纲，还应该考虑读者的水平，并据此确定哪些术语及方法需要定义或描述。

当然，正文的第一部分应该是引言。引言的目的是向读者提供足够的背景知识及设计思路，使读者们不需要查阅与此研究课题有关的出版物就能够正确了解和评价论文中的研究结果。在引言中还应该提出该项研究的理论基础。最重要的是，应该简要并清楚地说明写该论文的目的。审慎地选定参考文献以获得最重要的背景资料。

要写出一篇好的引言，建议遵守下列规则：（1）首先应该尽可能清楚地提出所研究的问（课）题的性质和范围；（2）为了适应读者的需要，应该对有关文献进行评述；（3）应介绍所采用的研究方法和手段，如有必要还应说明理由；（4）应介绍主要的研究成果；（5）应介绍由结果得出的结论。

材料与方法

在"材料与方法"部分应提供详细的实验细节。这一节的句子大多用过去时态。"材料与方法"部分的主要目的是详细介绍实验方案，以使有能力的研究人员可以重复这个实验。许多（可能是大部分）读者可能会略过这一节不看，因为他们在引言中已经知道使用的一般方法，也可能是他们对实验细节不感兴趣。但是，认真撰写这一节非常重要。因为科学方法的核心就是要求研究成果不仅要有科学价值，而且也必须是能够实践的。为了判断研究成果能否再次实验成功，必须为其他人提供进行实验的依据。不能再现的实验是没有意义的，重复进行的实验必须能产生相同或相似的结果，否则论文的科学价值就不大。

当论文被同行们审阅时，审稿人会认真地阅读"材料与方法"这一节。如果他对于实验能否再现这一点很怀疑，不管研究成果多么令人信服，这个审稿人都会建议退回稿件。

关于材料，应包括准确的技术规格、质量、来源及其制备方法等。通常还必须列出实验用试样或试剂的有关化学性能及物理性能。

至于方法，通常按时间先后的顺序来介绍。但很明显，相关的方法应该放在一起介绍，而不要总是拘泥于先后顺序平铺直叙。如果方法是新的（未发表过的），就应该提供所需的全部实验细节。如果一个实验方法已在正规的期刊上发表过，那么只要给出参考文献即可。

结果

现在进入文章的核心部分——数据。文章的这部分被称为"结果"。

"结果"一节通常由两部分组成。首先，应对实验进行全面描述，给出一个"大的轮廓",但不要重复已经在"材料与方法"一节中提到的实验细节。其次应该提供数据。

当然,如何提供数据并不是一件简单的事。直接将实验记录本上的数据抄到论文稿件上的做法是极少有的。在完成文稿时,最重要的是要应该选择那些有代表性的数据,而不是反复地罗列出所有数据。

因为"结果"是作者提供给世界的新知识,因此,"结果"一节应该写得清楚而简练。论文的前几部分("引言"、"材料与方法")告诉人们的是作者为什么和怎样得到了这些结果,而论文后面的部分("讨论")则告诉人们这些结果意味着什么。很明显,整篇论文都是以"结果"为基础的。所以"结果"必须非常清楚地表述。

讨论

与其他部分相比,"讨论"一节所写的内容更难以确定,因此,它是最难写的一节。不知你是否知道,尽管许多论文中的数据正确而有根据,且能够引起人们的兴趣,但讨论部分写得不好也会使其遭到期刊编辑的拒绝,甚至还可能会因为在"讨论"中所做的解释说明使得数据的真正含义变得模糊不清而导致退稿。

"讨论"部分的基本特征是什么呢?我认为它应该包括以下几个方面:

(1) 尽量叙述清楚由"结果"中显示出的原理、相互关系和归纳性解释。谨记:好的"讨论"应该是对"结果"进行讨论,而不是扼要重述。

(2) 要指出任何的例外情况或有关的不足之处,并应明确提出尚未解决的问题。千万不要冒大风险去采取另一种方法,即试图掩盖或捏造数据结果。

(3) 应说明和解释结果与以前发表过的研究结果有什么相符(或有差别)的地方。

(4) 大胆地论述研究工作的理论意义以及任何可能的实际应用。

(5) 尽可能清晰地叙述结论。

(6) 要简要叙述每个结论论据。

在描述所观察的事物之间的相互关系时,并不需要得出一个广泛适用的结论。你很难有能力去阐明全部的真理,尽最大努力所能做到的就是像聚光灯那样照耀在真理的某一部分,关于这一部分的真理是由数据来支持的。如果将数据外推到更大的范围,那就会显得荒唐,这时甚至连数据所支持的结论也可能会受到怀疑。

当叙述这一点点真理的意义时,要尽可能地简单。最简单的语言可以表达最多的才智与学识;冗长累赘的语言或华丽的艺术辞藻通常只能表达肤浅的思想。

参 考 文 献

[1] 陈统坚. 机械工程英语. 北京：机械工业出版社，2002.
[2] 颜国伟. 机械工程. 上海：外语教育出版社，1995.
[3] 刘振康. 机械制造英语读本. 北京：机械工业出版社，1988.
[4] 黄运尧. 机械类专业英语阅读教程. 北京：机械工业出版社，1997.
[5] Sergey Edward Lyshevski. Mechatronic curriculum-retrospect and prospect，Mechatronics，12（2002）：195～205.
[6] Masayoshi Tomizuka. Mechatronics：from the 20th to 21st century，Control Engineering Practice，10（2002）：877～886.
[7] 施平. 机电工程专业英语阅读（修订版）. 哈尔滨：哈尔滨工业大学出版社，2000.
[8] 张崎，杨承先. 现代机电专业英语. 北京：清华大学出版社/北京：交通大学出版社，2005.
[9] 汤彩萍. 数控技术专业英语. 北京：电子工业出版社，2005.
[10] 蒋忠理. 机电与数控专业英语. 北京：机械工业出版社，2004.
[11] Reno Filla and Jan-Ove Palmberg. Using Dynamic Simulation in the Development of Construction Machinery. *The Eighth Scandinavian International Conference on Fluid Power*. 2003（1）：651～667.
[12] 贺自强. 韩成石等，机械工程专业英语. 北京：北京理工大学出版社，1989.
[13] 司徒忠等. 机械工程专业英语. 武汉：武汉理工大学出版社，2001.
[14] 章跃. 机械制造专业英语. 北京：机械工业出版社，2003.
[15] 李俊玲，罗永革，现代汽车专业英语. 北京：北京理工大学出版社，2001.
[16] 蔡安薇，崔永春，汽车专业英语. 北京：北京理工大学出版社，2004.
[17] 粟利萍. 汽车实用英语. 北京：电子工业出版社，2005.
[18] 王锦俞等. 图解英汉汽车技术词典. 北京：机械工业出版社，2002.
[19] Serope Kalpakjian，Steven R Schmid. Manufacturing Processes for Engineering Materials. 4th edition. New Jersey. Pearson Education Inc. 2003.
[20] Fitzhugh L Miller. 3D production drafting and presentation with AutoCAD 2002. New Jersey. Pearson Education Inc. 2002.
[21] 张晓黎，李海梅. 塑料加工和模具专业英语. 北京：化学工业出版社，2005.
[22] Sixuan Zhong（钟似璇）. 英语论文写作与发表. 天津：天津大学出版社，2004.
[23] 唐国全，何小玲. 科技英语论文报告写作. 北京：航空航天大学出版社，2004.
[24] 方梦之，毛忠明. 英汉-汉英应用翻译教程. 上海：外语教育出版社，2004.
[25] 周志雄，孙宗禹. 机械设计及其自动化英语教程. 长沙：湖南大学出版社，2004.
[26] 马玉录，刘东学. 机械设计制造及其自动化专业英语. 北京：化工工业出版社，2001.
[27] Donald R. Askland and Pradeep P. Phulé. Essentials of Materials Science and Engineering. Published by Thomson Learning. 材料科学与工程基础——影印本. 北京：清华大学出版社，2005.
[28] Robert A. Day. How to Write & Publish a Scientific Paper. 5th Edition. ORYX PRESS，1998.
[29] 李红涛，费维栋. 材料科学与工程专业英语. 修订版. 哈尔滨：哈尔滨工业大学出版社，2001.
[30] 胡礼木，王卫卫. 材料成型及控制工程专业英语. 北京：机械工业出版社，2004.

[31] A. Aamodt, Explanation-driven case-based reasoning, in: Topics in Case-Based Reasoning, S. Wess, K. Althoffand M. Richter, eds, Springer, 1994: 274~288.

[32] R. Arkin, Behaviour-Based Robotics, MIT Press, 1998.

[33] R. Arkin, M. Fujita, T. Takagi and R. Hasegawa, An ethological and emotional basis for human-robot interaction, Robotics and Autonomous Systems 42 (3) (2003): 191~201.

[34] 王斌. AutoCAD 2006 实用教程. 北京：清华大学出版社，2007.

[35] Engineering Graphics-Supplement to the textbook, E. E. Pittman 2003.

[36] The Illustrated AutoCAD 2007 Quick Reference, Ralph Grabowski, Canada 2007.

[37] Engineering Graphic-a problem-Solving Approach Third Edition, 2006.

[38] D. Katagami and S. Yamada, Real robot learning with human teaching, in: Proc. of the 4th Japan-Australia Joint Workshop on Intelligent and Evolutionary Systems, 2001: 263~270.

[39] M. Kruusmaa, Global navigation in dynamic environments using Case-Based Reasoning, Autonomous Robots 14 (2003): 71~91.

[40] M. Likhachev and R. C. Arkin, Spatio-temporal case-based reasoning for behavioral selection, in: Proc. of the IEEE Int. Conf. on Robotics and Automation (ICRA), Seoul, Korea, 2001: 1627~1634.

[41] M. J. Mataric, Situated robotics, Encyclopaedia of cognitive science 4, 25~30, London: Nature Publisher Group, Macmillan Reference, 2002.

[42] Alan H. Epstein, MILLIMETER-SCALE, MEMS GAS TURBINE ENGINES. Proceedings of ASME Turbo Expo 2003 Power for Land, Sea, and Air June 16~19, 2003, Atlanta, Georgia, USA.

[43] T. C. Jen, G. Gutierez, S. Eapen. Investigation of heat pipe cooling in drilling application. Part I: Preliminary numerical analysis and verification. , p643~652. International Journal of Machine Tools & Manufacture 42 (2002).

[44] Lin Zhu, Tien-Chien Jen, Chen-Long Yin. Investigation of Heat Pipe Cooling in Drilling Applications, Part II: Thermal, Structural Static, and DynamicAnalyses. 2009 ASME INTERNATIONAL MECHANICAL ENGINEERING CONGRESS & EXPOSITION, Lake Buena Vista, Florida, US.

[45] 张芳，林良明. 微机械的基本特征、关键技术及应用前景，p25~33，传动技术，2001，15卷，1期。

[46] A. Faghri, Heat Pipe Science and Technology, Taylor and Francis, Washington, DC, 1995.